SPIRITUAL PARENTING

A Guide to Understanding
and Nurturing
the Heart of Your Child

HUGH & GAYLE PRATHER

HARMONY BOOKS   ❦   NEW YORK

To Scott, John, and Jordan
and the children
of us all.

———

Copyright © 1996 by Hugh Prather and Gayle Prather

*All rights reserved. No part of this book may be reproduced or
transmitted in any form or by any means, electronic or mechanical,
including photocopying, recording, or by any information storage and
retrieval system, without permission in writing from the publisher.*

*Published by Harmony Books, a division of Crown Publishers, Inc.,
201 East 50th Street, New York, New York 10022. Member of the Crown
Publishing Group.*

Random House, Inc. New York, Toronto, London, Sydney, Auckland

HARMONY and colophon are trademarks of Crown Publishers, Inc.

Printed in the USA

Design by REM Studio, Inc.

*Library of Congress Cataloging-in-Publication Data
is available upon request.*

ISBN 0-517-70385-8

10   9   8   7   6   5   4   3   2   1

First Edition

Acknowledgments

Hugh was a single parent for four years and although we have counseled many single parents and have worked with many more in our classes and relationship workshops, we wanted a deeper and more personal range of single-parent experience to draw upon to balance the "intact family" experience that we have had. We were exceedingly fortunate in finding Terrianne Jacobson and are deeply grateful for her contributions of ideas and essays to this book.

In these pages we have drawn extensively from our many years of association and friendship with Dr. Gerald G. Jampolsky. Jerry is a child psychiatrist and founder of The Center for Attitudinal Healing movement: free non-medical clinics for life-threatened children and others in crisis, now found throughout the world. He is the author of *Love Is Letting Go of Fear* and other best-selling books and is the recipient of many national and international awards for his contributions to identifying and improving attitudinal factors in the field of AIDS, for his contributions to world peace, as well as for his work with children. Jerry opened our eyes to the true nature of kids in the fall of 1978. When we were expecting our first child together, he introduced us to children at The Center for Attitudinal Healing in Tiburon, California (now in Sausalito), and showed us what miracles can flow from their innocent vision. He and his wife, Diane Cirincione, have been our friends, our teachers, and our soul mates for longer than time can quantify.

We have received a rich example and many invaluable insights from numerous other couples and single parents who also have loving and essentially fear-free relationships with the children in their lives. In more or less alphabetical order, a few of these are Susie Carter, Don and Josey Houser, Cherie and Jon Huntress, Kaaron and Randy Jorgen, Daniel Mauper and Carol Mothner, Donovan and Jill Porterfield, Cindy and Julian Silverman, Stacy Smith and Jeffrey Arlt, Bill and Maria Stennis, Barry and Joyce Vissell, and David and Susan Wilkinson.

Unquestionably our richest source of quotes, insights, wisdom, and encouragement is our boys Jordan, John, and Scott. Through them we experience God's oneness.

Contents

———

He said to his father, "All these years I have slaved for you, never disobeying a single order, and you have not given me so much as a goat for a feast with my friends. But now that this son of yours turns up, having squandered your money on prostitutes, you kill the fatted calf for him!"

"My child," replied his father, "you are always with me, and all I have is yours."

—LUKE 15:29–30

DEAR GUARDIAN OF
A CHILD OF GOD,

To benefit from this book, you need no faith in religious doctrine. Not even a *sense* of the One who is always with you and will never abandon you is required. We can assure you that if your child—whether baby, toddler, tween, adolescent, or adult—becomes your greatest pleasure, you will have lived a successful life, and the ramifications of your generosity will never end.

This, then, is a parenting book and not a book designed to reform the faithless or to correct world attitudes, if that were even possible. However, our personal distress over the world's treatment of children is unquestionably a primary reason we write about how to be a real mother or father, because it is our opinion, our faith, and our guidance that every parent who chooses to go against the present tide and approach the care of children as sacred work has an effect that reaches far beyond the boundaries of his or her family. The time has come for us to be immediate and reliable parents, as immediate and reliable as the Mother-Father we call God.

A quarter of a century ago Jonathan Schell, in referring to the My Lai massacre in Vietnam, said, "If we can accept this, there is nothing that we cannot accept." Perhaps we have all seen the pictures of the little boy running across a bridge in Sarajevo clutching his dog to his chest while snipers try to shoot him down. Before that we saw mothers and fathers rushing to the bomb site in Oklahoma City to discover that their worst nightmare had come true. Since the advent of television we have seen children being incinerated, bombed, and shelled in innumerable war zones. And from the turn of the century, in newsreels and on the covers of newspapers and magazines, we have been shown the fly-covered faces and bloated bodies of a thousand starving children.

The statistics on the number of children who are shot each hour, who are raped by relatives, who are homeless in our richest cities, who are exploited worldwide in factories and sweatshops, who are demeaned in "legitimate" ads and "adult" fare, and who are hit and abused by their own parents, read like a science fiction account of a planet gone mad. But this is *our* planet, and it has indeed gone mad.

We write this book not to call for still more outrage and payback, but to call for the beginning of sanity within our own homes and with our own children. How can we thrive as a people if our very offspring continue to be treated like lesser humans, like afterthoughts, and all too often, like refuse? Even more important than how at ease we are with what is going on around us is the question of our spiritual survival. Unless we heal our attitude toward children, the human race will end up so gutted of its decency that it will little matter whether it physically survives or not.

If the world wanted to feed starving children, it could do so easily. If the world wanted to outlaw acts of war against children, it could do so easily. If the world wanted to provide homeless children with shelter, it could do so easily. But children are not a priority in the world, and they never have been. Experience shows that we can't look to our world leaders or our religious leaders to cleanse our collective soul and redirect our energies toward children. That leaves you and me and our God.

We don't need to start still one more angry movement, or one more angry letter-writing campaign, or one more angry march on Washington. We must simply begin—today—to cherish and protect the children in our own homes, our own schools, and our personal lives. Within a world that has done very little for children, that is at least something. It's a starting point. And who is in a position to know the effects of just one parent, or one couple, or one schoolteacher learning to see and enjoy children? If God is the splendor that joins us all, who can place a limit on a single decision made in that Love?

This book reflects our deep personal conviction that parenting is a spiritual path, a form of worship. We believe that one's attitude toward children either is or should be at the heart of any reverential approach to life. In many ways a teacher is a parent; a coach is a parent; a counselor is a parent; a politician is a parent; even a mere voter is a parent. We should all think of ourselves as a parent in the gentlest sense of that term—as a guardian of the young. To put it another way, an aunt, uncle, stepparent, primary caregiver, or merely a citizen of our country or member of our society should seek the well-being of children above all else. If our relationship with children is a sacred trust—and that is the premise of spiritual parenting—in no circumstances can anything be more important than protecting and nourishing the children in our care. Those are the functions of the adult in all species. And we are not an exception. None of the heinous acts recorded in human history would have occurred if children had been the world's priority.

While discipline in the sense of a sustained commitment to a goal is a strength worth pursuing, this is not the way the term is most often used with regard to children. Discipline usually means punishment, a concept that is not entirely useful for those who wish to approach parenting as a spiritual path. If your most deeply held desire is to know God, to make all that you do an act of worship, then the guidance you give your child will be more like the light touch of a butterfly on a flower than the heavy hand of domination that "breaks the will" of a weaker ego. Rather than dispensing rules, regulations, and righteousness, you seek to *assist* your child to see the path clearly. After all, we are all on this journey together, regardless of our age.

As parents we should consider ourselves more like a Sherpa guide than a trainer or commanding officer. As one who has greater experience, but not greater value, our function is to climb the mountain beside our child, providing direction wherever we can, but above all offering our constant support. Then as we near the peak—as the child becomes an adolescent and then an adult—we stay back and let him or her pursue the dream, asking not even for credit for how much we helped along the way.

Before that time comes, we are willing to act as porter, chauffeur, companion, or nurse—when our child needs this. We are willing to provide whatever facilitates our children's ascent of the mountain, and since we are always beside them in this endeavor, we advance also. Our function is not to push, force, bully, or terrorize, because the mountaintop is an attainment of the heart. Only peace leads our children to peace; only love can find the place of Love.

*   *   *

When you kneel before your God in prayer, one question at least is always answered: You are loved. Wholly and forever. Nothing you can do could possibly turn the heart of Love against you. This you can feel in a moment's stillness. And as you rise and begin your day, you perhaps can sense that there is One who walks beside you. One who is more interested in your current efforts than your past mistakes. One who is committed to helping you find your way back home, no matter how often you have rejected home or how unworthy of a home you think you are.

We owe our children nothing less than what we ourselves are given. Since God loves all creatures great and small, it seems arrogant and conceited for us to say that we can pass judgment on our children when God does not judge them. How can we *know* that our disapproval and irritation is justified, when the Master himself taught with his final breath that even the destruction of the body does not justify anger?

All that we teach our kids by consistently trying to correct them in anger is that we believe deeply in anger as the most effective approach to difficulties. Is that what we want to model? Is that what the saints, the holy ones, the teachers of God, have modeled for us? Parents and stepparents who get angry with their children and won't give a birthday present; who stop coming to their games and ceremonies; who go for hours or days refusing to speak; who start showing more love for a grandchild than a child; who kick their teenager out of the house because she won't clean up her language or he won't clean up his room; who show more loyalty to their adult child's ex-partner than to their child; who won't let their kids come home for the holidays; who write a child out of a will—these parents must remember that it is not now, and never has been, our heavenly Parent's function to turn against us. Likewise, **it is not the parents' function to turn against their child. It is the child's**

function to turn against the parent—if that is what happens. And very often adolescents and adult children appear to do just that, even as we have so often rejected the One who never rejects us.

As we indicated earlier, you need not believe in God, or have any position on that word one way or another, in order to be a real parent. But if you are to see your child from a perspective greater than your ego history, you must approach child care as holy work. Which means happy work. If you can relax and *enjoy* your child—instead of straining against the burdens of child care—you are doing all any mother or father ever need do. You have, in fact, begun the healing of the world.

For many parents, enjoyment comes more easily when their kids are young, when they are little dolls who can be picked up and put down at will, and especially before they have developed a strong personality and a "mind of their own." The all-too-common experience of tweens and teens is to see their parents' disapproval of them build until finally they are rejected by the very ones who ushered them into life, who shared with them their blood and the genetic pool of their identity, and who once silently pledged to God never to abandon them.

Instead of eternal commitment, within the hearts of many parents today, there is the growing sense that their child is turning into a stranger. This perception is nourished by the my-needs-first philosophy of our times, strengthened by semiscientific pronouncements about the overly needy, controlling, power-hungry impulses in every child's heart, and sustained by the skewed and sensationalized reports of each misdemeanor and crime committed by a minor. Eventually the guardians of children hear themselves think the words they never thought they were capable of thinking: "I don't know you. What happened to the child I once knew? You are no longer my child."

Haven't you and I done a hundred dark deeds we once thought we were incapable of? And yet each time we turned to God, we were never once scolded and punished, and we certainly were never rejected. What we received was simple correction. To be like the One who never leaves us comfortless, we must now shift from a pain-inflicting, fear-inducing, mistake-oriented approach to child rearing to a loving, transforming, answer-focused form of guardianship. Do we really know better than God the attitude that heals? Can't we now trust enough to give to our children what we ourselves have been given—guidance that leads *forward,* that loosens us from our old unhappy patterns and sets us free to be as we were created to be? Can't we now love our children in the way God loves us?

You don't want to let your focus as a parent slip until one day you find yourself trading complaints about two-year-olds or adolescents or adult children with other alienated parents. "They should just put two-year-olds to sleep until it's over." "If I have to hear about one more pimple I'm going to scream." "I've been telling him to brush his teeth since he was four. Well, they can just rot out of his mouth for all I care." "She knows the facts of life. If she gets pregnant she's on her own. I'm not raising another kid at my age."

Nothing justifies anger toward your child. You may get angry—most of us do quite frequently—but never is it justified. There will be times when you need to be firm even with an infant, times when you must intervene in your teen-ager's life and say no, times when you will have to pick up your three-year-old and carry him or her kicking and screaming from the room. But there will never be a time when you *must* speak or act from anger rather than love. No matter how long you have pursued an arbitrary punishment or how deep into an abusive lecture you have gone, it is never too late to change your course. Do it right on the spot and return to God's attitude.

As a parent you will have internal consistency or external consistency. But you will not have both. If over and over you choose the love you feel for your child, and consult this rather than the latest child-rearing philosophy, you will *not* behave consistently. The picture of external consistency is highly valued in our culture, but for parents it is a meaningless value. Certainly you never want to change your course out of fear of a child's anger or disapproval, but when you change because you have remembered love, you teach your children the greatest lesson you can give them: that the voice of God speaks quietly in their heart and in stillness they will hear the answer.

Many of us summon our spiritual strength, or at least ask for guidance, when we and our child are in a crisis. However, the more difficult challenge of spiritual parenting is remembering to turn from our conflicted mind to our peaceful mind when making the little everyday, undramatic choices that have such a powerful, cumulative effect on our children.

At this writing Jordan has just turned twelve, John is sixteen, and they live with us in Tucson. Our oldest son, Scott, is thirty-six and lives outside of Los Angeles. About six months ago Jordan spent the night at his friend Jason's house. Jason's room has nice thick wall-to-wall carpeting, and the next morning Jordan phoned us from Jason's and, as he had on several occasions before, told us that he wanted a rug for his room. Only this time he was very insistent.

Our house has bare tile floors because, in the past, Jordan has been very sensitive to the kinds of allergens that rugs and carpets tend to collect. In the last year or so he has begun to grow out of this sensitivity—a fact he is well aware of—and he had been lobbying for a rug in his bedroom for several weeks before this occasion.

When Jordan first brought this subject up, we made the mistake that many parents make. Instead of considering the request strictly on its own merits and out of our desire for what was best for Jordan, our unconscious response was "Oh, one of our sons wants something. How can we use this as leverage?" Most adults are actually far more manipulative than most children. Using our kids' desires as leverage is just one of many ways we manipulate them, but it is a particularly unloving way because, in a sense, we are asking them to sell their souls. We hold out something they want and say "You can have it as soon as you become the person I want you to be." As soon as you become a neat, tidy person; or a more outgoing person; or a punctual person; or an academically oriented person; or a "respectful" person. The truth is that many of the world's geniuses, mystics, and greatest innovators were not tidy, outgoing, punctual, or especially polite. Jesus was not respectful of authority; Einstein found school boring and showed little scholastic ability; and Buddha rejected his father's idea of family duty.

Usually it's because they still have some degree of inner strength and integrity, and not because they are perverse, that children fail to live up to the so-called negotiations or contracts adults make with them—the terms of which, in reality, are conceived of and imposed by adults and are not "agreements" at all. In many instances children are fighting for their identity and not "waging a power struggle" when they deviate from a parent's understanding of what a child "agreed" to do. Often they are withstanding a basic misuse of parental authority and power.

When we lived in California, John had one friend whose parents would make him do all his chores before they would allow him to come over to our house. Once they even joked that because their son loved coming over so much, they had been able to increase the number of chores he would do. They didn't realize that they were passing on to their son their high regard for extortion. When we knew him, this boy had not rebelled against what his parents were doing. But if he does, most of the adults around him will probably consider him undisciplined, ungrateful, perhaps even destructive, depending on how he acts out his revolt.

Ironically, the week before Jordan spent the night at Jason's, we had advised a father who had come to us for counseling not to do what we ourselves were about to do. We told him not to consider his adult son Robert's disapproval and resentment when deciding whether to pay off a creditor who was making his son's life miserable. The father had said, "Ever since he went into therapy three years ago he's been angry at me. He never calls or comes by and he's said some horrible things about how his mother and I raised him. Why should I give him the money he wants?"

We told him we didn't know whether he should give it or not but we did know that he had to make his decision strictly out of love for his child. First he had to feel the love again, then he had to ask himself what he *believed* would be best for Robert—without being influenced by his son's present attitude. After only a moment's consideration, the father's eyes began to moisten. "I remember how much I loved that little kid. If I just look at that, there's no question what I want to do. I want that damn creditor off Robert's back."

"And do you have a feeling, a quiet sense, that's what would be best for him?"

"If some wild animal or some wacko jumped on him, I wouldn't hesitate to throw it off."

"But what about the fact that Robert got into this mess by himself? He's an adult now. He's the one who wasn't financially responsible, not you."

"Do you know how many times I've been financially irresponsible—especially at his age? And you know what? A few of those times my recklessness actually *made* me money. My parents never helped me out of any fix I ever got into and that didn't make me one bit a better person. It just made me feel abandoned."

This father's decision to pay off his son's debt did *not* eliminate his son's disapproval of him. It could have but it didn't. There is never any assurance that what we do out of love will bring about the changes we think we want. As parents we act from our better self because that is how we wish to live our lives and not because this approach magically transforms other egos or the objectionable circumstances of our lives. Despite what a few individuals within the New Age, New Thought, or other metaphysical movements like to claim, a spiritual path assures you no reward or special protection in the world. That should be obvious. Even Jesus' life did not go well. If you seek to know God you can be certain of one thing only: You will know God. And if you seek to respond to your kids out of the part of you that is deeply connected to God, you will see them as God sees them and know their destiny with certainty and peace.

How quickly ministers forget their own advice! It was only a few days after our talk with the father about his son that Jordan spent the night at Jason's. The next morning, when he phoned us about the rug, we said that as soon as he demonstrated that he could keep his floor clean for one week, we would get it for him.

Jordan answered that he had been keeping it clean.

We explained to him that while he was at Jason's we had been up until 3:00 A.M. scraping little bits of food off the floor and polishing the tile.

Jordan said, "If you'll get me the rug, I'll keep it clean."

We said, "No, first you have to keep the floor clean for a week."

Later that morning we were at Home Depot buying some gardening supplies when we saw a rug that was perfect for Jordan's room—it was vomit colored. A very *attractive* vomit that matched the tile. And it was on sale.

We realized that we had at least three options. One was not to buy the rug. The second was to buy it and store it in the garage until Jordan completed the one-week condition. And the third was to buy it and put it in Jordan's room. Ah, but to do the latter would be inconsistent with what we had just said. He would lose respect for us. It would teach him that nagging works. He wouldn't learn responsibility. And certainly he wouldn't learn to keep his room clean, which he had failed to do for over eleven years.

Yet his brother John learned to keep his room clean, despite the fact that we stopped making any demand in that respect when he was about six. Magically, at fifteen, right at the time when most teenagers are in full revolt, John started keeping his room clean. He even began cleaning the bathroom he uses.

And Gayle keeps her room clean, despite the fact that her mother periodically would get angry about the state of her room and insist that Gayle clean it up—but then would forget to follow up this demand. And despite the fact that she shares a room with Hugh who creates messes *that are not her responsibility.*

And Hugh keeps his room clean. He is also the one who makes the bed—without being told—despite the fact that he was never asked to keep anything clean in his entire life. And also despite the fact that he shares a room—and a bed—with Gayle, who creates messes *that are not his responsibility.*

So if all this were true, and if we had rarely made "contracts" with our kids before, what was this "one week first" all about? we asked each other. Then it dawned on us. (Yes, revelations are possible even in Home Depot.) It was about *our* having been up until 3:00 A.M. cleaning and polishing Jordan's floor! (Something we did because *we* had wanted it clean.) And it was about semantics: "Clean floor . . . clean rug." That sounds connected and related. It sounds like part of a "logical consequence," which is the big tenet in the disciplinary religion of our times. What modern parenting book wouldn't say that if your child doesn't keep his room clean "he should learn the consequences of his actions"?

But *do* actions have consequences? Do adults even believe this? Do they believe it if they get back more change than they should have? or if they go through a stop sign when there is no car in sight? or if they fill out their income tax when they are mad at the government? or if they are offered a once-in-a-lifetime sexual opportunity when they are being "emotionally starved" by their spouse? or if they are asked by a rich aunt whom she should leave her money to?

What adults actually believe is that *getting caught* has consequences, and even then you still may "get away with it"; you may even turn it to your advantage.

The fact was that "clean floor" had *nothing* to do with "clean rug"—unless we made it have something to do with it, and this we were doing because we were still tired and irritated from having gotten to bed so late.

So we bought the rug and put it in Jordan's room.

When Jordan got home that afternoon from his friend's, he first went to his room as he ordinarily would. Then he bolted out and ran to our room, where he peeked in the door. We were asleep.

Jordan, who usually never disturbs us when we are sleeping, ran into the room, jumped on us, and gave us each an enormous bear hug, then ran out.

The following day—without the subject of the rug having once been mentioned—Jordan announced that from that time on neither he nor his friends would be allowed to eat in his room. That was six months ago, and the rug still hasn't a spot on it.

So much for conventional parenting.

Which is precisely the point of this book. From twenty years of counseling families—first as authors on the subject, then as Crisis Intervention counselors, then as ministers—we can tell you unequivocally that there are no rules, no magic formulas, and especially no doctrine, science, teaching, or philosophy that you can safely consult about what to do in *this* situation, on *this* day, with *this* child.

Don't you want to hear the voice of God? Then consult your love for your child. Because God is love. And God is now. In the stillness of your heart you will always find a gentle option or two about what you might do and especially about how you really feel. God has entrusted this life into your hands and your protection. All that is asked of you is that you think of your child and look at your child and treat your child as if this were God's child also. Don't be afraid to trust yourself as you have been trusted. You are indeed caring for God's own child. This means you've got a lot of help.

Part I

—

MAKING THE COMMITMENT TO PARENTING: THE EARLY YEARS

1

THE INNOCENT VISION

A CLEAR HEART SEES CLEARLY

When we moved to California in 1987, for the first time in our family's history we found ourselves living in a house that had a lawn. One day soon after we moved in, Hugh was out mowing the grass, trying to get it done before he had to leave for an appointment, when John came outside and asked him if he could help run the gas-powered mower. The mower was safe but Hugh was in a hurry. He hesitated, then reluctantly let John try. However, he hovered over John and got progressively more irritated with each little mistake.

Finally, John had had enough of Hugh's attitude and walked back into the house. About ten minutes later he came back out. As Hugh watched him approach, he braced himself for John's anger.

17

John walked up to Hugh, handed him a folded picture that he had just drawn, then turned and walked away. Hugh opened it and there in a field of grass was Hugh holding John's hand. In the picture John was smiling, and over Hugh's head he had drawn a brilliant halo.

John had just turned seven when this happened. Today we are told by many parenting authorities that little children are attention-needy, manipulative, and dependency prone; that they are out of touch with the real world and must learn that "behavior has consequences"; that they are morally unformed and have to be taught right from wrong. Yet how many adults would spontaneously react to mistreatment the way this little child did? Instead of getting angry at him and confirming his false nature, John simply reminded Hugh of his real nature. Which is exactly the reminder that shines from the heart of God on all living things.

John didn't think his response through or consult a book about what to do when parents misbehave while mowing. From his goodness he merely did a good thing. And Hugh carried this reminder with him until, several years later, it finally fell apart. Every time he would take John's picture out of his wallet and look at it, tears would come to his eyes, for he knew that John had seen something in him that he had yet to see fully in himself.

On another occasion, when John was fourteen, Gayle was driving him to a soccer game when John suddenly asked her, "How did Dad get to be so pure?" When she reported this question to Hugh, he again was reminded that even a teenager could still see his core more clearly than he could, for he certainly did not think of himself as pure.

As parents we *start* by recognizing children's nearness to God. That doesn't mean kids don't need firmness, correction, and guidance, but it does mean that we are not in a position to judge them. We guide them not because they have basically shabby motives but because they lack the one strength most of us have: awareness of the world.

An infant of just a few months may yank her own hair or pull her own eyelid and howl in pain, not fully realizing that she's causing the sensation herself. Yet no one would accuse the child of masochism. But when slightly older children act in this way toward others, adults tend to attribute adultlike motivations to them. In truth, children simply lack full awareness of other people's feelings, especially in the first years of life. As soon as they are physically able, most kids will scratch, poke at eyes, kick, spit food, pull hair, or bite, and often they continue some of this into their twos and threes. It should be obvious that malice does not motivate these acts, and yet adults frequently misinterpret them.

Little kids lack awareness and yet in most situations display remarkably little ego. The large entrenched egos that so many adults have usually don't develop even during the teen years. Naturally, the egos of most adolescents are very active. They are at the height of differentiation. In fact, most teenagers are completely preoccupied with the process of leaving behind their childhood beliefs, associations, and relationships, and defining who they will be. They can turn on old friends easily and in extreme cases will murder to attain the new associations offered by a gang. As parents, we strive to do nothing that would make our children's egos grow more rapidly than occurs naturally, which is another way of saying that we do nothing to increase our children's fear, misery, or isolation. Thus, wise parents don't become combative with their teenager's ego, nor do they feed the ego inclinations in their younger children that they may find personally pleasing. For example, a real parent would not encourage a child of any age to feel superior to others merely because he or she has a great talent or gift. Yet all the while we are careful of how we handle our children's egos, we encourage their awareness of the workings of the world, including the effects of its evils and dangers.

*   *   *

In this book we use the term "ego" to indicate a false sense of self, which is how it is used in many religions and spiritual teachings. This sense is false because it feels unconnected to other people, to God, and even to our deeper being. Believing it is alone, the ego's basic emotion is fear.

Like an imaginary playmate, the ego is an imaginary identity, and just like the child's imagined companion, it seems to be autonomous, to have its own thoughts and feelings, and above all, to be defensive.

Identification with an imaginary playmate gives the child a sense of companionship, but it does not produce an actual friend. Likewise, our ego gives us a sense of identity, a sense of self, but it can't open us to the experience of Love, and it can never return the memory of who we are.

Our culture's general philosophy of parenting is based on observations and beliefs about how children's egos develop and not on what they bring with them spiritually when they come into the world. Many parents have felt the presence of a child before it was conceived. Sometimes this experience is quite dramatic. And certainly many parents have felt their son's or daughter's presence after the child died.

When Jerry Jampolsky (see Acknowledgments) and Hugh accepted an invitation to meet with parents of a number of African American boys who had been murdered in Atlanta, Jerry's plane was delayed and Hugh arrived before him.

When he walked to the front of the room, Hugh had no idea what to say. Here he was, a white middle-class father who had never had a child murdered—or even die—standing before a group of grief-stricken mothers, most of whom lived in one of the poorest sections of any city in the country. To Hugh it seemed as if they were staring at him in angry silence, daring him to begin.

Then it occurred to him that he was familiar with

one experience that some of them may have had. But he wasn't certain of this, because all of these parents' children had been murdered, and he didn't know how this affects the connection bereaved parents feel with their child. However, he decided to take a chance and began to tell stories he had heard from parents in the grief support group that he and Gayle led in Santa Fe. These were accounts about the humorous ways children had come back after their deaths to let their parents know that they were all right. Hugh had told two of these and had started a third when suddenly one mother interrupted with her account.

Her large extended family lived in two small houses that were just a few feet apart. The homes were of similar design and you could look through the windows of one house into the windows of the other. They kept their only TV in one house, and in the other, their only refrigerator.

One night, when they were all watching TV together, they looked up to see the shadow of the murdered boy creep past the window in the adjoining house. His mother jumped up and said, "I know what that boy's up to!" and they all ran over to the other house. Sure enough, he had once again sneaked in and drunk the family Kool-Aid, just as he had gotten in trouble for doing so many times when he was "alive." Partly because it was so funny to them, the family's grief was greatly lessened.

When the mother finished, it was as if a floodgate opened and the other mothers poured out their own accounts of the amusing ways their murdered children had come back to reassure them. As widely covered as these murders were, we know of no instance in which even one of these accounts was reported. Our culture simply does not believe that children are more than their bodies, as healing as this truth is.

Before we started the grief support group in Santa Fe, we would not have expected this tone of communication to a grieving parent. We would have guessed that the

contacts are sacred and serious. It would never have occurred to us that so many of them are amusing. But the basic
nature of children *is* humorous and playful, and the fact that
these assurances often come in this form makes them even
more meaningful and healing to parents. The playfulness is
usually very specific to that particular child's personality or
habits, and as far as we have been able to determine, reassurances of this nature are a universal experience throughout all cultures.

For the first few years after he founded The Center
for Attitudinal Healing, Jerry Jampolsky periodically invited parents in the Bay Area who were grieving the loss of
a child to come to his home for the day. He tried to provide
an atmosphere where these moms and dads could, in his
words, "feel free to be crazy" and say things they ordinarily
would never say to anyone else. The families would bring
food and spend the day talking about how they were feeling
and about the kinds of things that had happened to them
surrounding the death of their child and since that time.

These were people of different races and nationalities and from all walks of life, and yet Jerry was struck by
how much they had in common. When I spoke to him recently, he said that the stories he heard of children letting
their parents know that they were all right had the same
characteristics that we had noticed in our own work: Usually the deceased child came to the parent in some nonverbal way and frequently there was a sense of fun or merriment
in what happened. The child's favorite toy would keep coming on in some funny way; the kind of food that the child
liked to feed the cat would be found in the cat's dish several
times in a row; the rearview mirror would be turned the
way the child used to turn it; a favorite garden hose that the
child used to forget to turn off would be found running; or
the child's kiss or special way of touching would be felt by
the parent.

Quite naturally, there is no room for these occurrences in child/developmental/educational/instructional
psychology. The "science" behind current beliefs about
parenting acknowledges only what can be observed, tested,
and duplicated, consistent with other objective phenomena.
Parents who can look at their children only the way the
physical sciences look at them will see little more than the
development of an unformed ego and its body. But all parents have the capacity for what might be called spiritual
vision.

There is certainly nothing wrong with studying the
dynamics of the ego and the development of the brain and
body. But as a parent you will have many experiences that
most psychological, academic, and medical literature will
not support. We urge you to take your experiences of your
child's deeper nature into the quietness of your heart and
learn from them. Each time you will see the same obvious
truth: that everyone is held in Love and that your child is as
deeply connected to God as you are. These experiences may
take any form—suddenly knowing that your absent child is
in danger, foreseeing something before it happens, being
able to read your child's thoughts or someone else's
thoughts toward your child, glimpsing a previous relationship that you had with your child, or the more complete and
inclusive experience of seeing your child's innocence.

Remember, however, that you were not singled out
for spiritual honors and distinctions. Your experiences of
oneness do not make you special or prove that your child is
special. You are merely seeing the face of God where it always was and always will be. So we urge you not to talk
about these occurrences with other people, unless you are
certain they are fully aware of this other side of children. **It
is always a mistake to cite a spiritual experience as a means
of winning an argument, changing someone's mind, or im-
pressing others.** If you persist in misusing these experi-

ences, you will stop having them. Each time you try to use oneness to overcome separateness, you "prove" that separateness is real and strengthen your belief in it.

Jerry Jampolsky delivered his first baby when he was a fourth-year medical student at Stanford-Lane (now Presbyterian Medical Center). The delivery occurred around 2:00 A.M., toward the end of a twenty-four-hour shift. When it was over, Jerry felt profoundly rested—and transformed. He now knew that something else—something deeply powerful and good—was present in children that had not been acknowledged in his medical studies. From that time on he was never again able to see children through the lens of conventional psychiatric theory or to believe that their deepest impulses are negative and destructive. There was an unmistakable light in children. He had seen it and felt it for himself.

Jerry's second two-year residency was a fellowship in child psychiatry at Langley-Porter Psychiatric Clinic, where he worked with autistic children from the ages of about four to thirteen. His perception of children was dramatically enlarged when it became obvious to him that although these kids couldn't speak, they often could communicate telepathically. Realizing that all children must have a similar intuitive side, he began helping parents understand and deal with a set of abilities that most of them had lost and forgotten they ever had.

Even in adolescence most kids have a degree of intuition and insight that is far greater than their parents realize. Parents assume that their child is reacting to other people and places with likes and dislikes similar to their own. Since they are more experienced and their preferences are better informed, parents tend to dismiss their child's reactions as immature and inferior. This can be a mistake, and sometimes a very serious one.

Our children are not infallible oracles but their intuitions are often more relevant than the family dog's, which many adults closely heed. Kids often pick up on hidden thoughts and motivations in their relatives and their parents' friends and acquaintances. They can be very sensitive to unseen atmospheres at parties, in stores, or while visiting a new school or child care center. Notice, for example, how many children are not happy at "the happiest place on earth" or other large amusement parks.

Even older kids often have difficulty articulating what they are picking up. Children's overall state of mind is a better indicator of what they are aware of than their words. Many couples have noticed how their children act out because of the unspoken tensions between their parents, and perhaps all mothers have noticed their infant react when they are upset even though they have done nothing outwardly to convey this.

CHILDREN ARE BETTER HUMAN BEINGS

Although it comes during the darkest time of the year, Christmas is the brightest and merriest of Christian holidays. In part, perhaps this is because it celebrates the birth of a child—and the circumstances of that birth are so lovingly recalled that it honors the coming of all children into the world. Several years ago this quote from McEdmond Donald appeared on the cover of the *Presbyterian Outlook* for their Christmas issue:

> When God wants an important thing done in the world or a wrong righted, He goes about it in a very singular way. He doesn't release thunderbolts or stir up earthquakes, God simply has a tiny baby born, perhaps of a very humble home, perhaps of a very humble mother. And God puts the idea or purpose into the mother's heart. And she puts it in the baby's heart, and then . . . God waits.
>
> The great events of this world are not battles and

elections and earthquakes and thunderbolts. The great events are babies, for each child comes with the message that God is not yet discouraged with humanity, but is still expecting goodwill to become incarnate in each human life.

Jerry has tried in many different ways to bring the simple goodness and wisdom of children to the attention of adults. Several years ago he realized that if he could get world leaders merely to listen to children, it might have a profound effect on how they governed their nations and especially on their decisions about war and peace. He put together small groups of kids of many different nationalities and races and began traveling to various capitals.

All of the children he took were under twelve. Contrary to the assumption found in most parenting books—that children's moral sense is weaker the younger they are—Jerry has found that by the time many kids reach twelve, this sense has *diminished* to the point that often it is no stronger than the average adult's. When asked if world peace is a practical goal that we should all work toward, kids under twelve usually say yes, whereas kids over twelve often share their parents' position: for example, that universal peace is not obtainable and that some wars are good.

Interestingly, it is around this age—the very time when their kids are becoming more like them—that many parents begin to turn against them. During the onset of adolescence, just when kids most need someone to remember their goodness, parents tend to become more judgmental and pile on more "responsibility."

Although many leaders did take the time to meet with Jerry's kids, most adults, including world leaders, find the simple, straightforward goodness of a young child difficult to receive in any deep way. One head of state got into a conversation with a little girl about whether you should fight a war against "a bad guy." He told her that it was sad that so many people had to die, "but some men just have to be stopped." The child answered, "Don't kill all the people, just get the bad guy." While this was a remarkably simple suggestion, he merely explained to the child why she was wrong. Rather than question a system that makes killing thousands of conscripted young people and uninvolved civilians the only viable option, he cited international laws against "getting the bad guy."

Jerry and his kids visited several countries that, at the time, were considered enemies of the United States, including the then Soviet Union and China. He also took children to talk to several men and women who were instrumental in forming our foreign policy toward those countries. Twenty years as a child psychiatrist had convinced him that if young kids were simply in the room when heads of state were deciding whether to attack another nation's population, no buttons would ever be pushed and most wars would never be fought. When discussing war with one world leader, a nine-year-old boy said, "As long as I live, I hope I never kill or hurt another human being."

Yesterday Gayle got a call from a man who said that his marriage had finally broken up and that if he had just listened to his three-year-old daughter, it wouldn't have. He said that she used to run back and forth between her mother and him saying "Mommy, don't fight . . . Daddy, don't fight." But he thought he knew better. He thought he knew that "this" had to be settled right now, whatever it was. He thought he knew that problems had to be jumped on immediately. His very integrity and autonomy depended on it. Now he can't even remember what most of the fights were about. Through her three-year-old eyes his daughter saw clearly that the fighting was worse than the issue.

He also told Gayle that he had always believed that they had owned an awful dog. No matter what he tried, the dog just wouldn't obey. But his little girl would say to him

"Daddy, don't kick the dog, don't kick the dog." This is a good man at heart and he has helped many people in very important ways, but he now recognizes that his daughter was a better person than he was.

This same little girl used to pull the dog's tail when she was two. She was not yet aware of the dog's feelings. Like many adults, this father had mistaken lack of awareness for lack of compassion. Now he knew they are not the same. Children need to be shown how to extend their goodness, but most little kids are not lacking in goodness. Their hearts bubble over with it. Their eyes shine with it. The very fact that their egos have *not* yet developed is what allows this to happen.

Most older kids also retain much of the goodness they started life with. Gayle was recently in the car with Jordan and his friends Tim and Dusty. As she began to approach an intersection, she saw past the cars in front of her that there was a man in dirty clothes standing at the corner with a sign saying he was hungry. She asked the boys whether she should give him some money. All three answered yes. Gayle said, "But what if he's going to use the money for drugs, or what if he's a pro just pretending to be hungry?" Tim answered, "Yes, but what if he *is* hungry?"

In following up Tim's comment with more questions, she realized that all three boys thought that the risk that the man might genuinely need food was more important than the risk that he was an addict or a fake. If he got more drugs, then he simply continued being an addict, but if he needed food and didn't get it, he could die. They didn't think that adults' fear of being taken advantage of (a fear most children don't share) was a good reason not to give someone money. So Gayle circled the block and gave the man five dollars. The man said, "God bless you," a reminder worth every penny of what she had given.

The point here is not that it's always best to give someone who looks homeless money, but that even older children often are more motivated by compassion and less motivated by fear than adults.

Over the many years that we have been giving talks and workshops, we have noticed that audiences composed mostly of parents are usually happier and laugh more easily than the ones made up primarily of single adults or couples without children. As a group, childless adults are freer to concentrate on gratifying themselves, and yet adults who are weighed down with the burden and expense of raising kids often have a lighter spirit. Naturally, we also have seen exceptions to this generalization, but for most people the parent-child relationship can serve as a shortcut to spiritual advancement simply because we are predisposed to commit ourselves to it.

Your commitment will of itself bring your child's goodness into your heart and you will be transformed by it. To be one with your child is to be one with your child's spiritual strengths.

Our recognition of oneness—the essential of all spiritual growth—often comes more easily when we are dealing with someone of a few years rather than many. Although it's definitely beginning to have its effect, the ego-enhancing psychology that has gutted so many marital relationships has not yet completely undermined the parent-child relationship. For instance, oneness often can look like dependence to those who are not really looking. Yet as parents we recognize that we are physically stronger and more experienced with the world than our children, and thus we see that our children's "dependence" on us is not a pathology. Actually, it's a spiritual necessity.

Our spiritual unity with our child is the reality that allows us to love our child and our child to love us. This connection exists between all living things, but within the parent-child relationship most adults tend to be more open to the ancient mystical insight that to give is to receive, that what is truly in another person's interests is in our own as well. We also tend to be more aware that our thoughts and emotions are not "private," because we continually see our inner state reflected back in our child's behavior.

God is the river of light in which you bathe. This brilliance flows through the core of every living thing and certainly through your child. Nothing within the warring, separated images of the world reflects the unity of God, and yet the unseen waters of Love surround you in all circumstances, no matter how petty or shameful or tragic they may be. The uncomplicated reason that the experience of God will follow your decision to put your child first is that God *is* Oneness. God is that which creates and sustains and joins the spirit. God is what connects our hearts and minds. Although within the world God goes unrecognized, **those who see their oneness with just one other living thing cannot fail to see God.**

THE UNSEEN SIDE OF YOUR CHILD

We were standing in the hall of our newly bought house outside Patagonia, Arizona. Gayle said, "I don't like Jordan. He doesn't fit in this family. We were happy until we had Jordan." She looked at Hugh hopefully, waiting for him to say something spiritual that would change everything.

Gayle had just come from another battle with Jordan, who was almost three. He had refused to eat the same lunch she had made for John. This was just the latest of a series of problems we had had with him almost from birth.

Hugh said, "I don't like him either."

After a moment of shocked silence, Gayle said, "We've got to do something. It isn't fair to Jordan. This simply can't go on."

Hugh said, "You're right. Let's sit down and pray about it."

When we "pray" we sit in a quiet place, still our minds, let go of our opinion of what we think the problem is, then ask for help. The guidance we receive comes as a joint sense of what we should think or do. After many years of making decisions in this way and teaching others this simple and ancient process, we have learned that any two who first take a moment to admit that they could be mistaken about what is in their own best interests and then truly open themselves to the leadings of Love will feel a gentle leaning, a peaceful preference about what direction they should take. This path of peace was always before them, as it is before everyone, but now their willingness to be still and open allows them to see the obvious.

On this occasion, our prayers brought us a new determination to accept Jordan completely. We decided to set aside two periods a day during which the two of us would come together to picture Jordan in the light of God and silently speak to him from our hearts. We also decided to treat these times as sacred and do everything we could not to skip one.

Many weeks passed before we got a breakthrough, but when it came it was dramatic. Suddenly we began to see *Jordan*. And he was a wonderful kid! We began noticing his exuberance, his insightfulness, his offbeat creativity and inventiveness, his delightful sense of humor, his mental toughness and centeredness, and many other qualities that we had been blind to—merely because he didn't share the easygoing personalities that the rest of us had. Jordan has never been one to suffer in silence, but we saw that this was actually a good balance to have in our family. We needed Jordan. We needed his directness. It was no accident that he was in our lives.

This change in our perception allowed us to relax and *enjoy* Jordan's differences. He went from a project to a pleasure. Our two-year battle to change him had made him only worse in our own eyes. Undoubtedly it had not been easy for him either. The lesson we were forced by our frustration to learn was that **children and parents must change together.** Parents are not in a position to dictate a deep, meaningful change in their children. They are not in a position even to see what changes are needed—until they themselves are ready to grow spiritually along with their kids.

There is a very simple reason why it works this way and why trying to change our children without changing ourselves does not work: **A parent and a child are not separate.** A bat can hit a ball and change its direction without the bat having to travel along with the ball, because the two are separate entities. They have no shared spiritual core. In fact, a batter can change bats or a pitcher can change balls and a hit will still be a hit. Not so on a spiritual level. And real change takes place only on that level.

In reading through large numbers of parenting books, we have been distressed to observe how often the deep, untouchable connection between parent and child goes unacknowledged.[1] Often these books contain a discussion of concepts such as "bonding" or "attachment" or even "imprinting," but this form of joining usually is described as a mental or emotional shift confined to one individual at a time. No inherent union or oneness is acknowledged; love is merely a "learned response." If you slight or ignore any of the necessary steps (your face should be within twelve inches of your baby's face; your eyes should be rotated to the same vertical plane; you should talk in a high-pitched voice; and the like), your baby may not bond adequately. Thus you may end up feeling bonded to your child but your child may not feel bonded to you. Or the bonds you each feel may be of different and incompatible intensity. Or there may never be a bond because yours is an adopted or step- or foster child. Or the bond between you may be irreparably damaged because your infant was incubated, or you didn't breast-feed long enough, or you got pregnant again too soon, or you left your child in day care too long, or you broke up your child's home, or a hundred other factors.

Bonding obviously *does* operate on the ego level somewhat in this way. And, indeed, the bond between two egos is fragile. Yet there is another link between parent and child that is far more than an instinctual potential that must be carefully triggered and maintained. It is the divine or spiritual or soul connection between you and your child. Once you see this bridge clearly, your way of relating to your child will begin to change. **You can experience the eternal unity of you and your child at any time, regardless of what just happened between you and no matter how disturbed or lacking your history is with each other.** The door remains forever open to love because God is the door-keeper.

Our oldest son, Scott, didn't come to live with us until just before his fifteenth birthday. Hugh had married Suzanne, Scott's mother, when they were both twenty, and Hugh had spent very little time with Scott during the first year of his life, which turned out to be the last turbulent year of Hugh and Suzanne's marriage. After that, except for a few scattered visits with Scott, Hugh was basically absent from his son's life until we gained custody of him.

Nothing had happened between Scott and Hugh to fulfill any condition necessary for bonding. Then, when Scott came to live with us, he was so angry about being suddenly abandoned by his mother and we were so inexperienced in the ways of children, still no bonding in the traditional sense occurred.

When Scott was thirty-four and living in L.A., he was hospitalized for a brief but very serious illness. He called Hugh the morning he was released and told him what had happened and that he had been too sick to call him earlier. Hugh said, "I know you don't believe in this stuff,

but Gayle and I are going to surround you in light today."
Scott laughed and answered, "Okay, as long as I don't have
to do anything."

The next day Scott called and said, "I had the most
remarkable experience yesterday. I was coming out of an
office building and as I stepped onto the sidewalk everything around me was covered in holiness. 'Holiness'—that's
the only word I know to describe it. It covered me and every
building and every person I saw. I have never had a more
beautiful and peaceful experience. Were you by any chance
surrounding me in light then?" He told Hugh the time. After checking with Gayle to be sure he was right, Hugh told
Scott that he and Gayle had sat down to hold him in light at
just that moment.

To our egos this is a classic "So what?" experience—
because nothing changed in the world. There was no physical healing. A pedestrian was not miraculously snatched
from the path of a speeding cab. The sun didn't even break
out of the clouds. Only Scott's perception changed. But,
significantly, it changed when ours changed. That is the importance of this type of experience, which is so familiar to
those parents who habitually turn their own minds to God
in order to help their kids. And it happens because minds
are joined.

The mere existence of the quiet, harmonious link
between our children and ourselves calls out to us to take a
radically different approach to parenting than is currently
being practiced in most homes. But we must remember that
the difference called for is not to be permissive or to be
strict. It isn't a behavior or an appearance. Spiritual parenting is based on the river of God, the love that flows between
hearts. It comes from love and reflects love. It does not come
from adult importance or parental righteousness or the latest rules about what to say when your four-year-old throws
food on the ceiling or your teenage daughter comes in
twenty minutes past curfew.

GOD DOES NOT PLAY FAVORITES

Before Jordan was born, Hugh and Jerry Jampolsky traveled together for about three years giving lectures and workshops together and visiting children in hospitals. Jerry often asked children profound questions about world peace and human relations. More often than not, these kids would give remarkably wise answers.

On one occasion, when Hugh had returned from one of these trips, it occurred to him that if he asked our son John a question, maybe he could get him to say something spiritual as Jerry was always getting kids to do. He asked, "John, what happens after you die?" John, who was three at the time, answered without missing a beat, "You're swept up by the street cleaner."

Though John has never said anything "spiritual" on demand, many things he has done have affected us deeply. In our experience, **the light of God shines through most children's attitudes more obviously than it does their words.** If you wish to hear the echoes of Heaven when your kids speak, you can listen for it in the overall tone and purpose of their chatter and laughter rather than in the literal meaning of what they say. However, unless you have shed all the usual adult conceptions of what spirituality looks and sounds like, to try to force yourself to hear something divine in your kids' laughter or see it in their actions can quickly lead to disillusionment. **Never look for confirmation of your child's spiritual core in his or her behavior.**

Many parents see their children's deeper nature when they are born, then lose sight of it after a few months of full diapers, colic, and fitful sleep. If that doesn't blind them, the terrible twos usually will. **If you stand back and wait for your children to prove their spirituality, you will never develop complete faith in them, never become their absolute friend, and never learn how to enjoy them.** Only by *first* having faith in your child's purity and then by refusing to allow that faith to be shaken will you see it. The proof of your child's closeness to God is overwhelming—but you must let it come to you in its own form. This book can only describe the attitude you need for spiritual vision, but your children will present their core in their own way.

In 1978 Hugh awoke one morning realizing that he had just had an unusual dream. It was different because he knew that he had been given a message.

We had never paid much attention to dreams in those days; we didn't describe them or discuss them with each other; and none of our friends seemed particularly interested in dreams. Yet this dream had the feel of guidance. In it Hugh and Gayle and their baby were living in their present house, and they were all very happy. Period.

We didn't then have a baby, but dreams very often don't reflect reality. Hugh couldn't understand what made him think that *this* dream was a kind of instruction, almost an order, to have a child. Instruction from whom? Neither we nor any of our friends believed in God or the supernatural.

At that time in our lives, we and all our close friends not only didn't have children, we were prejudiced against them. Kids were not a part of a fun, sophisticated life. We often would complain to one another about parents who brought their noisy kids into restaurants and theaters. It disturbed *everyone's* enjoyment. There should be a policy against it! Most of us liked and owned dogs, but we all agreed that children were a nuisance. It was understood that none of us would ever succumb to the patent stupidity of having any.

Hugh was therefore embarrassed by his dream and decided not to tell Gayle about it. But by that afternoon the whole experience had begun to fade and seem a little ridiculous to him. He and Gayle were in the car driving to town when he said, "You know, something really funny happened last night. I had a dream that you and I were supposed to have a baby." He then described the dream. Gayle said, "I had the identical dream last night."

Now it wasn't funny. In fact, it was a little horrifying. So we came up with a plan whereby we could prove that we had misinterpreted the dreams. If Something could tell us both to have a child, that same Something also could get Gayle pregnant in just one try. We would not use birth control for one night only, and if Gayle didn't get pregnant we would know that the whole thing had been a coincidence and we could continue our carefree life without guilt.

But Gayle got pregnant.

The next unusual occurrence was that we were unexpectedly reminded of an experience we had had a few months before, one that we had already discounted. We had met a couple and a few weeks later had dinner with them and a woman who was a friend of theirs. After dinner, more or less in the tone of a game or entertainment, one of the women offered to lead us all through a procedure whereby any who were no longer in the world could give us a message if they so wished.

In the last message that came that evening, Hugh and Gayle were told that there would be "great joy" in their life in connection with the number eight. They were not to look for this number and certainly not to make any decision based on a number, but simply to notice this happy coincidence when it occurred.

As Gayle's due date approached, the number eight began popping up in numerous ways in our life. In the final days of Gayle's pregnancy, and especially during the drive to the hospital, there were so many eights everywhere we looked that we began laughing about it. In a dramatic finale, we walked into the hospital and the large clock on the wall read straight-up eight. John, of course, was delivered on the eighth.[2]

The message dreams, the immediate conception, the

coincidence of all the eights, and several other unusual occurrences surrounding John's birth did not have a good effect on Hugh once he began thinking about them and trying
to read a meaning into all that had happened.

We now realize that we merely had been reassured.
Despite our considerable fear at the time that children ruin
people's lives, we were "told" that it was just fine to have a
child. But that's not the way Hugh looked at it at the time.
And consequently he fell into a very common trap.

Hugh convinced himself that we had been singled
out to receive a very unusual and special child—a child who
was somehow more important than other children. John is
indeed a wonderful kid—in fact, we can't imagine any children being more wonderful than our three boys. But they
are not musical or academic or any other kind of geniuses.
They are just good, kind, bright kids like millions of other
children. Yet when the mundane fact finally began to dawn
on Hugh that John posed all the problems that kids always
pose for their parents, he lost interest in John, and it was
only Gayle's patience and Hugh's deep devotion to his spiritual path that eventually brought him back to his senses.
Fortunately, that didn't take too long (about two years), so
John was not damaged, as he could have been if Hugh's lack
of commitment had gone on for many years.

In the eyes of the world, ranking is a fact of life.
There are important people and unimportant people and
many levels between. These rankings are always shifting,
and nothing is less reliable than your relative importance
today. But in the heart of God, no child is assigned a role
that is spiritually less important than the role of any other
child. God does not have pets. We now both realize that
children offer us and every guardian far more than the possibility of special worldly honors and attention. They offer a
way to walk gently out of the grip of the world and into the
freedom of God. There are a thousand other forms this free-

dom can take, but in the truest sense of the term, children are God's gift of salvation.

CHILDREN'S USE OF WORDS

Adults tend to use words to separate, to contrast themselves, to create boundaries, to set themselves apart, or to win. Kids tend to use words to *include*—especially to include others in some game or childish humor. Even on occasions when adults are relatively happy—for instance, when parents sit around a backyard pool and watch their kids play—you can hear or feel a subtle difference in the *purpose* of children's chatter, especially when compared with the adults' conversation. Just close your eyes and listen to the tone of each group's interaction. Ask yourself what is being said by this adult's tone of voice, and this other adult's tone, and that child's tone, and so on. The underlying agenda of each group should become clear.

While they relax, perhaps snacking and drinking together, the parents might first talk about a local politician, then comment on a large purchase someone just made, then analyze a mutual acquaintance's behavior the night before, then make jokes about a certain profession, then give their opinions about the new school administrator. Although topics such as these are innocent and unavoidable, they do tend to emphasize the distinctions and differences between people. Certainly they don't generate a sense of oneness with the human family—but in normal adult conversation, this mild separation is virtually inescapable.

As these and other subjects are pursued, most of the adults present are also aware of how their bodies, their clothes, their senses of humor, and their opinions compare. They are conscious of who agrees with whom; who is listened to respectfully, who, dismissively; and the up or down direction of their lives.

Meanwhile, the kids also are using words—perhaps yelling "Marco Polo!" or talking about "Who's it?" And although there may be some screams of "Don't splash me" or "I was on the raft first," these grievances are forgotten remarkably quickly. If the kids are young enough and if the adults watching over them are not too rigid and controlling, their words will be used mostly to express exuberance and excitement, to set up funny predicaments, to make childish jokes, and to initiate joint projects of sheer silliness.

Many adults have forgotten the joy of silliness. They have replaced it with self-importance. To them silliness is much too rooted in the present. It doesn't honor the past or respect how the future can be used to build a more glorious past, used to generate still more "meaningful" accomplishments. And it deflects attention away from adults' important goal of building up their egos. Even on a beach, where kids supposedly have full rein to be kids, most adults can get very irritated if their important work of getting a tan is interrupted—or even threatened with interruption—by running, shouting, sand-spraying, ball-throwing, happy children.

If you say to most adults, "Why are you so happy today?" they can give you a reason—the one they have just been thinking about. But if you ask young children the same question, they often seem caught off guard by the notion that you need a reason to be happy. Little kids simply don't analyze why they feel happy, or why they make everything into a game, or why they see the difference between fairness and unfairness so clearly. To varying degrees, **children come into the world carrying the light of happiness with them.** Even in detention camps, areas of mass starvation, war zones, and areas of extreme poverty and squalor you usually can find at least a few children playing, a few children who are happy.

In the presence of a world stooped by crushing problems, childish behavior often appears insensitive, selfish, rude, or deliberately tormenting. At best it seems foolish. "Good" children are children who are "emotionally balanced," "responsible," and "well adjusted." They "present few problems" because they do "what the situation requires." And yet, the "obvious demands of the situation" are obvious to only one person. Ten other adults would interpret the same circumstances ten other ways. Even the same adult in a different mood would read the situation differently.

Situations are not logical. They don't "dictate" a given response. And the younger children are, the more likely they are to respond to their core rather than to the "logic of events."

About fourteen years into our marriage, Gayle developed severe hypoglycemia, which went undiagnosed for several years. Periodically she would collapse, too weak to get up. Her heart would beat irregularly and she would lie wherever she was, in great discomfort and fear, until either she was discovered or the attack passed. Once this happened when she was at home with John. He was one and a half at the time and discovered her in the bathroom lying on her back and moaning. He went to the shelf where we kept various medications and brought back a tube of CortAid. He opened it and started rubbing the ointment on Gayle's forehead, saying over and over "Poor Mommy. Poor Mommy."

On the level of "what the situation requires," John's actions were foolish. Gayle's problem had nothing to do with the skin on her forehead, and any adult would have recognized that. And yet, while the doctors, Hugh, and all of Gayle's adult acquaintances had stood by for two years doing nothing—because they said they didn't know what to do—a little child had acted unequivocally and had done so with gentleness and love. The result was that Gayle's strength started coming back almost immediately and she was able to crawl to the phone to call for help.

Most adults have very rigid ways of identifying goodness and spirituality, and these definitions blind them to their children's obvious strengths. We suggest that you consider doing what we have done for several years now: Take long moments to sit back and watch your and other people's children in stillness. Whenever we are around a child, especially in public places—restaurants, stores, parks, car washes, movies—we become inwardly still the way a birdwatcher might become when catching sight of a rare and beautiful specimen. "Here is a visitor from heaven. What does this child have to teach me?" Then we watch closely and try to take in the child on his own terms, not on ours.

This last summer Stacy and Jeff took their boys, Collin (sixteen) and Sean (eleven), to see the Grand Canyon. Jeff and Stacy are old friends of ours and probably the wisest parents to walk the earth in ten thousand years. Our family met theirs in Sedona on their way back to Santa Cruz, and they told us about their trip and several interesting insights they had gained about children and parenting. Having a book to write, we were all ears.

Stacy and Jeff's boys were not particularly excited about seeing the Grand Canyon ("Who wants to drive for days to see a big hole?"—Collin), but it was an opportunity to connect with two other couples and their kids that they didn't get to spend much time with. And, besides, all the parents thought it would be "good" for the kids to see the Grand Canyon ("How does it make us good?"—Sean).

The parents (not the kids) chose the North Rim, which is considered to be more spiritual by many adults because fewer adults come there. And because it doesn't have all the fast-food restaurants, tourist shops, and other things that kids like. What it has is camping and hiking, which make adults feel spiritual just thinking about them ("What's the big deal about camping? I'll just sleep in the car."—Collin).

The first morning, the parents woke up all the kids while it was still dark and announced that they were all going to hike to Bright Angel Point to watch the sun rise. Not one of the kids wanted to go. They all wanted to sleep (not spiritual) and then play cards (definitely not spiritual). But the adults knew what was best for them, and so off all three families went.

When they got there they saw that Bright Angel Point included a huge rock and that the children of all the other parents who had come had escaped and were climbing all over it. Jeff and Stacy noted that not one child ever looked at the sunrise except for a few obligatory seconds whenever one of the parents would yell at them to look at it.

None of the adults seemed able to get comfortable the whole time that the sun was rising. Inconsiderate Mother Nature had not provided any rock La-Z-Boys, and then there were those pesky, unappreciative kids of theirs whom they thought they had done a better job of raising than this. Leaving the whole uplifting experience—which the adults knew was over because the sun had risen but their unenlightened kids thought was not over because they were still having fun—Stacy and Jeff saw one irate mother dragging her three-year-old girl by the arm and yelling "It's erosion! It's erosion! Your problem is you have no appreciation of beauty!"

The next morning someone suggested that they should all go to Sublime Point (we're not making these names up), but by then Stacy and Jeff had learned their lesson. They said they would stay with the kids and play cards, which they did and were far happier than they had been the morning before. As a result, they decided to spend less time at the Grand Canyon and instead stop at Whisky Pete's, a casino in Nevada, which has no hiking or camping and where you have to stretch your neck around a building in order to see a sunrise. What Whisky Pete's has is a gigantic swimming pool with water slides, a Ferris wheel, a log ride, and a huge roller coaster that goes right through the casino. Stacy and Jeff didn't gamble at Whisky Pete's; they didn't even have whisky. But they did feel the circle of God's light that binds their family, and it was larger than the Grand Canyon.

Nothing is happier than the experience of God, and if you will relax and simply drink in your child, you will see that you have been sent a playful, happy, and very very funny little person. If your child is much older or if you have in your care an emotionally or physiologically damaged child, your peaceful watching can still unveil the glow of God's presence, although you may have to look gently past a great deal of ego nonsense, or even destructiveness, before this other part of your child comes into focus. However, once you recognize it, you will understand why children are in a position to be our teachers and guides as surely as we are in a position to be theirs.

ACHIEVING ONENESS WITH OUR CHILDREN

Oneness is not easy to experience within a culture that believes as strongly in separation as ours does, but it *is* possible. For those of us who are parents, a growing sense of where minds join is perhaps a little less difficult to achieve within our relationship with our own kids than it is within many other types of relationships. However, in order to experience God, it is never necessary that the child to whom we commit carry our blood. All children—whether they are adopted, step, or foster; whether we are their coach, teacher, in-law, or faithful friend—are equally endowed with the potential to transform us, to lift us straight into what has traditionally been called Heaven or the knowledge of God.

Obviously, many parents will find it easier initially to love "their own flesh and blood," but this reaction is not universal and certainly is not a "natural law." One father, whose mother had been adopted, who had grown up with an adopted sister, and who now has an adopted daughter of his own, told us that he believes it's easier to love an adopted child. He said, "I feel more responsible for her because she was abandoned, as, in a sense, are all kids put up for adoption. I also feel that I owe her a great deal because I *intervened*, even though she was merely the child who was assigned to me, the one who happened to come up at that time. But no one forced me to take her. I stepped forward and *chose* to undertake her care, to assume complete and final responsibility for this particular child." He also added, "I think it's easier to love an adopted child in a *pure* way because you aren't tempted to believe you are loving yourself."

The temptation this father speaks of—the desire to add to, to extend, to "fulfill," the ego—lures many people into having children for the wrong reasons. They think, "I have a right to experience anything I want to and this is an experience I haven't had." Or they think, "Our relationship has gone flat; maybe a baby would breathe new life into it." Or they think, "I have low self-esteem and I need someone who will love me, someone who will think I'm the most important person in the world." The dictate of the ego-centered psychology of our times is that our first consideration must be our own ego needs, not our concern for children.

We met Terrianne Jacobson when she became Jordan's second-grade teacher. In California, Jordan's first-grade teacher had taken an early dislike of him (perhaps unconsciously, judging by our conversations with her) and had worked to turn his classmates and the parents of his friends against him. Fortunately that teacher left in the middle of the school year, which was about the time we were thinking of taking him out of that school to get him away from a destructive situation that we seemed unable to change. The teacher who took her place saw, without our ever having to mention it to her, the mistake the first teacher had made and went out of her way to heal the damage.

The public school in Tucson that Jordan entered for the second grade has a principal who is more open to parents than some others we have known, and we were able to talk to her about Jordan's history and the kind of teacher we hoped he could have. She assigned him to Terrianne's class.

The school initiated a two-year continuation program at about that time, and Jordan was able to have Terrianne for the third grade as well. We realized early on that she was an unusually gifted teacher. For Jordan's sake as well as for our own enlightenment, we spent as much time in her class and with her personally as we could. In the classroom she was able to create what we as parents must create in our homes: a true family from which no member felt excluded. That becomes possible only when the importance of each child is recognized.

The essence of this kind of parental attitude is beautifully interwoven into the pages Terrianne wrote for us on the subject of the single mother's dilemma over day care. As we read this we were struck by the absence of distinction not only between her biological child (Mark) and her adopted children (Kolby, Jamie, and April), but between her feelings for her own children, for herself, and for the children of others. Real love jumps the perceived distance between all living things. Within families, this happens automatically when the needs of children are cherished as deeply as the needs of adults. When parents adopt this attitude, their life is made a little easier, but it is not made easy. In Terrianne's words:

Kolby and Mark were nine and nineteen months old, and as I was preparing to go back to work, I was forced to admit that although the sitter I had been using would never hit or abuse them, my boys were now at an age that demanded a more stimulating environment. They also needed a caregiver who could recognize their dear and emerging spirits. And yet I felt the heavy pull of inertia and hopelessness. Like countless mothers, I was in the horrible situation of needing to return to work regardless of the cost to my children, and yet for my own peace of mind I had to find a good child care setting and find it quickly.

I began an almost frantic round of phone calls to friends and acquaintances for recommendations. I begged one dear friend to quit her job and take care of my babies. I felt a deep terror that left my heart pounding as I realized I was being forced to leave my babies in a situation that I would not have adequate time to assess. Who could possibly step in with such short notice and give my boys the adoration and acceptance they deserved? Doesn't the deep love that allows us to treasure our children despite full diapers, dirty faces, wet beds, spilled milk, and temper tantrums, have to grow over time? Is this relationship guaranteed merely because we pay someone to care? Merely because it's their job? Obviously not.

When Mark and Kolby were tiny infants, they spent a lot of time asleep on my chest. Their little baby-fat bodies melted into my ample bosom. I would marvel at the sweet peace of those times. I could tell that they were absorbing love from the very tissues of my body and soul. They were surrounded and engulfed in love. They knew nothing else. I noticed, too, that when someone who did not particularly care for them held them, they did not relax and soon fussed to be returned to me. It was not reasonable for me to expect a paid baby-sitter to give them the same quality of care I could give.

Nevertheless, I had run out of money and had to go back to work. At the suggestion of several people, I visited a popular day care center in Tucson. I had heard many good things about it. They had a program for little babies like Kolby and a high adult-to-baby ratio. There was also a toddler setting for Mark, and this is where we spent our time observing. What I saw made my heart ache, and even now, two years later, it can still bring tears to my eyes. I did not see any children treated harshly. I simply saw ten one-to-two-year-olds who were strangers to their caregivers. The children were not cherished; they were a commodity. When they came in from the sandbox, they were all placed on chairs around a table and water bottles were put in front of them. No one talked to them, or asked if they were thirsty, or encouraged them to have a cool drink.

I was struck by the children's silence. I remember one little girl in particular. She sat on her chair, looking like a doll. She didn't drink water. She sat through the scheduled diaper changes. She sat through hand washing. She sat as plates of food were placed in front of each child. She didn't eat. She didn't move. Because she made not a sound and did nothing else to attract attention, she sat alone on her chair without human contact. No one spoke to her, no one said her name, no one looked into her huge brown eyes. And of course no one realized that she had not eaten. When the plates were cleared away she continued to sit. She was waiting, barely breathing. She was waiting for her mama. She was waiting, and in the meantime she was invisible. She had taken her bright little soul, the treasure of herself, and hidden it away from those who did not know her. I wondered how many weeks or months could this little star remain in a day care facility before she became dull and the twinkle of her being just disappeared?

The room where these children stayed was filled

with bright baskets of toys, tumbling mats, and climbing equipment. Naturally drawn to these wonderful playthings, Mark tentatively reached for a basket of toys. Although no one said anything to him, I saw him pull his hand back and decide not to play. He felt the rules in the room. This was not the time to play. At nineteen months he felt that he could do something wrong. As we left the building, quiet tears ran down his cheek and I knew he had also felt the unbearable loneliness.

Though I eventually found a baby-sitter whom Kolby and Mark came to love, I could not escape my perception that leaving them for eight hours every day was unnatural. I continued to suffer, despite the good care they were receiving, and I felt jealousy and guilt when I talked to mothers who were able to stay home with their kids. At this same time, I also began noticing the differences in children at the school where I taught. Although there were exceptions, most of the kids who had a parent waiting for them at home seemed decidedly lighter and brighter in spirit. They left their classrooms at the end of each day with excitement and anticipation, whereas the children who had only day care to look forward to lingered and seemed reluctant to move on. Naturally, at the end of a long school day, they were tired and wanted to go home.

I have had several opportunities to observe Jordan Prather's homecoming at the end of a school day. Although the bus lets the kids out only two blocks from his house, Hugh and Gayle always walk down to meet him, the only parents who do so at that bus stop. They are obviously delighted to see him and eager to hear about his day. Their home is infused with a sense of welcome and of Jordan's importance. I would find myself comparing this to my own children's after-school hours.

Unlike many single parents, being a schoolteacher I at least was able to stop work at the same time my own children got out of school, but then I had to dash to the sitters to pick up my two boys, drive a very long distance to pick up my daughter Jamie in her after-school program, then I had to run my errands for the day, hoping all the while that my oldest daughter April would be home when we got there and not off with friends or at some neighbor's house. Finally we would arrive home, tired, hungry, and with no welcome. All I wanted to do was put my feet up and watch the news. But that was never possible. I had dinner to fix, and yet the babies always seemed to fuss at this time of day. In trying to get my girls to help out, I would end up snapping at them.

I didn't have the energy to provide anyone with a sense of welcome. We were all hurting, bristling with the effects of separation, and missing the welcome mat and the peace of a homecoming. It all felt wrong to me. The need for a steady income was mixed up with the need to be a complete mother to my children, especially since I was the only parent they had or probably ever would have. Yet until I could figure out something else, this was simply the situation. If I was going to improve our after-school relationships, I had to start where I was and not divide my focus between what I had and what I regretted not having. What I had was four wonderful children. That is where I decided to begin.

Terrianne eventually worked out a way of earning a living without having to leave her home for long periods. It took her many months to accomplish this, and she believes that if she hadn't first focused on improving the after-school atmosphere among the five of them, she would have lacked the motivation to do it. Remaining in the present generates great energy, as little children themselves demonstrate. The improvement came because she made it her priority. She was clear about just what mind-set she wanted during these difficult periods.

Terrianne was able to come up with alternative jobs not only because she was determined to do so, but also because she is an unusually talented and energetic person. Most of us do well just to keep the job we have. However, we all can work to improve the tone within our home. Doing so is largely a matter of recognizing the importance of children, a subject that is given lip service by almost everyone but has never been deeply addressed by our culture.

THE HIGHER CALLING OF CHILD CARE

The unimportance of children is evident even in minor aspects of our society. For example, we have had to look for a home several times since our boys were born. During this period we have seen the relative size of children's and adults' bedrooms change to the point where the "master bath," or even sometimes the "master walk-in closet," is now almost the same size as the standard child's bedroom. In the house we now rent, which was built as a spec home, all three children's bedrooms would fit easily into the "master suite."

Ostensibly because of the increased danger of children being outdoors, the trend in middle- and upper-income homes is to make children play in their rooms. Yet adults, who are free to leave home without permission, are provided not only with a huge bedroom that goes unused during the day, but a separate den, living room, or library. Even the kitchen in many households is essentially a private playroom for adults only. There is no rationale for dividing and using space this way except children's unimportance.

In many homes children are not prized as much as the family pet. Just before we moved to Tucson, John's friend Tony was grounded for "snapping" at his father. Because there was a "family" rule that Tony was never to talk back to his parents, John was deprived of the opportunity to say good-bye to his best friend. We tried to intervene on John's behalf, but Tony's mother said that he had to "learn responsibility" and that maybe he could call John in Arizona.

John, who was eleven at the time, noticed that

Tony's parents made allowances for a dog that they didn't make for their own child. The small terrier mix that they had purchased before Tony was born had not just "snapped" at but had bitten two people that very week. Fortunately she was small enough that the damage she inflicted was minor.

In both instances the parents had excused the dog and blamed the victims; in fact, they had even laughed about how terriers as a breed tend to bite and that "you would think that everyone would know this." You also would think that most parents would notice how much difficulty *adults* have controlling their tongues and make allowances for a child's occasional angry outburst. Tony's parents haven't made this connection because they don't think that childhood is a subject they need to bother thinking about.

Gayle was in a supermarket recently and the woman who was pushing a cart about halfway down the aisle in front of her suddenly noticed something she wanted. She left her cart in the middle of the aisle and bent over to try to read the label on a box of cans that was on the bottom shelf. Unable to see it clearly, she started to kneel down on the floor. She was in the process of doing this when she looked up and saw Gayle. Immediately she stood and apologized for blocking the aisle, then moved away from her cart so Gayle could get by.

Two or three minutes later Gayle happened to be passing by that aisle again and noticed that the woman was on one knee examining the same box of cans. This time, however, a little boy of about three or four was standing a few feet away from her waiting to get by. Gayle watched to see what would happen.

A moment later the woman looked up at the boy and said, "Are you still there? Why don't you go around to the other aisle?" Which the boy promptly did.

Like many parents, if this woman had children she

probably would get upset if one of her kids got down on the supermarket floor. And being aware of her importance as an adult, she might become furious if a child who was on the floor blocking the aisle were to use the same words and tone of voice on her that she had used on the little boy. The reason is clear. Since children are not important, their needs and desires are not important.

Because it doesn't lead to money or success, child care is so looked down on by our culture that, in terms of the actual number of hours spent doing the job, a beginning teacher is paid less than many *unskilled* manual laborers. Those parents who stay at home to care for their kids— sometimes at enormous sacrifice—are considered unemployed. This means that in most people's minds they are doing *nothing*—regardless of the hypocritical nod that our society now gives to this "occupation" in modern census and survey forms.

It's unrealistic to think that you are not personally influenced by this attitude and that it has no effect on the limits of your patience with your children. But what if God were to appear before you and say "Your child is your way home"? God *is* before you, and that is the call you have already heard in your heart. Are you not a child of God? Are *you* not held in the arms of God? Only if you see child care as a sacred calling will you rise completely beyond the effects of the widespread indifference to children.

Remember that the call you hear applies no less to your teenager or your adult child than to a passive infant you can play with when you are in the mood. No natural limit has been placed on your capacity to love any girl or boy you choose to love. Your previous history with this child is irrelevant. Whether the two of you bonded at birth is irrelevant. Nor is there any law as to how long it must take you to begin experiencing oneness with this child. Because you are cherished by God, you can cherish a child of God. Some circumstances are more difficult than others; some will seem almost impossible; but never is this because a force, or condition, or law, exists that requires the difficulty. Miracles of love are possible because God's heart is your heart.

Creating a bond with our children is not up to them; it's up to us. This doesn't imply that we must neglect our own needs. (See Chapter 3, "Meeting Your Needs.") In fact, it implies no particular effect or behavior of any kind. But it does require us to recognize that within this one instant, our capacity to love is limitless and that any effort we make to look gently upon a child will not be made alone. All the host of Heaven will assist your every gentle impulse.

Nothing in blood itself facilitates the experience of God. In addition to the physical and personality traits that we can recognize as coming from our own gene pool—traits so prized by our ego—our blood also can transmit "bad genes," addictive substances, harmful chemicals, lethal viruses, and numerous other damaging factors. Blood is manufactured by the body—not by the spirit—and it will have whatever meaning we want it to have.

Regardless of a child's genetic makeup or degree of birth trauma, parents who consistently look past the body to the spirit—who "honor the light, not the lamp shade," as Jerry Jampolsky says—will help dissipate their child's ego as well as their own. There is no higher calling or happier life work. From a spiritual standpoint, child care is as important as feeding the hungry, healing the sick, or raising the dead. You simply cannot honor your God without putting your child first.

2

WHAT ARE PARENTS FOR?

OUR BASIC PURPOSE

Because they have a superior knowledge of how to play a team sport, most coaches assume they also know best how to motivate the kids who come out for the team. This is similar to the assumption many "breadwinners" make. Because they bring the most money into the marriage, they assume that they know better than their partner how to spend, save, or manage that money. It's also like the attitude that partners who bring a child into a marriage (from a previous marriage or through giving birth) sometimes have: They think they know better than their spouse how to guide, correct, comfort, or nourish that child.

Because this type of assumption can be so strong, it came as a surprise when a baseball coach in California (we'll call him Art) turned to us for advice. His pony-league team (a nonschool league for young teenagers) was near revolt. It was the most talented team he had ever coached; it had the best record at this point in the season; and he believed it had an excellent chance of going to the state championship and winning. However, the more games the team won, the "crazier" the kids became. At the time he called us, the team was in emotional chaos and several of the boys were threatening to quit.

We agreed to give him our thoughts, and after observing several practices and a couple of his games, we made some suggestions. We include these in this chapter because **the basic *nature* of the relationship an adult has with a child should remain the same regardless of the context of the relationship.**

From our observations, it appeared that Art's way of relating to his players suffered from the same disruptive factor that we have observed within many parent-child relationships: a conflicted purpose. He had opposing aims and yet seemed unaware of this. He would call a boy a "wimp" and a moment later would pat his back in apparent contrition. He would scream at his kids to slide during practices—even though the field he used was very rough—then would seem genuinely concerned about the gashes they got. He would badger, sometimes even humiliate, his infielders to step in front of a sharply hit ground ball (so that if they missed, their bodies would block it), yet we knew that the previous season he had spent three days beside the hospital bed of one of his players whose cheek and eye socket were fractured by a wild pitch.

Just as this man had never asked himself in any deep way "Why am I a coach?" most parents are very resistant to looking at the question "Why am I a parent?" They believe that they are already operating from proper motivation. They would feel insulted if anyone directly asked them, "Do you know why you are a parent *today?* Do you know what desires influence you *today?*"

Parenting is the outcome of moment-by-moment decisions. Moms and dads who remain aware of their ego are conscious of the many impulses or "voices" within them on which they can base these choices. They *want* to know from what feelings they are about to act. It is second nature for them to ask, What is a parent for? What is a parent's purpose and function? What do I *want* to guide me in this situation today? And yet, just as this coach had never deeply considered why he coached, most parents *never* search their hearts with this type of inquiry. They not only assume that they are already doing it right, they think that the questions that plague them are perfectly understandable: "Am I too permissive?" "Is my husband too strict?" "Should I get flash cards for the baby?" "Will our seven-year-old end up living a life of crime?" "Will we make our daughter financially dependent if we support her after her divorce?"

But note that all these worries are directed at outcomes, at consequences, at appearances, at "how things will work out." None of them addresses the question of the state of mind, the state of heart, of the parent now, today. Returning to our example of Art, the baseball coach, his conscious concerns did not relate to the well-being of his kids but to how aggressively they played; whether they got to practice on time; whether they stepped into the pitch when they hit; whether they "got their butts down" when they fielded; and especially whether, at any given moment during a game, they were ahead in runs.

Before we tried to help him discover his most deeply felt purpose in being a coach, we encouraged him to explore his concerns about results. We asked him what he was trying to *accomplish* as a coach. He said, "Well, I'm trying to get the boys to play better baseball. God knows they make enough mistakes. That's what a coach does; he teaches basic tactics and skills."

Many coaches assume that is their main role, just as **many parents assume that their primary function is to teach**

**their child how to approach life successfully in the real
world**—in other words, how to "grow up," how to feel and
act "like an adult." So we began by exploring the goal he
had stated.

We asked Art questions about the outcomes he personally expected to come from his kids' improved skills.
Did he think, for instance, that he would assist in the development of a major-league ballplayer? If he believed that was
a possibility, what about the other kids on his team he knew
did not possess that potential? What was his purpose in
improving their skills? What did he expect learning to play
better baseball to do for his *average* kid—and, more to the
point, what did he expect it to do for *him*?

We then had Art consider how important his status among
parents and other coaches was to him. We wanted him to
think about the following scenario. If his team made it to
the state championships and if his only good pitcher was
slightly injured, would he have the boy pitch and risk permanently damaging his arm—even if the risk was small and
even if not taking it would mean losing the championship?

We knew that Art's answer would be no if we simply
asked this as a quick, hypothetical question. In fact, the situation we described was very close to one that existed on
Art's team at that time. He had several good pitchers but
only one of them was overpowering, and that boy had
proven to be the most injury prone. So we guided Art
through a fantasy about making the kind of decision that
might come up concerning this boy.

We described the day of the championship as vividly as we could so that Art could feel for himself his resistance to protecting one of his players when so much was at
stake. Under circumstances like this—even imagined circumstances—any normal person will feel some resistance,
but we also wanted Art to recognize that resistance was not
all he felt.

When we had led Art up to the point of making the decision whether to put this boy in to pitch, we asked him to pause and look directly at his resistance—his resistance to putting him in and his resistance to not putting him in. We also asked him to attempt to feel what fears were behind all of this. In other words, was there anything about these choices that scared him?

For most coaches to admit that they are afraid of anything is not easy, and this is also true of most parents. "Of course I'm not afraid! How could I be afraid of something that involves a mere child?" Yet you can be certain that an unconscious fear is behind any resistance you feel. Don't hesitate to look at it; simply looking at it is often enough to allow you to make your decision in peace.

What Art saw was that his fear wasn't losing face within the fraternity of coaches, it was losing his "backbone," his "guts," his identity, his core. If he succumbed to compassion, he was afraid he would begin "walking down the road to Wimpsville," as he put it. The very meaning of being a man, he explained, was dependent on making "hard decisions." But now he realized that his ego had only one definition of "hard," and that was "compassionateness." The really hard decision, he said, would be *not* to put the boy in. Now he would truly be a man, because **true men are men that boys can trust.**

On a smaller scale, choices that are intrinsically the same as Art's come up for parents throughout the day: Should they insist that their daughter complete an "important" homework assignment even though the hour is late and she is tired and emotionally upset? Should they make their little boy change his "inappropriate" shirt even though he picked it out and got dressed all by himself? During a "crucial" soccer match, should they yell out to their goalie daughter that she is standing too far back in the goal, even though they know that this would embarrass her?

Mothers and fathers who monitor their feelings can

spot these moments easily and thus be in a position to make each decision without conflict. Unless they are aware of their superficial feelings and the fears behind them, they are likely to be controlled by them. But **it is never necessary to battle your ego emotions. Doing so will only strengthen your belief that they characterize your identity.** All you need do is pause long enough to experience a deeper, more central level of feeling than fear. Having done that much, you now have a choice as to which level of feeling you wish to act out.

The mind is always capable of producing conflict—in fact, a part of our mind is always in conflict. Nevertheless, any decision can be based on peace and clarity—*if* we consciously choose that ground to stand on. When parents sacrifice their child's well-being to some other consideration, they will always lose their peace.

First, they need to be aware of their ambivalence. Second, they need to become deeply conscious of the fear behind the ambivalence. Third, they need to make the most loving choice they are capable of at that moment. And fourth, they must honor the goodness or holiness of the process they have gone through and not reconsider. Only if the situation itself changes do they reconsider.

As with all spiritual guidelines given in this book, making a decision from peace or declining the temptation to sacrifice the well-being of our child does not translate into behavioral rules. For example, this does not mean that we must continue to enforce a rule that isn't working, or that we must never be firm in the face of our child's anger, or that putting our child in a difficult situation is always a mistake. Kids need to get shots, go to the dentist, go to school, brush their teeth, get up in time for appointments, and a hundred other necessities that are difficult for them and that they may not like doing. A true guideline is always an internal one and usually boils down to this: Look closely at the conflict, then take the time to be clear about what you want to do.

This rule is so vital to spiritual parenting that we elaborate on it in many ways throughout this book. But we want you to know that we have failed to follow this advice on several occasions, especially when we were younger and didn't fully understand its importance.

THE ONE-MINUTE SACRIFICE

One such instance occurred when John was ten and Jordan was five. We had scheduled a new and well-recommended baby-sitter. However, when we met her, both of us felt that there was something a little off about her. The feeling was not strong; we didn't plan to be gone long; the social engagement we needed to attend was important; and we didn't have time to get another baby-sitter. So, after giving her instructions that she was not to let the boys go outside, we left.

When we returned, we discovered that not only had she let them go outside, but Jordan's dog, Tigger, who was his best friend and constant companion, had been run over and killed as a result.

When we had felt uneasy, if we had taken a moment to become clear about what we wanted to do, perhaps we would have decided not to go; perhaps we would have taken the boys with us; perhaps we would have given the baby-sitter instructions so strong and unequivocal that she would have followed them; perhaps we would have thought of still another alternative. But we didn't sacrifice that one minute; as a result, it took us six years and several false starts before we found another animal (a Siamese cat named K.J.) that Jordan bonded with as deeply as he had with Tigger.

At the time, our decision not to pause and pray seemed an insignificant betrayal of our kids. Likewise, most of the choices parents are presented with throughout the day seem of little or no consequence. And, considering only the outward results, that may be an accurate assessment. Obviously, acting in conflict usually does not produce an outcome this dramatic, but on a spiritual level the effects are cumulative and strong. Whenever we make anything more important than our child, we take another step back from love and therefore back from the experience of God.

At the conclusion of the guided fantasy, Art told us that he would not allow the injured boy to pitch, but he also said that he was surprised that while imagining having to make such a decision, a question arose in his mind about what course he wanted to take. The fantasy allowed him to recognize at least a little of his conflict between his fear of losing his identity or manhood and his deeper desire to protect and care for his kids. The resistance he felt informed him of the tension between these two motives.

As a way of allowing him to explore his feelings for children more deeply, we followed the fantasy with a series of questions.[1] Here is a condensed version of the exchange:

Q: Again, Art, why do you want to coach baseball?
A: Well, I love baseball, and I like helping kids get better at it.
Q: If you would close your eyes and picture your kids getting better at it . . .
      Now that you can imagine your kids improved, with your eyes still closed, say to yourself, "Now that my kids are better at baseball, what else do I want as their coach? Is there anything else I want for them, for me, or for anyone else?" Please take all the time you need to sense what the answer would be.
A: Yes, I want them to get still better.
Q: Okay then, imagine them getting better and better until they are as good as you could ever want. (*Art does this.*) Now say to yourself, "What more do I want as

their coach? Now that my kids are so good that I can't imagine them getting any better, what else do I see myself wanting, what else do I *feel* myself wanting?" Take your time. . . .

A: Well, I want them to win games. They don't have to win all their games, but I'd like them to have a winning season, maybe go to state and win there too.

Q: All right, imagine them winning all the games you could possibly want, and when you can picture that, ask yourself, "Now that they have won all the games I could ask for, what more do I want as their coach?"

A: (*After pausing a moment, Art laughs and opens his eyes.*) I want them to be happy. You'd think I would have thought of that before. But I do want that. I love baseball. I want them to love it as much as I do.

Q: Let's follow this up in the same way, Art. Picture all the members of your team very happy and really loving baseball. . . .

A: Yeah, I can see that now.

Q: Okay, now that they are happy, what else do you want—either for them, for yourself, or in any other way?

A: I want to enjoy it myself. I haven't really enjoyed coaching the way I did when I first started—with the little tykes, you know. They're so funny. We had fun. Even the parents had fun at that level, the T-ball level.

Q: So you would like to enjoy it. Sounds like you'd like the parents to enjoy it too. (*Art nods.*) So now we've got you happy, the kids are happy, and the parents are having fun too. Take a moment to picture what that would be like, to feel what it would be like, then ask yourself, "Now that I have this, what more do I want?"

A: Not to sabotage it. Boy, do I do a lot of things that keep this from happening. There's no need to get angry at them all the time. It doesn't make the parents feel good either. That's what baseball is all about. It's a great, great game; it's not a fucking war.

Q: Okay now, Art, we've made a lot of progress here, but please close your eyes and see your kids with good skills, winning games, enjoying it, you enjoying it too, even the parents enjoying it—and you don't do anything to reverse that. Spend a moment imagining such a scene, then ask yourself, "Now that I have all of this, what else do I want?" (*After a few minutes of silence, Art slowly opens his eyes.*)

A: Peace.

Q: Just peace?

A: Just peace. I would really like peace.

Q: I think you can have it, Art. I think you've already got a pretty good idea how to go about it.

A: (*Art is now very softly crying.*) Yep, I guess I always did know.

A coach who would cry in front of two parents is a very unusual one. Even a coach who would ask for comments about his team's state of mind is highly unusual. But the deep feelings that most adults have for children—feelings that at first seem lost to so many but are actually just below the surface—are universal and very strong. In a sense, this is what unites us as a human family. For thousands of years it has been understood that we work for our children; we save for our children; we protect what we have for our children; and at the end of our lives, all we have is passed on to our children.

Of course, the mistake we made in the past was applying this ideal mainly to money and property. But actually it has been so much more than possessions that we have longed for our kids to have. Because we are the keeper of their future, we want them to have a family they can rely on. We want them to grow up in a real home. We want a safe world where they can live out their lives. We want a healthy environment where they can stay healthy. We want them to have a good and faithful partner. We want them to be financially and emotionally secure. We want them to know a wisdom that will guide them well, that will steer them around so many of the mistakes we ourselves made. And underlying everything that we can imagine about their *situation* in life, we want more than all else for them to come home to God, where we will wait in peace for their return, each and every one.

How do we work to bestow such an inheritance on our children? We love them; we understand them; we respect them; we honor them. We commit absolutely to never losing sight of their basic nature, no matter what age or stage they are in. We do this even when as adolescents and adults they forget who *we* are. Perhaps they turn against us for unjustifiable reasons. Even then we don't turn against them. We do not forget who they are.

Unless there is at least one person who has unshakable faith in the core of innocence with which the child came into the world, the difficulties that are erected against that child's spiritual development are enormous and may not be overcome in a lifetime. This friend, supporter, believer, faith-giver, can be a brother or sister, a grandparent, an extraordinary friend, but by far the most natural and likely source is the individual's own parent or guardian. We agreed to this role when we chose to be this person's keeper, and our own spiritual completion is blocked as long as we fail to fill it.

PARENTING AS A SPIRITUAL CALLING

We have known Jon and Judy for many years, and we remember well the week they were given the news that Cynthia, their new baby girl, had a degenerative and inoperable heart defect. Their initial reaction was one of intense shock and confusion. They emotionally clung to Cynthia and to each other. They got second and third medical opinions. They cast about in their minds for someone to blame. But the diagnosis remained the same.

Then a curious thing happened. As the reality of Cynthia's condition sank in, they found themselves inwardly turning away from her and at times wanting to hold back even from touching her. They talked about this and realized that, as insane as it seemed, they felt betrayed by her. Judy said, "It was like being given the brightest star in Heaven but told that if I got too close it would turn me to ashes."

Judy and Jon are deeply devoted to their spiritual path, a type of Buddhism that teaches awareness and compassion. They already had some degree of awareness — they were aware of their resistance to loving Cynthia— but they had not yet opened their hearts to compassion. They explained to us later that instead of being moved by the fact that their child was dying in discomfort, they were more concerned with their own "imaginary suffering" over her death—"imaginary" because they had not yet suffered this loss.

After meditating on the nature of compassion as they had been taught, they decided that they would care for Cynthia as if every loving effort they made was a gift she could carry with her when she left and not a hollow gesture that would soon be rendered meaningless by her death.

When Cynthia turned two, Jon quit his job in a highly competitive and quickly changing area of computer programming. It was "career suicide," his immediate supervisor told him, but Jon felt that the time his work was taking away from being home left him, as he put it, "with no other moral choice." He started working from home, selling novelty telephones through the mail and over the phone.

Judy also quit her job as a teacher at a community college and began doing typing and writing grant proposals from home. Neither her nor her husband's business grew substantially, but they did remain stable sources of income. By selling their house and moving into a trailer park, they got by.

Jon and Judy's "sacrifice" lasted four years, almost twice as long as any doctor had predicted it would take for Cynthia to die. To their surprise, they didn't experience this period as a sacrifice or even as marking time. They have remarked frequently that in many ways, this was the happiest and most satisfying period of their lives. The love between the two of them also grew stronger, even though they had very little time for each other and their sex life was virtually put on hold.

It hasn't escaped Judy and Jon's attention that this period was also the time they were the most focused on giving happiness rather than getting it. In interviewing and working with parents in grief, we have heard many couples and single parents make similar remarks about the final weeks, months, or years that they gave to their dying child. Even in the midst of what was for many of them a nightmare, it was as if another story were being told that had a depth and beauty these parents will never forget.

Three days before her death, when both parents were in her room, Cynthia sat up in bed and spoke to them. That in itself was not remarkable; she could talk quite distinctly up until the day she died. What amazed them was how she spoke and the words she used. "It was not the voice of a four-year-old; it was the voice of wisdom," Jon told us.

Cynthia said, "I came to remind you. You remembered when you loved me." Then she lay back down and once again seemed to become a four-year-old. They told us that since her death, her words have "spread over all areas of our lives." Now they understand that "the memory" is in every person and in every situation. Or as they put it on another occasion: "Love has eyes. We see the divine where we already are—if we *express* the divine."

Because they are exposed to so many news stories, dramas, and books about individuals who become bitter and vengeful after the death of a loved one, many people might think that this was an unusual legacy for a couple to receive from a dying child. But it's not unusual, and that is the significance of children: They are much more than the world believes they are.

Several parents have told us stories similar to Jon and Judy's. For just a moment the dying child sheds its little costume and speaks the truth directly. Many parents also have experienced something similar when their kids were very young, and suddenly they say or do something that belies their age.

One evening, when Jordan was four, he complained about having to go to sleep. He said, "I wish God would stop talking to me at night." Gayle said, "But, Jordan, this is wonderful. It's wonderful that God talks to you." Jordan said, "No, it's not. He talks too long and he's got a weird name."

Hugh often put Jordan to bed, and when Gayle told him about this comment, he began asking Jordan what's-the-meaning-of-life kinds of questions. He discovered that if he asked these when Jordan was a little sleepy, he would give wise and helpful answers. These exchanges continued until he was almost seven. Jordan enjoyed doing this, and in fact would complain to Hugh if he went too long without "consulting the great Jordan."

Hugh had been telling Gayle about Jordan's answers for several weeks before she decided to ask a question of her own. First, she recited a very long list of her current problems. Then she said, "So, Jordan, what should I do?" Jor-

dan answered, "Problems do not exist. There are no
problems in God."

WHERE LOVE'S GUIDANCE LEADS

A thousand stories have been written about God's power.
And indeed Love is the only true and lasting force. A thousand hymns describe the wonders of God's creation. And
indeed all things eternal and real come from Love. In our
houses of worship we shout praises to God's name; we sing
of God's unfathomable wisdom; we preach the consequences of disobeying God's will. And in the sanctuary of
our minds, we dwell on the many ways we are not in accord
with the everlasting and we note each instant that we fall
short of the perfect and the pure.

This form of faith comes easily to us because it seems
to support our sense of how separate we are from God, how
small and different we seem compared to "the Almighty."
And surely nothing is more apparent in the world than our
separation from God! But is this, perhaps, an adult's idea of
worship, the notions of those who have long forgotten the
child's way of "receiving the kingdom of God"? Is it possible that these are not as much God's priorities as they are
the priorities of a worldly parent? So often we forget to
cherish our own children, so we think we must ask God to
remember to cherish us. We demand thanks and acknowledgment from our own children, and we assume God demands this continually from us. We insist that our own
children bow to our wisdom in all their ways, so surely God
insists on this same show of "obedience" from us.

And yet what could be more impossible than Love
forgetting to love? Even we do not forget *our* children. Of
all the worries we might have, none is more unnecessary
than the thought that Love could leave our side. Often we
feel like the last sheep, and yet God has promised that not

only will Love's heart be open forever, Love itself will lift us up and carry us home.

Perhaps the faithful within all the world's religions experience a similar difficulty in acknowledging that of all God's attributes, "the greatest of these is love," that love is God's first commandment, and that Love is God's very name. Whether this is true in other religions, certainly within Christianity the trouble we have believing that God loves us and that no matter how far we wander, we cannot pass beyond this Love, is particularly ironic, since the core event and forming image of our doctrines and rituals is a demonstration of God's love for *people*.

Perhaps if we look at this seminal event in mundane terms, we can grasp a little more of its meaning for us individually. Let's say that you have been my lifelong friend but that one day I betray you. This mistake, this "sin," makes me very sad indeed, but there is really nothing I can do, or so I believe. Although I long to mend the bond between us, there is no way to undo what I have already done.

But you come to me and say "Don't you realize that you are my friend? Don't you realize there is no mistake you could make that could stop me from loving you?"

"The betrayal was too great," I reply. "You may say that you have forgiven me, but you haven't. What I have done is impossible to forgive."

But you answer: "Since you don't believe my love for you, I will show it to you in a form you cannot deny. I have a child, my own flesh and blood. My child and I are so close that everything I know, my child knows. He is my joy, my completion, and my meaning. And yet I love you no less than my child. To prove to you that I forgive you, I will give you my child. I want you to kill him, and as you are killing him, he himself will tell you that I forgive you."

A love this great is beyond human comprehension. It is so far outside what we think we are capable of that at first it seems bizarre. Yet in the Bible this is precisely what God does. He gives His child to be crucified so that His love for us can never again be questioned. And as he hangs dying from the cross, His son evokes the complete and eternal forgiveness of God, not only for those who had betrayed him, but even for those who were mocking and torturing him at that very instant.

Maybe one of the reasons we can't imagine a love this deep is that in the Bible it appears that God's love is being compared to the love between a parent and child—and *that* is a love we think we know something about. We ask: "How could God be willing to give up His own son? How could any loving parent send a child to be destroyed?" Whether we are Christian or some other religion or no religion at all, the answer to that central question is what we fail to see as parents, especially in this culture and within the climate of our times.

The answer is that love does *not* sacrifice and it does *not* destroy. It doesn't harm the one who gives love, and it doesn't harm the one who receives it. Yet today we have come to believe that loving our children imperils our personal freedom and even our identity and risks making our child a weak, dependent nonperson. Anxiety has become the driving force of our parenting—and there is no love in anxiety.

We are all too familiar with "parental concern." We fear that having children will demand of us endless sacrifice: No more free evenings and weekends. No more leaving and returning as we wish. No more spending money on ourselves alone. No more time to pursue our long-term goals. In short, no more us. Once we have abandoned our dreams and succumbed to parenthood, we discover that our fear level has not decreased: A mistake in our child's nutrition could lead to a fatal illness. A mistake in discipline could create a sociopath. A mistake in education could wipe out entire career opportunities. As our children mature, we worry that if we don't push them out of the nest quickly enough, our sons will be emasculated and our daughters will become "caregivers." And once they are adults, we agonize over how little to advise them and how much to support them.

The biblical chronicle reflects real life far more accurately than does the current psychology of fear. This greatest of all love stories at first appears to be headed toward disaster—but it does not end there.

Before it is exercised, while it is still being merely contemplated, love will *always* appear to be a sacrifice. But the story will never stop there. It doesn't in the Bible and it doesn't in life. The Father's child is *given* but is not destroyed. God did not ask Abraham to destroy Isaac and God did not destroy Jesus. God does not lose His child, and His child does not receive destruction but instead receives everything. As was promised in Jesus' parable of the prodigal son, a parent's commitment *cannot* be broken: "My child, you are *always* with me, and all I have *is* yours."

The plain fact is that our kids can teach us things about the Place they have come from more easily than we can teach ourselves. Little children not only love their parents, they know with all their being that their parents love them. In working with families, especially families in which there is abuse, time and again we have been awed by the power of children's perception of the spiritual bond between themselves and their parents. Even when they are being horrendously mistreated, they refuse to believe that their parents don't love them. Each time we observe it, the amount and duration of abuse necessary to convince these kids otherwise amazes and inspires us all over again.

Judging by how many adults seek to go back and reconnect with parents who abandoned them, searching sometimes for years to locate them, we suspect that the spiritual knowledge of the connection between two people is never completely lost to anyone. It's interesting how often the adults who undertake these searches are happy with how their adoptive or foster parents have treated them. Being raised lovingly appears to make us *more* likely to seek out other love connections. These adult children often do not have childhood memories of the lost parent, but they will say, as one man was recently quoted in our local paper, "I will always think of [his adoptive mother] who raised me as my real mom, but I still want to find my natural mother." The untouchable connection between spirit and spirit, between soul and soul, between God and the children of God, is a gentle memory that lies quietly in every heart. When we choose to do so, we can awaken it and know love.

Does any of this mean that because you have a child you now must give up all the things you love to do? Does it mean you must let your child become a tyrant, the cruel princess or prince of your household? Does it mean that every whim and proclivity that kids have somehow carries more wisdom or spiritual correctness than the thoughts and desires of adults? Obviously not. But it does mean that there will be many times when it will *appear* that you must sacrifice your adult wishes for the welfare or happiness of your child.

The mistake we are now making is in thinking we know what giving *looks* like. Giving isn't getting on our hands and knees and wiping up the footprints of a little saint. It isn't necessarily more giving to say yes than to say no, to be permissive than to be firm, to disregard our own needs than to meet them. In fact, giving is not a mere behavior; it is a quality of the heart and mind. But the fear we now have about that quality is crippling our chances for personal happiness and growth; it is, in fact, keeping us from experiencing the kingdom of God.

In eternity, giving and receiving are one, but in the world of time, giving comes first. Eventually we see that where we expected sacrifice, our child left a gift; where we expected boredom, our child engendered a new interest;

where we expected a dead-end day, our child transformed it into fulfillment. In making these seemingly endless sacrifices, we received a reality far more lasting than we would have had we gone about our usual adult life in our usual adult way.

Children named the day of crucifixion Good Friday because they knew it was not the end of the story. And it was of children that Jesus said, "The kingdom of God belongs to such as these." It doesn't belong to those of a certain age but to those of a certain attitude: "Until you welcome the kingdom of God like a little child, you will not enter it." It is that simple.

PARENTING, THE IMPOSSIBLE TASK

This gentle rain of children has poured from the heavens for thousands of years, but as yet the world has not received it and been nourished. The soil of our hearts is very hard and resistant. Perhaps this is in part a result of the extraordinary difficulty the task of parenting presents to adults. Given the circumstances and mind-set that most adults are in when the time comes to have children, in many ways the newly arriving child asks the impossible. She asks the adult to change.

Consider for a moment the coming together of these two realities—the reality of the child and the reality of the adult. On the one hand, you have this little uncredentialed individual, this little nobody with obviously impaired physical and mental abilities, having no experience of its own from which to communicate, a mere child with a child's mind—a child's sense of fun, a child's sense of time, a child's sense of priorities—coming into the world wanting so fervently to be with his parents, to be loved by them, to play with them, to be friends with them, in fact caring about nothing else in life as much as his parents.

On the other hand, with remarkably few exceptions, by the time they reach the age to have children, adults have lost their child's mind, have developed a busy and complex life, have made past experience more important than present experience, have gotten caught up in many goals and desires in which children don't figure at all, have by now developed a radically different idea about what is fun, about how time should be spent, about what love looks like, about what life is for, and about the relative importance of this relationship that the child so ardently wants and, furthermore, expects!

Is that not an impossible situation? Adding to the problem is the fact that most parents enter some kind of midlife crisis right at the time their kids are entering adolescence. Later, adult children often ask for financial assistance after older parents have retired or have lost much of their earning potential.

To do the impossible and receive the gifts your child has brought you, *you* must meet your child on your child's level. You must at least *accept* his or her sense of love, time, fun, priorities, and values. And above all, you must see and work within your child's view of *your* function.

Don't be afraid to be the parent your child wants you to be. You don't have to wait to be asked. Furthermore, you must not make the mistake that most parents make and believe that your sense of reality is the only one that is valid and, therefore, your function is to make your child attitudinally and emotionally "mature" as quickly as you can.

The older parent should look carefully at the question: *What is money for?* Many moms and dads who have been generous all their lives suddenly become fearful and tightfisted at the end of their lives. This may be understandable, but is it God's guidance? Don't be afraid to pray about anything, to look deeply in your heart, and to receive your answer from the stillness of your being.

THE LEAST YOU CAN DO FOR YOURSELF

To our ego—that small, lonely part of our mind that focuses only on what it isn't getting, only on I, me, and mine—the concept of "oneness," even oneness with our own child, sounds like gibberish. Oneness is physically impossible and spiritually perplexing. In the world there has never been a single image of eternal oneness, and there never will be. This is the place of time in which all things end. However, once we had a general belief in the *possibility* of oneness, in the possibility of lasting unity and love. It didn't take us far, but it was something.

In the second half of the twentieth century, our society began to divide increasingly and deliberately along the lines of race, faith, gender, political party, and age. Religious leaders, cultural psychologists, prominent politicians, and speakers for various groups and causes took up the mindless battle cry that we must all separate from one another still further. Our faith in love, in devotion to one another, in simple generosity and fairness, has now become a strong distrust.

In fact, today it is fashionable to speak, sing, joke, and write quite forcefully against any reconciling approach to friendship, business, politics, homemaking, worship, and the care of others. Personal power, spiritual fulfillment, and financial success are now thought to flow from increased separation, "individuation," and selfism. And this unhappy shift in our thinking, which has almost destroyed meaningful marriage in this country, is beginning to infect the sacred bond between parent and child.

Since the 1960s, there has been a dramatic increase in runaways; parents are now giving back their adopted children in record numbers; kids are being quickly and repeatedly transferred from one foster home to another; the number of reports of child abuse has exploded; more fathers than ever are abandoning their families, never seeing their kids again, never even helping monetarily; mothers who are in a financial position to stay with their children are increasingly choosing not to; parents are reporting their kids to the police; and kids are beginning to sue their parents.

Yet all the while many authorities on children, religious authors, and the nameless thousands who call in to talk shows continue to equate love with authoritarianism, rigidity, and corporal punishment. The basic message that our culture gives to parents is slowly becoming: "Use whatever means you must to defend your own time and pleasure and don't hesitate to hammer your children into the shape you want. If this doesn't work, kick them out, turn them back, or at least shut them out emotionally. It's the least you can do for yourself."

This book is a call to parents to stand firm before the tide of me-ism and keep safe the one remaining relationship this philosophy has not polluted fully. At this time the call to give vent to our egos is very strong, but let us at least draw the line when the subject becomes our own children. We can see for ourselves what works and what doesn't. Surely we don't have to snatch the latest belief from the air and impose it on the most basic and intimate of all relationships.

Any two who look into their hearts will see that this child, this wonder who has come from their love for each other, unites them with something greater than themselves and thus can teach them as much about what is real and important as a thousand prescribed acts of prayer and contrition or ten thousand self-esteem workshops. Whether it is fostering, or fathering, or adopting, or bearing, within the experience of the coming of a child into one's life God stands before us and says, "There is indeed a place where you are not alone, and I have sent this little one to show you where it is."

Naturally, in the incredibly difficult and confusing task of rearing a child, we can quickly lose sight of this experience. But the memory of oneness is available to any parent in the most petty problems and distasteful decisions, and the light of its truth is an unfailing guide.

3

MEETING YOUR NEEDS

ACKNOWLEDGING YOUR LEVEL OF LEARNING

Our friend, whom we will call Joanna, is one of the most compassionate and balanced mothers we have ever known. In fact, she is so good at parenting that those who know her well affectionately call her Mother Guru. And yet, when her oldest daughter was fourteen months, Joanna tried to kill her.

Joanna and her husband, Kent, have a daughter who is four and a boy who is six. They also have a ten-year-old girl named Leeanne whose father, Joanna's first husband, died when Leeanne was just a baby.

Joanna was living in a one-room, half-bath apartment; her husband had been dead a year; she was trying to put food on the table by working at two minimum-wage jobs; and Leeanne would not sleep through the night. Every night she would wake up two or three times and call to her mother. Even if Joanna didn't get up, once she was awakened she couldn't get back to sleep. One morning, utterly exhausted, she was bathing Leeanne in the bathroom sink, trying to get her ready for day care, when she snapped. She had dunked Leeanne under the water to rinse out the shampoo. Then she watched herself remove her hand from her daughter's mouth and nose. And she watched herself continue to hold the child under water. She had made no conscious decision to kill her; rather, it was all happening as if someone else were doing it.

Just then the phone rang and Joanna took her daughter with her to answer it. The call was a wrong number, and when she hung up, Joanna fell to her knees, clutching Leeanne to her breast. She was shaking so badly that she fell to her side—but she didn't let go of Leeanne.

That day and the next Joanna spent on the phone. She called almost every church, temple, child-oriented charity, governmental agency, and friend that she had in the city. With the exception of the agencies, in each phone call she stated that she was so out of her mind with exhaustion that she had just tried to hurt her daughter, whom she loved more than anything in the world, and she desperately needed relief. By the end of the next day, Joanna not only had several people who were scheduled to relieve her periodically from child care, she even had backups. She also received some unexpected financial help.

This is an extreme example of what can happen (or almost happen) if we ignore our needs and let them build up. Often our reasons for doing so are well meant. We want to fulfill our ideal of what good parenting looks like, and taking time out to meet our own physical or emotional needs is not part of this picture. It seems self-indulgent and petty, and we think that if we just persist in the face of these inferior urges, we will suffer no bad effects. In other words, we make the very innocent and common mistake of believing we are spiritually further along than we are.

If you make this mistake in any form, you now want to remedy it, not only because of the delaying effects it can have on your spiritual progress but also because until you do so, you also will expect your children to be further along than they are. Knowing well and **being comfortable with your own ego is essential to seeing your children compassionately.**

WHAT ARE NEEDS?

The meaning of the word "need"—as used in everyday conversation—has expanded over the years to include almost all human motivation and emotion. Once the term referred mainly to "basic needs": psychological and physical instincts or drives. Now we hear phrases such as "I'm not getting my needs met" or "I have needs too!" Or more to the point: "That school doesn't understand children's needs" or "Is your relationship meeting your needs?"

The term "need" now covers nearly every interest we have or lack we perceive—even those suddenly hatched in our mind by a magazine article or a talk show. However, there are some impulses that our culture doesn't like to think of as needs. For example, a young woman and a young man fall in love and get married. Perhaps the young woman admires and adores the young man, and so he assumes the role of mentor or teacher within the relationship. As time passes, she begins to see weaknesses in her husband and also starts to feel boxed in by her role of pupil and devoted follower. The young man, on the other hand, has grown comfortable with his role, and when his wife tries to change the way they relate, he resists her.

When this dynamic plays itself out in the usual way, we might say that the young woman has a need for boundaries, to individuate, or to self-actualize. And in attempting to fulfill these needs, she may feel an additional need, the need to manipulate her husband in order to get her way. Manipulation is the need so often attributed to children, even though most kids lack the sophistication and deviousness necessary to be truly manipulative.

For his part, the husband might be characterized as having a need to control, to dominate, to be passively or actively aggressive. Or we might say that he has shown himself to be a rageaholic and has a need to be angry.

Interestingly, we don't say that at the start of the relationship the young woman had a need to admire or a need to adore or that the young man had a need to provide "the needed balance" to the relationship. Today, a need to admire, for example, would not be considered a "legitimate need," even though it is widespread and highly motivating. The need to *be* admired comes much closer to how we like to use the term.

If he were less typical, when his wife began to change, the young man might feel strongly that she should be allowed her freedom. We have known several married women and men and several parents of both younger and older children who have felt a strong urge most of their lives to give others their freedom, even including a misbehaving spouse or child. This urge sometimes outweighs the individuals' "better" judgment, and they act on it rather than from "common" sense. Surprisingly often, decisions so motivated don't have the disastrous consequences that friends or counselors predict they will.

Like all the impulses our culture treats as needs, this one also can be thwarted. For example, a father may not share a mother's urge to give their teenage daughter the freedom to dress and to style her hair as she desires. If he controls the money for clothes, allowance, activity fees, and so on, his wishes may prevail. Yet the mother's urge to give freedom may be as strong as the father's "need to control."

Despite the strength, persistence, and motivating

power of this urge in many people and despite the fact that it can be thwarted by external circumstances, there is no general recognition of the "need" to give others their freedom. Yet there are probably as many freeaholics as shopaholics or rageaholics.

These few examples by no means exhaust the ways that the term "need" is inconsistently applied in everyday speech. Our culture's classification of needs simply is not reliable. You may not have a need that a hundred parenting books assume you must have (for example, the need to get away from your child), and yet you may have other feelings that have not been singled out for attention, such as those we have just mentioned. Please do not worry about whether some persistent feeling you have is a "legitimate" need or whether it is negative or separating enough to be classified as anything at all.

MISCONCEPTIONS ABOUT THE NATURE OF NEEDS

Needs Are Not "Basic"

A lioness feels a need to kill, stalks and charges her prey, then makes the kill. She eats and shares the meat with other members of her pride. This need satisfied, she then lies down and dreams of fulfilling her next need: a new Lexus and a beach house in Malibu.

No?

Humans, however, can feel driven to climb an endless ladder of needs. This happens whenever our egos become fixated on any area of our lives. Perhaps it begins with a nagging question: "How can I have a better self-image; how can I increase my self-esteem?" We look at our body and see that the problem is we are overweight. So we lose ten pounds, but suddenly we become aware of our lack of muscle tone. So we join the spa and after weeks of pumping iron, our abs, 'ceps, pecs, and buns have increased definition, but we see that our teeth are not their whitest, our skin could have better texture and tone, and certainly our wardrobe is no longer worthy of our improved body—not to mention our somewhat frayed spouse, who doesn't seem to compare well to the newer, sleeker model one of our friends just got.

Likewise, when one's attention turns to having a child, ego needs often grow and proliferate. Let's say that a woman thinks that her biological clock is running out and she begins yearning to have a baby. Although she tries to get pregnant, she soon realizes that she is having unusual difficulty. So she studies the subject and learns how to pinpoint her ovulations. She sends her husband to a clinic that can determine his sperm count and suggest ways to increase it. Someone advises her that stress may be the problem and she reorganizes her day into a less stressful routine. She even makes a pact with God. Finally, she succeeds in getting pregnant.

Is she now content and free of needs in this area? No. As the weeks go by the woman begins feeling a new desire, the desire for a *healthy* baby. "If it can just have all its fingers and toes, I'll be happy," she says. So the woman gives up smoking and drinking and changes her diet. She schedules an ultrasound test and then an amniocentesis. She spends an hour a day "visualizing" a healthy baby. She makes a new pact with God. The baby comes and it seems normal in all respects.

Now is the woman content? Not if she is like most of us. A few weeks later she begins to feel a new yearning, one for a rash-free baby who sleeps through the night. . . .

We are used to thinking of our needs as no one's business but our own. Yet in the example of having a child we can see that our needs also have everything to do with our child and everything to do with the tranquillity of our family. First, we want a precocious one-year-old, then a tranquil two-year-old, then a smart three-year-old, then an outgoing four-year-old, and on and on. And so the running battles begin—because our child simply *cannot* give us everything we need and demand. Our sons or daughters have their own individual natures, and to a large extent they will be what they will be, regardless of what we need them to be. Is this an impossible situation? If we think that our child must change in order for a yearning we feel to be met, the situation is impossible. If we think that a need is as real as a child, the situation is impossible.

Needs Are Not Stable

In terms of day-to-day feelings, needs simply don't operate as permanent currents running through our bodies, like some congenital pacemaker that forces us to move to a certain beat. As children we had the need to run around and scream. As adults we don't. As adolescents we needed to be rebellious and secretive. Now we don't. In our teens and early twenties we needed to experiment with different personality types, to "try on different costumes." Later on we are more comfortable with whatever personality we have. Only a few years before, we needed lots of possessions and accomplishments. Now we feel a growing need for simplicity.

Many parents, especially during these my-needs-first times, worry unnecessarily about what has not yet happened and what is clearly not happening this instant. Obviously, parents shouldn't neglect the needs they have, but they also don't want to fear enjoying the many moments when they are relatively need free. You can't know peace in the present if you are continually asking yourself "What haven't I been given?" "What am I not getting now?" "What must I have next?" The relevant concern is "How can I enjoy where I am now?" "How can I enjoy what I already have?" "How can I enjoy my baby or my teenager this instant?"

Parents should guard against building a story

around a certain need and thereafter reacting to it as if it were permanent. Take, for instance, the rageaholic. For an individual to see where within his childhood these feelings came from can be helpful, but it is not infinitely helpful. A time comes when reconstruction of the past turns into monument building. What happened to you during your formative years obviously generated certain needs that you can still feel echoes of today. Sometimes very loud echoes. But the *story* has ended and you don't have to spend the rest of your life embellishing and updating it. If you look closely you will notice that even your old patterns and emotions are never quite the same each time they reappear. And they will continue to change. Only the names for them remain the same.

The past is no longer here to hurt you. What happened then is simply not happening now, and you can safely look at a need the way it is this morning or this afternoon. You are not an abused child or a neglected child or a spoiled child or an abandoned child or a thousand other classifications. You are what you are today. God's name is I AM, not I WAS, and God is your strength and your peace. If an accident had given you permanent amnesia, would not God still take your hand and walk with you all the way home? Remembering the past is not a spiritual necessity.

Ego Needs Are Never Met

Another misconception that can cause parents to appraise their needs unrealistically is the myth that an ego yearning can be wholly satisfied. We all know people who are consumed by the drive to be a success and have always been consumed by it. No degree of success satiates them. Each new success, in fact, seems to fan the flames of their discontent still further. Not only do needs tend to proliferate, the earlier need, from which the later needs grew, is never perfectly quenched.

On the most basic level, we feel hungry and we eat. Regardless of what other needs that leads to, is our ego now satisfied on that one level? No. If we merely ask the question, we see that the meal was not completely satisfying. It had too much salt, or not enough salt. There was too little of one dish or not enough of another. The vegetables weren't fresh enough or were not organic. The seasoning was a little off in the sauce. We ate too quickly and now we have a stuffed feeling. Or no dessert was included and we are left with a slight sugar craving.

Again, the ego part of us is *never* satisfied. It has judgments against even what it thinks it likes. This means that your partner will never give you a perfect sexual experience and your child will always disappoint you in some way. That is, as long as you look at your life through your ego.

Each instant of the day we have a choice. We can see what is before us with our unpeaceful mind or with our peaceful mind. When we view our children with gentleness rather than fear, we still can see what they need, what mistakes they may be making, and what would be most helpful for their growth. We see these things more clearly because we see them without distortion. Likewise, when we look at our body and its emotions with peace and affection, we can tell how best to keep it content—not perfectly content, but adequately content.

When we fear our body and its needs, it becomes an uncontrolled and unpredictable factor in our lives, as any alcoholic, for example, knows well. When we *identify* with our body, we free our mind to use it lovingly and intelligently. This should not be a confusing concept, but for those on a spiritual path it often is. Just because you identify with your body does not mean you become ruled by it or that you forget who you are spiritually.

Those people who identify with their pets are more intuitive about their pets' needs and take much better care of them than those who dislike their pets, fear them, or are indifferent to them. Think of your body as a pet that has needs that you as the owner must take care of. Identifying with a body, like identifying with a pet, is not a spiritual danger. For example, if you identify with a poodle, you are not in danger of thinking you are a poodle. You simply see the poodle with more affection and therefore respond to its needs more quickly.

You take your dog for a walk because it *needs* exercise—but you are careful where it sniffs. If it gets too interested in the wrong thing, say a dead bird or a dangerous rottweiler, you move it along—because you identify with it. You see that it doesn't *need* a dead bird or a fight with a larger dog.

Likewise, you look calmly at what your needs are now and take care of them with affectionate awareness. If you need a nap, you set the situation up so that you will not be disturbed and you rest your body well. However, you don't stay in bed all day if that isn't what your body needs.

If you will identify with your body, you will begin to anticipate needs before they ever arise, and you also will sense the moment when a need has been adequately satisfied. No matter how good the food is, many animals will not eat when they aren't hungry. This is the sense you want to develop about any current need you have. But if you are scared of your needs and push them out of your mind, or think that you are too spiritual to concern yourself with them, you either will overreact to them or underreact.

Needs vs. Appearances

To our egos, appearances are everything. Merely change the appearance and the ego thinks something meaningful has happened. This is why, for instance, parents think they can tell their child that they aren't angry—when in fact they are furious—and the child won't know they are.

The ego belief in appearances pervades all aspects of our culture. We think that if we look orderly and composed when we leave our homes in the morning, we *are* orderly and composed. It's enough that our clothes, shoes, even our underwear, *look* smooth and comfortable on the outside. Unless you pay extra, flannel pajamas are made with the soft part of the flannel facing out. Our politicians need only paint unattractive word pictures of their opponents in order to get elected. And we instruct our children not to brag, but don't teach them what true humility is and why it is a wisdom worth developing.

An effective guardian recognizes that attitude, not appearance, is everything. Your child learns from how you feel about things, not from how you act like you feel. If we silently believe that our race, income, sex, genes, or family name makes us important, our kids will start out their adult lives believing the same and will apply these values, or will react against them, when choosing friends, a spouse, or a job. If you were physically handicapped and couldn't communicate verbally or even visually with your children, they would still receive their basic lessons about life from the underlying tone in your home and not from the picture your family presents to other people.

Jordan recently celebrated his twelfth birthday. For his party he wanted to have a paint-ball-gun war. During his freshman and sophomore years in high school, his brother John had been invited to paint-ball-gun wars sponsored by the local Fellowship of Christian Athletes as a part of their recruiting program.[1] Knowing how much fun John thought these "war games" were, Jordan now believed that he had reached the age when he should be let in on this fun.

Since we didn't know how old kids had to be, we contacted the business that organizes these games in Tucson and were told that there had never been a serious injury to anyone in any age group they had supervised. For eleven- and twelve-year-olds, they said that they reduced the velocity of the guns; they shortened the length of the games; they provided full protective gear to every kid; and the paint they used washed out (mostly).

Phone calls to parents revealed that a few would not allow their kids to participate on the grounds that they would be playing with toys that looked like guns, in games that looked like war. It was interesting to us that these three boys were also the angriest of the group that Jordan had invited and had the worst histories of bullying other children or of being inordinately self-critical. Naturally they were made even angrier by being told they couldn't go.

These boys' parents certainly meant well—they didn't want their kids to do something that would lead them into violence. They merely made the mistake that most of us make in one form or another: Their decisions were based more on appearances than on reality. It should be obvious to any who care to look that play and fun don't lead to violence; anger leads to violence. The stepmom of one of the boys frequently hits him, even in public, and another boy's parents lecture him in front of his friends and punish him for a surprisingly long list of minor infractions. The third boy who couldn't come has a dad who on more than one occasion has joked to others in front of his son that his wife's pregnancy was a mistake and his son was unwanted.

As parents we have no secret needs. Your children can sense—even if they can't put words to it—what you long for. If there are some longings you don't like having, the solution is not to pretend that you don't have them— nor is it to announce in misguided honesty every need you think you have. The solution is to look at how you are now and teach by example that feelings are not final and that **spiritual progress can be made from any starting point.** In taking this approach, however, you must not ignore your urges in order to make it appear that you don't have any. You don't want to be a pretend parent. That wouldn't give your kids anything they could use. You want to be a real parent with real problems—but one who also demonstrates how growth takes place. You don't have to talk about this process in order to teach it, but you do have to live it.

HOW TO MEET YOUR NEEDS

Whenever possible don't allow yourself to enter a child care period low on gas. Doing so does not serve your child, your marriage, or your God. And it certainly doesn't benefit you. If you want to be an effective parent, if you want to raise a loving, happy, decent human being, then you must have several safety valves available to you and you must use them.

Aside from the higher needs we feel toward our children, such as yearning to be close and connected to them and yearning for them to be happy, perhaps the most common ego need we have as parents is our periodic desire to get away, to be left alone, to have time by ourselves. Many parents try to meet this need by becoming irritated at their kids. They "snap" at them, they "look daggers" at them, they "bark" at them, they talk to them "through clenched teeth"—in other words, in these and a hundred other ways, they try to drive them away. And this does work—but only at great cost to the relationship with their child and to their own peace of mind.

Instead of relating in this way, plan out how you can meet such a need, then do so quickly and easily and return to the present. For example, if you know that when your kids get home from school you "don't get a moment's peace," yet from experience you also know that by meditating or reading or working out or taking a walk or doing some other activity that releases tension, you will have greater reserves with which to deal with your kids, then stop what you are doing and take a sufficient break. This is not selfish indulgence; it is maintenance and repair. And once you are with your kids, if you see that it would help your frame of mind to be by yourself for a moment, as you step back physically from your children, step forward mentally—that is, maintain your sense of oneness with them by reminding yourself that your reason for taking this break is to make it easier for you to remember that you love them.

*   *   *

The ego mind-set is like the mind-set of a dream. We want a dream to feel and look real, so we design it to resist the intrusion of any other perception that would puncture its illusion of reality. You might say that a dream, just like an imaginary playmate, and just like an ego, has survival instincts.

So, for example, when children are going through the transitional period between wetting their beds and waking up to go to the bathroom, the dream mind-set works against their desire to awake by incorporating into the dream the sensation of their full bladder and adding a vivid experience of their urinating somewhere else besides their bed. Later they wake up to realize that their dream tricked them and that, once again, they wet their bed.

One of our boys saw this dynamic very clearly and when after one birthday he announced that he had now stopped wetting his bed, the handful of times that he later slipped didn't count, he said, because of the circumstances his dream had manufactured. He would then recount in detail how his dream had tricked him. And his assumption was entirely accurate.

Eventually, of course, he trained himself to recognize when his dream was trying to trick him. In very much the same way we as parents learn to recognize when our ego is tricking us into believing that we want to turn against our kids. This is never what you truly want—but you must be prepared for the little twist that your ego will put on your needs to make you *think* this is what you want. You too must train yourself to recognize these ploys and plan how to circumvent them.

Thus when you feel "I need to be by myself," do not let your ego add "and get away from my child." Obviously you will separate yourself *physically* from your child, but that is a far cry from turning against your daughter or your son within your own heart. And yet most parents in one way or another do turn against their children when they feel this need. This mistake has far greater spiritual consequences than if, for example, as an adult *you* were to wet your bed.

As part of this self-training, many parents we have counseled have found the following approach helpful.

Get by yourself and physically act out any feeling of dislike, distrust, anger, irritation, or disapproval you catch yourself feeling toward your kids. Do not treat a feeling of animosity toward a child lightly. Do not dismiss it unless you are ready to dismiss it entirely and replace it with the memory of your love. Turn your mind and look directly at the feeling and then act.

For example, go outside or get in your car and yell out exactly what you are feeling toward your child. Doing so is not negative. You already feel this way, and you are simply becoming aware of the dimensions of your feelings—out of the sight and hearing of anyone else, especially your child.

Then, perhaps, act these feelings out in some additional way. Take a picture of your child and tear it up while you scream or hiss your displeasure. Rip up an old phone book or newspaper. Hit or kick something as if you were doing this to your child—all the while looking at your thoughts and emotions very bluntly.

Here is what you will see for yourself: Your need is *not* directed against your child. Your ego thoughts are actually the opposite of your true feelings. In the midst of harmlessly acting out your ego position—if you do so thoroughly and honestly—your love and God's gentle perception of your child will flow back into your heart.

In attempting to set up a program for meeting your present needs, it's important for you to distinguish between the actual need and how you, your partner, or other parents commonly meet it.

For example, during the early years of parenting,

loss of sleep, loss of time, changes in hormonal production, and a strong shift in interests can have a dampening effect on your spouse's libido. As a result you may soon discover that your need for a sexual outlet is building. One common way that people meet this need is by having an affair or by considering leaving their spouse. This is not a safe or fulfilling way to handle your sexual drive and is not your actual need. If you look closely, you will see that decreased sexual activity between you and your spouse is *not* a decrease in the love between you—although you can definitely get your friends to argue that it is. Nor is it a decrease in the spiritual appropriateness of your marriage and family, although, here again, many authorities today make the mistake of linking sexual intimacy with true intimacy. You can have terrific sex with someone you don't even like, and you can have numerous sexual problems with someone you love deeply. Love and sex simply are not the same, and in many relationships they don't even overlap.

Another common example is the misperceived desire to hurt one's baby. The sound of a baby crying can indeed fray the nerves and shatter the mind of almost anyone, if it goes on long enough. In a sense, it can make you temporarily insane. There is a body of scientific, biological evidence that the human organism is genetically programmed to react strongly to a child's cry of distress. Like the pain that comes if you back into something hot, this genetic program is designed to catapult you into action. It is therefore entirely normal for this particular sound to affect you deeply.

If your baby cries more than you can take, the need is not for you to be rid of your baby, but to be rid of your baby's *noise*. Your need is never to scream at, strike, or shake your infant. In fact, dealing with the problem in this manner will merely shatter your mind further, because it is a betrayal of yourself and your child.

A third example is the need to relieve the unpleasant

sensations and effects of depression. The sometimes crushing burdens of child care can certainly cause depression, and yet drinking, a common way of attempting to alleviate depression, does not work. The need is to change a set of emotions and sensations, not to drink.

Likewise, overeating is not a healthy way to lessen anxiety and is not the actual need.

In these and countless other examples, seeing the distinction between the true need and the misperceived need is a necessary part of an intelligent response. The actual needs themselves can be met adequately in numerous ways, and so you must first open your mind to all options. Never is there only one way to proceed, but some ways are definitely less destructive than others.

Four years ago Carol was the single parent of a three-year-old boy named Todd. At that time she worked for a housecleaning service, a job that gave her the income and flexible hours she needed. She had grown to enjoy the strenuous work and the companionship of the other women, but she had a strong need "to do something creative" that was not being fulfilled.

As a child, Carol's great love had been to help her mother prepare elaborate dishes for the parties she often gave, and before her husband left her, she used to entertain a great deal. She received much praise from her husband and their friends for the unusual taste combinations she came up with and especially for the striking ways she presented and served her dishes.

Then came the divorce. Todd was two at the time, and after the family split up, her husband moved out of state and got his child-support payments reduced to almost nothing.

After a year of single parenting and housecleaning work, Carol felt a desperate need to cook. For many months she denied this because it seemed like such a silly need and one that was embarrassing to talk about with her women friends. But it didn't go away.

When she came to us for help, the first thing we did is ask her to keep a record of every time she was aware of this need. She was to write down exactly what it felt like (what sensations it was composed of and where in the body they were located) and what thoughts were in her mind when it surfaced. One of the first insights Carol had from doing this was her suspicion that it was the preparing of the food and not the parties that she missed. To test this idea, she gave a party for her friends at her apartment. The event, although not expensive, cost her so much of her meager savings that she realized that she would not be able to meet her need in that way. However, she did notice that she was happiest while she was fixing the food and serving it.

The next thing Carol tried was joining a catering service owned by a man she knew. This required only one or two evenings a week, and at first she thought it was the solution. Soon, however, she discovered that the clients seemed more interested in controlling and criticizing the service than in enjoying the food. The owner didn't care as long as he was paid, but Carol realized that people's reactions, although not as satisfying as the time she spent preparing the food, were nevertheless important to her.

Carol had several other false starts in her attempt to satisfy her need before she finally came up with a satisfactory solution. Today she writes a column on food presentation for a small magazine in which she gives her E-mail number. She writes in her spare time, and she loves hearing from her readers and giving them advice. She even makes enough money from the magazine to throw a party occasionally!

Carol's approach to meeting her need was excellent on several counts. First, she studied the need until she could distinguish it from the way she had always met it. Next, she opened her mind to any option that might work. Then she tried out these possibilities one at a time until she came up with an adequate solution.

If *any* feeling is disturbing you, it is also disturbing your relationship with your child. Your purpose as a parent is to see your particular needs clearly and meet them as best you can in the simplest, most peaceful way possible—especially those needs that you may be neglecting because of the demands of child care. It's important to look carefully at any persistent desire, buildup of emotion, nagging distress, or growing sense of deprivation. You want no blind spots in your awareness if you are going to be a real parent to your kids.

Obviously, for you to be increasingly resentful, wistful, agitated, discontented, or preoccupied works against your well-being and the well-being of your child. Although you definitely may feel them, it is never necessary for you to be *dominated* by any of these moods. **Your ego is always feeling something,** but your internal reality includes far more than the offerings of your ego. The deeper side of you—the side that is quiet and whole and never needy—can be invited into your mind at any time.

If you are on a spiritual path, you don't deny your needs, and certainly you don't fight them. You add God to the needful state. This frees you to act, if action would be helpful. Eventually we all learn that although we are feeling, say, discontent, that is not *all* we are feeling, and that we can open our hearts to a gentler set of emotions. As a first step, we see that we can be peacefully depressed, peacefully sad, peacefully sexual, even peacefully irritated. **There is nothing in your heart that you need to get rid of before you invite God in.** And once you have remembered God, it is normal for there to be a period when you will seem to feel both—both the ego emotion and the comfort of God. Stay with this and God's peace gradually will blossom within you.

With a good understanding of the nature of needs

and with plenty of practice in holding to your purpose in the face of ego impulses, eventually you will be able to see the need quickly and take care of it. To be a consistently good parent, **you want "meeting your needs" to become like brushing away a fly or removing a pebble from your shoe.** You do what you need to do effortlessly, undramatically, and unmemorably.

HEALING THE NEED FOR NEEDS

Bringing peace into the mind alongside a need is the first step toward lessening the strength of our needs overall and of eventually eliminating any but the simplest of them. However, we can take an even more deliberate step toward healing, one that is at the core of this book. It is still a form of turning to God, but on the surface at least, it involves our kids more directly. Simply stated: **We consciously give our children what we ourselves failed to receive as children.** Ask yourself, What attitude would I have liked my parents to have had in this situation or in that? Then practice being the "good parent" that your childhood indicates would have been helpful for you to have had.

This works because so many of our problems as adults are reactions to our own childhoods. If we can choose to be damaged by our past, we also can choose to be healed by it. Our childhood is not causing the problems—because our childhood is over and no longer exists—but our reactions to it continue in the present. Because our reactions are within our control, healing is always possible.

This is not a new principle, but it's usually acknowledged only in its negative form. If we were hit as children, we are more likely to feel a need to hit our own kids. If our parents tried to solve their problems by drinking, we are more likely to feel the need to drink. If lying was a family practice, we are more likely to feel a need to lie. And so on. Thus we re-create the past within the present and carry on the same miserable patterns from generation to generation.

As adults we like to think of our lives in terms of our accomplishments. We recently heard a man talk proudly of having fully funded his pension. He had done this, he said, despite the financial machinations of his five wives. This was indeed a good accomplishment. But what if the destructive pattern of men abandoning their wives that had characterized his family for generations had ended with him? Now, that would have been a great accomplishment, and one that would have touched the world. It is fully within your hands and mine to accomplish something this great.

The quiet place of our being has no needs. Thus as we become increasingly interested in the part of ourselves that never left God and less preoccupied with filling the gaps in our ego history, all our human needs begin to lessen. At first, we notice that the edge has been taken off many of the old cravings and yearnings. Then, within our milling emotions, we begin to recognize areas of stillness or freedom where former needs once stirred. Eventually we find that unconscious motivation has largely dissipated. Now we see clearly the choices before us and gently decline to heed any voice but the voice of sanity.

4

WHAT ARE CHILDREN FOR?

IS YOUR CHILD A REFLECTION ON YOU?

Most parents hope that their kids will reflect favorably on them. This almost goes without saying. It certainly goes without question. But if you are to be a real parent to your child, you must ask how strong, how controlling, is this hope.

We now live in an area of Tucson populated mostly by lawyers, doctors, engineers, and professors. Here, aggressiveness and competitiveness are highly valued. When our family lived in a small community southeast of Tucson, those same qualities not only were absent but were viewed suspiciously. There, compatibility and steadfastness were the dominant values. The way our boys would have to think and behave in order to reflect favorably on us would differ radically in the two areas, and neither way would be relevant to their basic nature, their peace, or their connection with God.

What reflects favorably on us as parents is seldom in the best interests of our children. We think that our child holds one of the keys to our happiness, but the key is actually in our seeking our child's happiness. "To give is to receive" is a truth no less valid because it is ancient. God *is* happiness, and it stands to reason that the more like God we become, the happier we become. Regardless of how often they may have forgotten it, certainly this is a truth that many parents have experienced countless times.

Two Saturdays ago Hugh was finishing up writing for the day and realized that he had an hour or so before he needed to get to bed. The next day was Eastern Sunday, and he and Gayle would have to get up early for two morning sermons they had to give. So to relax a little before trying to get to sleep, he sat down in his favorite chair and opened a book.

Then he remembered Jordan. Jordan usually has lots to do, but this Saturday he had not been able to connect with any of his friends and now was in his room watching television.

"Well," Hugh thought, "that's unfortunate, but I've got to get up very early. And Gayle's at a meeting. So there's nothing to be done about it." He opened his book again.

"It's Saturday night and your son is alone." That thought returned with surprising force. And it ate at him until he got out of his chair.

Hugh went into Jordan's room and said, "Is there anything you want to do tonight?"

"What do you mean?" Jordan asked suspiciously.

"We can do anything you want. We can go bowling. We can go to a movie. We can go to Golf and Stuff. . . ."

"Golf and Stuff? Isn't that a long way from here?"

Hugh saw his mistake. He had meant to say "Funtastics," which was nearby. Golf and Stuff is on the other side of town.

"You're right." Hugh backtracked. "It would take us a long time to get there."

"But Golf and Stuff has batting cages," Jordan said, "and Funtastics haven't put theirs in yet."

So Hugh took Jordan to Golf and Stuff and spent two hours running back and forth between the batting cages and the token dispenser (which was in another building), getting snacks, and doing other miscellaneous errands for Jordan.

Jordan was happy.

And, Hugh conceded, he was happy also. He, the parent, was the reflection of his child.

Love is the great simplifier. As parents we must see our kids directly, which means we must see them kindly. And we must deal with only the tendencies that are obviously there. Never do we need to make an interpretation against our son's or daughter's core. **No child was ever helped by being judged.**

This approach is more practical because looking at our children through the eyes of love allows us to see their *mistakes* more clearly than looking through the eyes of disapproval. To this end, parents must learn to separate legitimate concern from competitiveness. As they grow older, we won't continue to cherish our children if at the same time we believe we are in competition with them either physically or mentally. And certainly we can't love our kids if we are always ranking them against the progress of our friends' kids. There's no place for rivalry or embarrassment in parental love, and the competitive emotions will not inform us whether our children are heading in a direction that is good for them. **The purpose of our kids is neither to add to our value nor to increase our**

self-esteem. Their function is not even to avoid embarrassing us.

We have followed with interest three other families whose boys are around the same age as ours. Two of the families put great pressure on their kids to stop wetting their beds (getting them up to go to the bathroom multiple times at night, drastic reduction of certain liquids, visits to new pediatricians and neurologists, drugs, large rewards, conditioning devices set off by moisture, and punishments such as creating the new chore of making their boys wash their own bedding). On the other hand, we and one other family did very little besides keep our children warm at night.[1] We were also especially careful to protect them from other children or adults learning about their so-called problem, since so many people are unreasonably emotional about bedwetting.[2]

Naturally it's fine for you and your partner to try things to help your child stop wetting the bed, especially if your child welcomes the help. But in our experience, you will get conflicted results if there is even a hint of condemnation or embarrassment within either of you. It's interesting that the boys in all four of our families stopped wetting their beds at about the same time—one at nine, one at ten, one at eleven, and one at almost twelve. *All* were well past the age that is considered "normal" by most authorities. Although there isn't necessarily a connection, the child who wet his bed the longest was in the family in which bedwetting was the greatest issue. His parents believe that the last thing they tried (a more sensitive wake-up device) was what worked. Whether it was or not, the running battle this family has had over this one issue has done much to destroy the love between them all. Our culture's preoccupation with bodily functions has made bedwetting a compelling issue in many parents' minds (and consequently the brunt of much joking—and shame—among children), but **no issue is worth destroying the bond between you and your child.**

At present, our four families are taking different approaches to our teenagers forgetting to clean up their rooms, take out the trash, and the like. This same couple, who believe strongly in discipline through punishment, have virtually ended all meaningful communication between themselves and their thirteen-year-old.[3]

Attack doesn't work. It may get temporary results, but it doesn't get the long-term changes of heart that parents seek. And it is not a necessary component of firmness, order, and clear guidelines. Because each child's personality is inherently special and different, the art of spiritual parenting is more like nourishing a seed than chiseling stone into a statue. All good gardeners are informed about the needs of plants at each period of their growth, but they never try to change one kind of plant into another kind.

Most parents pay remarkably little attention to the various normal stages that all children go through.[4] Some adults will not hesitate to study the breed of dog they are picking out, yet somehow they think they should intuitively know all the characteristics of the age or stage their child has just entered.

A good mother or father strives to understand. Spiritual parenting is a path of deep seeing, acceptance, and encouragement more than it is a path of altering, pushing, and re-forming. And yet most of the attention that parents give their children is directed at correcting them. Very little is devoted to appreciating them, playing with them, or merely stopping and talking with them.

As was true of us for several years, **parents usually praise their kids only when they ask to be praised, and except with babies and toddlers, adults rarely initiate fun and play.** They continue with what they were doing while they are being told something that is important within their child's world—a disrespect they would never show another adult—and they quickly and easily break their promises to their kids if "something comes up." Naturally there are exceptions, but **the majority of parents focus completely on their kids only when they are trying to change them.** Our culture's unquestioned and untouchable attitude is that adults and adults' work are more important than children and children's play.

Many people haven't seen how pervasive this attitude is in households, but sooner or later most parents should be able to witness it in adult-supervised sports, especially within those teams composed of kids approaching adolescence. Go to almost any practice of any sport and you will see virtually no tolerance for fun, happiness, or silliness. Furthermore, you will hear very little praise of the kids for their courage or their good play.

Coaches often turn to one another to acknowledge something well done by one of the kids—but do not say it to the kid. Likewise, parents will praise or brag about their children to other adults but not to their children. Obviously there are coaches who are not in this mold, just as there are parents who compliment their kids and tolerate—even join in—their children's exuberance and silliness. But overall, adults look askance at sheer enjoyment. Somehow it's not proper or respectful of the sport or sensitive to the world's misery or to "our life's work."

Our sisters and brothers within our human family— and certainly our children—do not receive enough acknowledgment and appreciation. What's so wrong with complimenting people liberally? Don't most of us try very hard? Don't most of us do the best we can? And can't we remember how hard it was being a child? Would anyone really want to go back and repeat all of that? We even know to praise our pets! But somehow we've gotten this notion that it hurts children's and even adults' *character* to be complimented. As if human beings just might get used to it, and then where would this world be?

THE FUNCTION OF CHILDREN

If a child's function is not to reward us, or to keep from embarrassing us, or even to refrain from inconveniencing us, what are children for? Hold in mind that all kids are already themselves. Their function is never to change into something or somebody else in order to conform to our personality—an impossible task when you consider that each parent, grandparent, and older sibling has a separate personality.

To see clearly what children are for, we must look at children, not at adults.

Children Are a Wanted Surprise.

They are a planned breakout from the status quo. The mistake we make is forgetting that their greatest value is in what still remains *untouched* within them. How can children possibly fulfill their function unless they are seen and appreciated and, as much as possible, allowed to be themselves?

LITTLE CHILDREN RUN AROUND AND SCREAM. Even in quiet zones. That is their function.

LITTLE CHILDREN FIND NEARLY EVERYTHING FUNNY AND AMUSING. Even "serious" problems and somber occasions. That is their function.

LITTLE CHILDREN HAVE BOUNDLESS ENERGY. Even at night and early in the morning. That is their function.

LITTLE CHILDREN THINK THE PRESENT IS MORE IMPORTANT THAN THE PAST OR FUTURE. Even when parents are running late. That is their function.

LITTLE CHILDREN MAKE A GAME OF ORDINARY EVENTS— eating, taking a bath, putting on pajamas, and flushing a toilet. That is their function.

* * *

The world has many dangers and is capable of many unfortunate reactions, and it should go without saying that parents must set limits on their kids' behavior. But a child's basic nature deserves to be prized—even during those moments when it must be reined in. Big people have overreacted to the world, and they badly need little people who underreact to it.

Children Are an Act of Faith

Parents, knowing how troubled the world is, nevertheless choose to bring children into it. Children are a profound expression of their belief that healing is possible. They are, in a sense, the parents' stand against cynicism.

Children are "the hope of the world." Who knows what miracle of change even one child might bring? Within this person is a new combination of potentials and talents, a new beginning, one who is starting fresh. Certainly the motives for the sex act are not often this pure, but when you consider the state of the world, what is more surprising than the number of unplanned births is the number of planned ones. Very few parents have a child—no matter how accidental its conception—without some degree of hope.

Children Are a Light in the Dark

In many ways a little child—full of laughter and fun, full of love and trust—is the opposite of the world. The light in a child's eyes and smile is so obvious that it is almost palpable. Because we have come to think of the world as normal, their lightheartedness makes them seem almost out of place. Here is a candle in the dark—and in their decision to give birth, parents light this tiny flame and set it gently down on the face of the earth.

Children Are Vulnerable

We need no other reminder that peace is more important than war than the existence of children. In the little

wars between mothers and fathers, in "great" wars between
nations, and in the thousand other conflicts that adults en-
gage in daily, children get hurt. It is not a child's function to
become a victim. We say "it can't be helped." But it can be.
If we simply look at all the ways that a child can be hurt—
and at who alone stands between the danger and the
child—it *will* be helped.

Children Love and Trust

Love is more important than hate. It reaches further
and lasts longer. It is healthier both mentally and physically.
It makes life easier. And it is much more beautiful. Just to be
around little kids feels better than to be around those adults
who are filled with grudges and opinions. Kids begin their
lives free of judgment and malice, and it shows. They will
kiss old people on the lips. They find deformities interesting
rather than repulsive. They will play with the "wrong" children. Obviously this is quickly lost, but it is lost a little more
slowly when we love them back.

You must commit deeply to your child's basic innocence
and goodness. You must never "decide" against a son or
daughter's nature or spiritual potential, never let the
thought seep into your mind that your kid is "a little off," or
odd, or twisted, or "a bad seed." You must continue to see
him as he is and always hold to the eternal truth that at his
core he is a child of God. This has nothing to do with rules
that you may need to make clear or steps you must take to
correct behavior. It is an act of the heart, not some current
notion of permissiveness.

You must never allow another's diagnosis or opinion of your child's personality, IQ, or health color your
knowledge of your own child's inner spirit. Whether the
opinion is that one of your kids has attention deficit disorder, attachment disorder, a terminal illness, "doesn't consequence well," is overly needy, is learning disabled, is a

bully, is possessed, is dyslexic, or is just "a little strange," don't start looking askance at your own child. No matter what is going on within his or her body or brain, in this child's heart there lies the quiet memory of God. That memory *will* eventually awaken.

THE GIFT THAT CHILDREN BEAR

As we have stressed before, our purpose is not to set forth a new system or still another set of rules or even fresh strategies for solving old problems. Rather, we hope that we can present a simple means of seeing a child clearly. When you see and respond to your child with honesty and acceptance, a third reality called "the parent-child relationship" is formed that will benefit you, your marriage, and your home long past this little period of childhood. Any kid who is honestly seen will positively affect the bond within the family of which she or he is a part. Your patient construction of a bridge between you and your child—which is actually a progressive realization of what is already there—can be the conduit of the greatest treasure you can receive in this world: the recognition of God or oneness.

About a year ago our boys played in a basketball and a baseball game within a week of each other. Because one was on the heels of the other, we were especially conscious of the differences in attitude of the parents, coaches, and officials at the two games.

In his game, John pitched for the city league team, which plays other Tucson teams in the fourteen-, fifteen-, and sixteen-year-old division. His coach had a standing "bounty" that several coaches of other school and Little League teams that John has played for also have offered: If a boy hits a line drive so hard into the opposing pitcher that he has to be taken out of the game, or if a boy fakes a bunt, draws in the third baseman, and hits a line drive so hard into

that boy that he has to be taken out, he gets a steak dinner. These coaches give their answer to the question "What are children for?" unequivocally. Clearly the purpose of the kids on their teams is to win the game for them at all costs.

At the start of John's game we found a place to sit in the bleachers that were nearest his dugout. Naturally, most of the people around us were parents of boys on his team. During the course of the game several fathers and one mother shouted insults at the boy who was pitching against our team. ("He's done—stick a fork in him." "Don't worry about where he's going to pitch it; he doesn't know himself.") John's coach periodically yelled out his displeasure at the two seventeen- to eighteen-year-old boys who were umpiring the game. ("Hey, blue, you're missing a good game." "Are you totally or just legally blind?") Parents shouted advice to their own kids. And the coach, in front of their teammates and parents, loudly announced each mistake his players made.

Then we went to Jordan's basketball game. His league is made up of eleven-, twelve-, and thirteen-year-olds, and his team is sponsored by the JCC (Jewish Community Center). So far this year, all of his games have been against various YMCA teams in the Tucson area. Although most of the parents of our team sat in the balcony, we sat with the parents of the opposing team because those seats were closer to the court.

During the opening minutes of the game we began to notice inappropriate clapping. At first we couldn't understand what these parents were doing, then suddenly Gayle said, "They're clapping for the kids on our team!" Anytime a boy on either team did something well they would clap or yell out a compliment, or if a mistake was made, they would shout encouragement. These parents were religiously and ethnically a diverse group—as memberships in most YMCAs and JCCs now tend to be—

and yet as adults they obviously felt protective of all children.

The teenager who was refereeing was with the JCC and was not known to these parents. Whenever a time-out was called, he would practice shooting baskets, and when he made one—which was most of the time—the parents would loudly clap, and the boy would laugh and bow. This continued even after he called a technical on their coach, the first such foul that coach had ever gotten. (His foot was inside the court when he called out a play.) And the father who was sitting next to Hugh made it a point to lean over and comment favorably every time Jordan made a good pass or shot, even though he was the parent of the opposing team's best player.

The adults at the baseball game clearly did not feel protective of all children. Actually, they felt hostile toward most of the kids, at times even their own, and they actively attacked children throughout the game. For whatever rea son, perhaps because the Oklahoma City bombing of the civil-service day care center had occurred just two days before, the parents at the basketball game were parents of all children—and that is how they behaved throughout the game.

Now, we want to ask you a question with a very obvious answer. It is because you already know the answer that we want to ask it. And yet it is the one question that is fundamental to parents receiving the gift that their children bear. It can be asked at any time you are with your child.

Which parents were happier and felt more fulfilled?

Obviously, it was the group of moms and dads who were protective of all children. They joked and laughed and smiled throughout the game. They were a pleasure to be around. And their children had more fun. It is also reasonable to assume that their children's love of basketball grew as a result.

The other group was angry, agitated, and not at all pleasant to be near. Their children's love of baseball did not grow. In fact, several boys on that team eventually quit.

When we yearn for or strive to get something from someone who isn't willing or able to give it, we blind ourselves to that person's goodness. **You can't help but be irritated at anyone you want something from.** Moms and dads who use a spiritual approach to parenting give guidance rather than want obedience. To give to children makes us happy. To focus on getting from children—whether it is getting a feeling of superiority in comparing ourselves to them, getting their absolute compliance, or getting a boost to our ego because of their performance—does not make us happy. Love sees each child clearly and so *receives* the child.

How could something so obvious be so universally ignored? And yet we as parents so often overlook the obvious. The mother of the girl who is trying out for cheerleader overlooks the obvious when she goes beyond merely helping her daughter to working to defeat other girls. The father of the boy who is struggling to become a starter on his team overlooks the obvious when he gets angry at his son for the mistakes he makes.

In our example of John's and Jordan's teams, both groups of parents were watching children play a game. Both groups saw their kids make mistakes. And both groups saw their teams lose on this occasion. Yet one group was upset by almost everything that happened, whereas the other group was delighted by almost everything. Even the usual mistakes that kids make while at play seemed funny to them. In short, one group received the gift that their children brought into the world; the other group did not.

5

WHAT DO YOU DO WHEN . . . ?

RULES OF BEHAVIOR—
RULES OF THE HEART

Generally speaking, there are no rules or natural laws governing what a parent should say or do about the typical problems that arise between themselves and their kids. Yet in the classes and workshops we give on marriage and parenting, more questions begin with the words "What do you do when . . . ?" than any others. And of these questions, most are about children, not about partners.

Many couples see that there is no perfect way of handling large, complex issues such as the discovery of an affair, the announcement of a firing, or the news of a terminal illness. Many couples even recognize that no magic answers exist for how wives should respond to husbands, or husbands to wives, when the toilet seat is left up, when issues are raised late at night, when socks are not turned right side out, when the question "Do you love me?" is asked during "fourth down and goal," when underwear is left on the floor, when "too much time" is spent on the phone, or when nail clippings are found in bed. Yet many adults assume there *are* behavioral answers to common problems with children!

This discrepancy comes in part from parents underestimating the complexity and individuality of their kids. To put it another way, it comes from a lack of respect. **Adults assume that young children, even adolescents, are so simpleminded that they can be manipulated by a few pat phrases or stock punishments.** They believe that children are so unaware of the random, inconsistent, and contradictory workings of the world that they can sell kids on the concept that "all our actions have logical consequences" or indeed that *any* of our actions have logical consequences.

Our counseling experience is that even when kids respond outwardly to disciplinary formulas in the way their parents hope they will, it isn't because they are naive. Today, as in times past, children eventually see through what their parents are up to. As evidence, look at one of the common routines of stand-up comics. They rely on the fact that their audience members all heard many of the same things during childhood and knew they were being manipulated. "Little brothers are not for throwing," we recently heard one comic say. Many of us remember that once popular way of talking to children. It's funny because it's so obviously formulaic.

Having a hidden agenda behind what you say to your child tends to create more distance and separation between the two of you. Be attentive to the uncomfortable sense that you are tricking your kids into doing something you want them to do. It's fine to *use* a trick, but you want to be very clear while carrying it out that you are loving, respecting, and enjoying your child at the same time.

For example, if you know that your child is scared of

the dark and you say, "You better get in bed because all the lights go out at nine o'clock," you are using a trick. A more honest statement of what is actually going to happen might be "If you are not in your bed by nine, I am going to try to scare you so badly that you will run for the covers and will remember to do so every night from now on when I threaten you." But to state this trick that honestly would not work as well, because your kid probably would start arguing with you not to turn out the lights quite yet.

A more loving and enjoyable variation of this trick that one single mom uses is to race her daughter to bed because "the monsters come out at night." As they run through the house, they squeal as they pass any piece of furniture that a monster could reach out from under. Some nights they even take more than one lap through the house just to get in extra squealing time. When they get to the mother's bed, they both jump under the covers and then her mom reads her stories until she drops off to sleep, at which time she carries her into her own room.

The mom herself sometimes gets scared at night, and so she has come up with this game of their being scared together. Every time her daughter has asked her if there are monsters or whether the monsters really come out at night, she has explained that no, this is just a game, there are no monsters, but that when she was a little girl she sometimes liked being scared, hearing ghost stories, and, when she had friends over, talking her dad into dressing up to scare everybody.

Parents need to be honest not in the sense of verbally mirroring their own ego emotions, but in the deeper sense of speaking and acting from their hearts rather than their egos. When little kids show their parents how high they can jump, how well they can stir the pancake mix, or how good they are at drawing pigs, parents are *not* responding from their hearts if they critique the performance. The child is asking for bread and is given a stone. Likewise, if your teenage daughter says, "I just made the JV softball team," you don't say, "You can't earn a living playing softball." This response may be "honest" but it is probably not from the heart and therefore not *truthful*, that is, not full of the truth of your real relationship with your child.

In the first half of the twentieth century, many parents told their kids that unless they behaved, "the bogeyman will get you," or "Santa will put ashes in your stocking," or "I'll take you to the orphanage." This is no less truthful than the more modern practice of telling children "Junk food will stunt your growth" or "If you don't do your homework you'll end up pumping gas." The purpose of both the old formulas and the new is not to convey truth but to manipulate the child into compliance. And the primary lesson that kids learn from this approach is that it's okay to say whatever you need to in order to get your way. Today couples routinely threaten each other with divorce during arguments, not because they really believe the issue is worth separating over but because they believe that using words as a weapon is an acceptable way to win. Many talk-show hosts, religious leaders, and politicians operate from the same premise.

Knowledge of several options of what to say or do in certain recurring situations can help parents, but only if they don't use the options as a substitute for focusing on their true goal as parents. If their purpose is clear at the time, whether they are familiar with many strategies or none at all, their actions will at least do no harm. However, if they are not clear, even a well-thought-out strategy can lessen the sense of oneness within a family.

Many parenting books have tips on, say, how to make dressing kids easier or how to help them better dress themselves. (Let a big outdoor thermometer, that you both read together, decide if it's take-a-coat weather. Have an important laying-out-the-clothes ceremony the night before in order to cut down on getting-dressed time the next morning when everyone will be rushed. Buy iron-on decals to cover stains or holes in the child's favorite shirt. Have little underwear drawers or colorful underwear boxes—one for each day of the week—to make changing underwear daily more appealing to your child.) Any of these tactics—if carried out with affection and fun—could ease a particular getting-dressed problem with a particular child. But once many parents know some options, the mistake they make is relying on the formula rather than on their attitude toward their child. A mom or dad can know hundreds of strategies for all manner of problems and still be very destructive. Study the problem area; open your mind to your intuition and creativity; read what other parents have found helpful; but always **treat any strategy you try as merely the box that you are putting your love in this time.**

A good example is having to deal with sibling rivalry. Books and articles are replete with suggestions: Never force siblings to share or to spend time together. Never compare children. Never encourage tattling. Before a child complains, she must say how she participated. Never try to determine who was to blame. Only intervene in a fight to protect life or limb. If possible, distract the children into doing something else.

These are all excellent ideas, but often there is also the subtle implication that sibling rivalry is a hassle that you don't need to have. Adults fight in a different manner, but they fight no less than children. If you look at your children gently and with understanding, you will see that nothing has gone wrong. Of course there is sibling rivalry. All egos clash. You will not solve this problem. Your job is not to reform egos, which is impossible, but to bring as much peace and safety to the situation as you can. Your job is physically to protect your children and to modify, plan around, or shorten the clashes when possible—but it is not to judge your children for clashing or to judge one child for the way he attacks.

Obviously, do not try just any gambit suggested in a

book. Many tactics are so symbolic of attack that most parents would find it impossible to use them lovingly. You want to feel *comfortable* about any trick you try. If you feel anxious or ill at ease, you may be acting against your higher sense of parenting. One popular book recommends doing to young kids what they do to you: Each time your boy hits you, hit your boy back a little harder. If your daughter bites you, bite her back or flick her on the chin. If your son pinches you, take his hand and make him pinch himself. If your girl uses a swearword, get close to her ear and yell, "That word hurts my ears." In our opinion, this eye-for-an-eye approach signals your mind that you are attacking your child. It would require enormous spiritual effort and concentration for you to do any of these things and still deeply enjoy and love your child at the same time. These actions may result in a quick change in behavior, but is that all we as parents can aim toward?

Again, it's more how you feel at the time than how you act that determines the nature of your influence on your child. Parental love—the experience of oneness with a child—will never generate destructive behavior in a child regardless of how much or how little knowledge the parent has of strategies. Therefore, learn as many ways of responding to your child as you can, but remember that unless you use them with God, unless you speak or act with Love, the technique you use will accomplish nothing of lasting value.

KNOWING WHAT TO DO

A social worker named Jill recently asked us, "What do you do if after a lot of work on your part the parents and their daughter have finally come to your office to talk; you have just gotten the parents to open up; and suddenly you notice that the girl has started peeling off little pieces of wallpaper from the wall you spent all weekend papering"?

How to respond to someone else's child is a common problem. More typically the situation involves people you have invited over who are not keeping their kid under control, but this social worker's story perhaps defines the dilemma even more sharply. It also illustrates that most real-life circumstances are too complicated and atypical to fit *any* formula. Probably you have already noticed that the rules of what to do that you read in many parenting books never quite fit the situations you actually find yourself in. Fortunately, to be a good parent doesn't require a set number of premade decisions. All we *must* know is *how* to decide.

Before we get to the answer that Jill arrived at herself, let's first explore a process for handling this type of question. Here is the essential first response to any question that begins with "What do I do when my kid . . . ?" **Always start by clarifying your purpose.** Once your purpose as a parent is clearly established in your mind—and is deeply felt—your behavior will naturally follow without your having to give much, or any, thought to it. As one mother recently put it: "Get your heart right and you'll know what to do."

Before you act, wait until you are at peace about what you are going to do to your child. The converse of this is: **If you have a question about whether you should do it, don't do it.** If you feel a sense of *urgency* about doing what you know in your heart does not have to be done immediately, don't do it. If you are *uneasy* about it, don't do it. Wait until you feel comfortable. Wait until you once again truly *feel* your love for your child.

Obviously this advice can be taken to some silly extremes. For example, if your child is in imminent danger, you don't wait to clarify your purpose before you act. Yet almost always, there is plenty of time to remember how much we love our children. So why *don't* we take the few seconds or the minute or two that this requires? Why do we feel an impatient resistance to using time to remember Love?

The ego's sense of urgency informs us what is at

stake: If we pause, we may continue to dissolve our ego.
Remember that we have set up this imaginary identity in our
mind to defend itself—just as a child's imaginary playmate
defends itself. The imaginary playmate—even though it is
produced entirely by the child's mind—will tell the child to
stay away from that new kid who just moved into the neighborhood. Why? Because it "knows" that real companionship will begin to dissolve its level of reality for the child.

Likewise, your ego "knows" that as you grow in your
experience of oneness with your child, you will feel the nature of your real self—which is at one with all living things—
and you will see that you don't need an imaginary self, a
separated self, a self that seems cut off from God and the
children of God.

Obviously Jill was asking about a situation that she had been
in personally. At the time that the scene she described happened, she was aware of the conflict between her sense of
urgency that she protect the wallpaper and her desire to do
nothing to sabotage the meeting. To Jill's great credit, she
did not act.

Jill had suspected that Donna, the seven-year-old
daughter, was being emotionally abused by her stepdad,
and this is why she had worked so hard to bring about this
meeting. For her to have corrected Donna would not only
have interrupted the stepfather and possibly returned him
to sullen silence, it also would have played into his belief
that Donna was "no good." When she saw Donna peeling
the paper (the girl was sitting slightly back and out of eyesight of her parents), Jill did not say anything to her. However, she became so distracted over what was happening
that, looking back, she now felt that the meeting had suffered as a consequence.

Note that it had not suffered because she failed to
correct Donna, but because she was so preoccupied with
the question of whether she *should* correct her that she

couldn't concentrate. Many authorities today would say that she should have gone ahead and corrected her. They would say that Jill had "so much energy around" the question that if she had just done it, she would have dispersed her excess energy. Then Jill would have felt freer to focus on what was important.

In other words, if you long to do something, yearn to do it, feel a "need" to do it, or are frustrated and are "holding yourself back" because you are not doing it, then, the philosophy of our times says, "Just do it." Taken at face value, this advice sounds reasonable.

When we were doing research for *I Will Never Leave You,* we were amazed to discover how many psychologists justified or even recommended that dissatisfied marital partners have affairs on these same grounds. In our research for this book, we have noticed this same above-all-else-take-care-of-your-needs type of reasoning in parenting books, articles, and on TV. For example, one popular children's authority admits that spanking, even one or two smacks, creates deeper problems than it solves and that it can teach children how to hate, fear, and seek revenge against their parents. However, she goes on to say that when parents really *want* to spank their kids and feel "antsy," "thwarted," or "a need to release tension," then they should go ahead and spank them in order to "clear the air."

In another book by a popular authority, a pediatrician, several pages tell why parents should not hit, whack, shake, or spank their kids, including medical reasons such as the damage a cuff near the ear can cause, or the damage to the spine that shaking or a slightly off-target swat can cause. He also points out that broken bones and even death have resulted from children falling because they were whacked when they were off balance, which kids frequently are. Despite all of this—including the risk of death—this authority says that if parents smack their child on impulse and "without any premeditation," this can have a beneficial effect on the parents' mental state and may result in an immediate improvement in their attitude toward their kid!

It's obvious that these and many other children's authorities have not dealt with battered women and batterers. During the years we were working in this field, we heard the same kinds of justifications: "It was just a little shove." "All I did was shake her." "I hit her once without thinking." And almost always, not only the man but often the woman also would describe how much better things usually are after the outburst—there is contrition and closeness and sometimes even "the best sex we ever had."

No authority would say that physical abuse of a smaller adult or even verbal abuse of our physically weaker partner is justified because of the frustration we feel before doing it and the release of tension and "improved" state of mind we feel afterward. Yet our children, who are even more physically vulnerable and whom we are morally bound to protect, are somehow acceptable outlets for our emotional needs. Obviously this is psychological insanity; it is certainly spiritual suicide. Nothing comes before our duty to safeguard our children, even if it is from ourselves.

Many parents, perhaps most, will at one time or another get so upset at their children that they will smack them, or shake them, or angrily set them down too hard, or scream obscenities at them, or flick their chin, or pinch them, or spank them. And yet, regardless of how commonplace physical displays of anger are, **no one who stays open to options and keeps trying can fail to move beyond *any* hurtful impulse.** However, if we justify the attack, we leave ourselves wide open to repeat it.

If as a parent you make a mistake, then you correct it. But do not believe any book or authority who tells you there is only one way to meet a need, only one way to release anger, only one way to dissolve frustration. There are a thousand ways, and your child does not have to figure in any of them.

It is therefore admirable that Jill did not correct Donna in front of her stepdad and mom. Her inaction did result in damage to her wallpaper, but that was a small price to pay for not risking damage to a child. During the meeting Jill felt her frustration grow, but she recognized that this emotion was a sign that she didn't know for sure what was in Donna's best interests. She didn't know that correcting Donna would unquestionably harm her, but she also didn't know that it unquestionably wouldn't. Therefore she did not act. The only thing she failed to do was to take the next step, which would have been to focus on her purpose. Naturally, she would first have to know what her purpose is.

To help Jill clarify this, we led her through a series of questions similar to the ones we used with the baseball coach in Chapter 2. At the end of the process she summarized her feelings by saying "I'm a healer. That's my purpose, to heal. That's all I want."

We then asked her to close her eyes and picture herself once again at the meeting and to recall the point at which she noticed what Donna was doing to the wall. When she indicated that she was imagining herself there, we continued our questions:

"What are you feeling as you look at Donna?"

"Horror! You have no idea how hard it is to paper a wall. And expensive!"

"But you don't say anything, so what else are you feeling?" (*Jill closes her eyes.*)

"Well, her stepdad is talking, looking mostly at his wife, but at least he's talking. Essentially he's telling us that Donna is a bad seed, that these things happen in nature. Even though he doesn't see it, there she is proving his point. But really I think she's doing it [peeling off the wallpaper] absentmindedly, like chewing on a pencil. So I don't want to take the chance of asking her to stop."

"So what happens next?"

"He keeps talking. She keeps peeling. But by now

I'm not hearing much of anything that's being said because I don't know what to do."

"Describe this feeling of not knowing what to do—what are the thoughts; what are the sensations?"

"It's almost physically painful to see her tearing off little strips. I keep thinking she'll look up and I can shake my head at her, but she doesn't. I also have this feeling that if I were any kind of therapist at all I wouldn't give a damn about some silly wallpaper. What's a little wallpaper compared to a girl who's probably being cut to ribbons by this man every day?"

"Now, still picturing yourself sitting at your desk with all this going on in your mind, take a moment to remember your purpose as a social worker. You said your purpose was to heal, to be a healer. Picture yourself taking a few deep breaths or closing your eyes or stepping out of the room for a second or two—whatever you need to do to focus on your purpose."

(After a moment, Jill opens her eyes.)

"All right, I've done that."

"Good. Now put yourself back in your office. . . . You are remembering your purpose. . . . And now, do not ask 'What should I do?' Instead, as you feel your purpose, just allow your body to do whatever it does. But whether your body acts or does not act, continue to concentrate only on your purpose. Do you understand?"

"Yes." *(Two or three minutes later, Jill smiles and opens her eyes.)*

"What happened?"

"I got up—I never break eye contact with the stepfather—and I go over to Donna's chair, sort of pick it up, and say, 'Sweetie, let's move you up a few feet so you can be part of what's going on here.' "

"What effect did this have on the meeting?"

"The stepfather liked it. I think he thought I was telling her to listen more closely to him—which I guess I was in a sense. And Donna did start listening better. I think she felt a little more included, a little more loved, at least by me. I had the feeling that the meeting was now going to end better than it had."

Pulling Donna's chair up is not something we would ever have thought to suggest to Jill. It also wasn't something that had occurred to Jill during all the time she had worried about the meeting afterward. And it's not a guideline that can be found in any book or article about parenting. It is what grew out of Jill's decision to stop thinking about what she should do and start thinking about why she was there. Perhaps Jill will never find herself in another situation in which pulling a child's chair up will make sense. But she will be in countless situations in which a purpose-centered mind can guide her.

MISPERCEPTIONS OF DAMAGED CHILDREN

Unfortunately, much nonsense has been written about the intrinsic virtue of all human beings, without any accompanying explanation or guide as to where this well of goodness lies or exactly how it can be used. Advocates of positive thinking often imply that all anyone need do is call strongly enough to another's heart and that person will respond. In practical terms this is not a workable approach. In spite of the spiritual or therapeutic strategies used, in countless cases destructive individuals have remained destructive. It does not follow, however, that they began their lives in "original sin" or as a "bad seed." The notion that some people are completely evil from birth is contrary to our experience and that of everyone we know who works with young children, and yet this is often how the villain or "heavy" in movies and novels is portrayed.

Children begin their lives with no malice and for a while are open to love and the peace of God. Genetic abnormalities or damage during pregnancy or birth can produce severe emotional or physical difficulties for an infant, but these cases are infrequent and the problems are so individual that we will not attempt to address these exceptions. However, it's interesting to note the shift in thinking in at least one such category. Many who have dealt with substance-addicted infants ("crack babies," for example) and have followed their progress, either in a professional capacity or as foster or adoptive parents, have changed their original view of both the nature and durability of the problem.

At first it was believed that fetal addiction somehow erased the child's moral sensibilities, that in a sense it stamped out that individual's spark of humanity. Now many observers are saying that in light of the fact that such a high percentage of these kids have developed into normal adults, it is likely that the caregivers' *perception* was coloring these early reports and, even more important, was causing some of the difficulty these kids were having. Knowing the tragic way the children had begun their lives, the caregivers looked for and found trouble in the kind of behavior that they ordinarily might have passed off as typical childhood antics. Not that these kids don't have special developmental problems, because most of them clearly do, but in the early history of this field, everything they did tended to be over-interpreted.

As a group comparison, if we again take the behavior of coaches as an example, we see some of the more prominent basketball, hockey, baseball, and football coaches of our day throwing chairs, spitting at fans, striking players and other coaches, chewing on towels, and exhibiting facial tics, inappropriate laughter, sudden uncontrolled tantrums, and repetitive mindless mannerisms—even though they are on camera at the time and stand to lose a high-salaried job. If we add to all of this their sometimes even more violent or disturbed personal lives, it would be difficult to say that these men are inherently more normal, more human, than individuals who came from their mothers' wombs addicted to heroin, cocaine, or some other substance.

The actual reason that one group is revered and showered with money whereas the other group is looked at with suspicion and kept at arm's length is the *perception* that the first group's success at winning what was originally a child's game is very important in itself. Because the public believes that these men are accomplishing much, their behavior is dismissed, tolerated, or looked on as merely "colorful," "competitive," or admirably "intense." In most instances it is not viewed with deep fear and mistrust.

If parents or other adults misuse a child—any child, regardless of the circumstances of his or her birth—the inherent open and gentle nature of that little person can indeed change, and by the prepubescent or adolescent stages, the child can become so locked into his or her ego that nothing short of a miracle can open that individual's heart. Miracles, however, are always a possibility, especially within the parent-child relationship, and therefore parents must not give up on their children or decide against *any* child's spiritual core.

Naturally, this doesn't mean that moms and dads should fail to protect their family from a biological, adopted, foster, or stepchild who has become physically destructive or in any other way threatens the safety of the family. We know one father of three kids who had to institutionalize his adopted son temporarily when at age ten the boy began setting fires in the house. However, he did not for one instant falter in his commitment to his son. He visited him daily, celebrated his birthday that fell during this time, and at the end of six months, when the therapists caring for the boy said it was safe, brought him back into the home. Today that boy is a kind and responsible young adult, as many other children would be if they knew that the answer to "What do you do when . . . ?" is always act from love, a love that never leaves.

6

THE PARENT-CHILD BALANCE

THE TRUE NATURE
OF PARENTAL ACCEPTANCE

When she was teaching in Togo, West Africa, Terri-anne Jacobson told us that she was struck by how different the family attitude toward the arrival of a new baby was compared to in our culture. A birth is announced to the community in terms of the "new guest" who has arrived. Instead of pride and expectation, the prevailing emotions are wonder and awe. Parents and grandparents seem to hold no dreams or plans of their own for this little one, but rather they await the unveiling of an entirely new individual whose uniqueness will slowly be revealed.

Contrast this to the arrival of children in our culture. More often than not we hope that they come with bags packed for some prestigious university or with a karmic passport to a remarkable career in hand. Parents look for signs of genius, physical precociousness, exceptional beauty, or advanced spiritual evolvement and are disappointed when other mothers and dads can point to more specialness in their child than they can in theirs. Thus begin the little wars with our children's personalities, propensities, and rates of development. We act as if an individual could be *pushed* to become someone of whom we can be proud, as if all children become who they are because of the decisions parents make.

Children are not given to us by God to mold and define. They are already created.

Some friends of ours who adopted a little boy at infancy were telling us recently about a family they know whose youngest biological child, a girl of nine, is in the same class at school as their boy. The girl's family is large and very talented. In fact, every member is considered a musical genius in his or her field, except for the little girl, who evidently possesses no musical talent at all. Our friends told us that this girl's life has been made a living hell by the unrelenting pressure her family has put on her to find some musical pursuit at which she can excel. Yet all the little girl is interested in is her friends.

Because she carries their genes, her family chooses to see her as an embarrassment, and the girl is clearly aware of this. She is starting to turn away from her family as a means of protecting herself from the pressures they apply.

In contrast, our friends, who are both professors in the math department of their university, are merely amused that their boy gets his lowest grades in math. They have a wait-and-see attitude about what his main interest will be and in what direction it will take him in life. They told us that they are dedicated to helping him develop in whatever ways he wants to go. Like the homes of many attentive parents, their house is filled with the paraphernalia from several old interests he has already pursued and discarded.

*   *   *

The child you have is a very interesting little person, and probably still a very good human being. If your child is older, as you now look back you can undoubtedly see that in many ways what your infant was at birth, he or she is today. Crying and fussing are not important indicators of the basic nature of a new arrival, but the essential character and spiritual essence of the person often *are* quite apparent, even at birth. From his first day, our middle son, John, exhibited a deep sense of purity, gentleness, and merriment. Jordan, our youngest, had a more difficult birth, and although he was uncomfortable and made this clear, his inner strength, clarity of purpose, and intense devotion to our family were evident right from the start. Scott, our oldest son, is from Hugh's previous marriage. Hugh was only twenty when Scott was born and because of the unusual chaos that surrounded that particular birth, he doesn't remember much of what Scott was like during the first hours of his life. All he recalls is that Scott was like a small peaceful haven in the storm. This sweetness of nature is still one of his most noticeable strengths.

It is not beneficial for parents to try to read the signs of their babies' genius or future greatness, because in all likelihood they will not turn out that way in the eyes of the world. Nor would it necessarily be a happy thing for them or their parents if they did, as is obvious from what we all know of the lives of people who attract considerable attention. What you want is for your children to grow up happy and strong, not merely to "make you proud." If you will look gently at your baby, toddler, tween, teen, or adult child, if you will see them from the stillness of your heart, you will recognize the part of them that comes from God, and this will be a vision you can safely commit to.

An older child still needs your unshakable commitment. Today many parents are making the mistake of not supporting their adult children in their life decisions. They somehow feel free to take hard stands against the spouse they choose, their occupation, their way of raising "my grandchildren," their faith, or their sexual preference. Many parents side with a former daughter- or son-in-law, declare a stronger love for their grandchildren than for their daughter or son, and even favor other relatives or friends over their own children in their wills.

No matter what your adult children have done, it can never justify your decision to stop loving them. This doesn't mean that you must agree with their opinions or disagree, invite them over or not invite them, phone or not phone them. Again, commitment is an act of the heart, and it is your heart that you must keep absolutely pure, not theirs.

There is ancient and powerful symbolism attached to births, deaths, inheritances, marriages, and the like, that loving parents take into consideration in deciding how to behave toward their children. For example, years ago it wasn't convenient for Hugh to attend Scott's graduation, and he didn't; it wasn't convenient for Hugh's mother to attend our wedding, and she didn't. Yet both of those decisions caused considerable and needless pain because they were not made from love and awareness. Now we try to attend every game and ceremony our children have, because in our culture such acts are the language of love. And we have occasionally given them money when "they didn't deserve it" because of how powerfully money represents caring and concern.[1]

The parable of the prodigal son contains a wise and gentle message about adult children. Clearly both sons in this story make mistakes; one "sinned against Heaven," the other was petty and jealous. Yet the father does not question their behavior. He doesn't pass judgment on it one way or the other. He simply reaffirms his absolute love and his eternal welcome, and he uses the symbols of his day to show that he means it. As their parents, **we must love our children even in their mistakes.** Unless we do this, we will not fully sense God's commitment to us.

As a good parent, you never lose sight of what this child is at heart, whether young or old. You strive never to make a harmful decision about this one who was delivered into your arms to cherish and believe in. Even a child who comes to you from another family already damaged and headed in a destructive direction still can be deeply seen, and this way of looking contains the possibility of healing.

As we said earlier, the fairly obvious fact is that most kids are better human beings than the adults who surround them. That can, and often does, change, but even as late as elementary school, a visit to most classes shows that the children who are being "molded" still have more innocence, happiness, and goodness than the adults who are doing the molding. If it were possible for you to visit a large number of households, as we have done as counselors, you would see the same pattern there. The conclusion is clear: Children are our teachers as well as our students.

Not long ago Terrianne Jacobson put this truth in lovely perspective: "I looked up and saw my two-year-old running in the yard with a long stick," she wrote to us. "He was growling and swinging the stick recklessly. I was afraid and started walking toward him. He would lose an eye or run himself through. As I started to speak I caught sight of his shadow, tall and bold, with the sword held high. And I noticed that he had just seen it too. In an instant his play changed from aggressor to sprite. He leaped sideways. So did his shadow. He turned around. His shadow nearly disappeared. He dropped the stick and cavorted across the yard in delight. I can't tell you exactly why I didn't speak— and I'm grateful he didn't poke out an eye—but I'm also glad I didn't choose that time to interrupt with a rule about sticks. He would have missed that playful time with his shadow. And I would have missed it too. This little boy, my birth child—but above all, my guest—reminded me that I too had a shadow, and I ran and laughed and jumped around the yard with a friend I had long forgotten."

WHETHER OR NOT TO INTERFERE

Children don't come into the world fully "actualized," requiring little more than someone to feed, clothe, and house them. All kids need to feel that their safety and health are important to their parents and also that their parents provide thoughtful limits to what they can do. While pushing to mold and change a child's basic nature is destructive, a laissez-faire attitude is equally injurious. Many New Age books foster the notion that children are already potentially perfect and should not be interfered with, that the parents' function is to "trust" and step out of their kids' way and therefore that they should be supportive of whatever their kids want to do. Parents who adopt this approach are often surprised to see their children become increasingly insensitive, self-absorbed, and mean-spirited.

Viewing a parent's role as a mere caretaker of a little god is intellectually appealing, but it's not based on experience. Children need their parents throughout their lives in numerous extremely important ways. Furthermore, when they are young they feel unloved without firmness and boundaries.

Vision and trust do not preclude parents involving themselves in their children's lives, nor do they preclude firmness and intervention when children get caught up in destructive or unhappy behavior. Most kids need to be encouraged to be thoughtful and conscious of others; they need to be made aware of the evidence that indifference and cruelty will not make them happy.

A child can feel the effects of other people's insensitivity and a loving parent can sense when and how to point out "how this feels." Thus kids gradually learn that they don't want to be the cause of making others unhappy in the ways that they themselves have been made unhappy in the past.

Once one of our boys was not understanding the effect he was having on the whole family by refusing to do little things for the rest of us. He would not bring back plates and glasses he had taken to his room, objected to our making another stop when bringing him home from one of his activities, would not look for us when a phone call wasn't for him, kept up the parent who needed to help him with his homework by not starting it early enough, and so on. Our many talks with him had little effect. So we finally sat him down and told him that for the next two weeks no one in the family was going to inconvenience him- or herself, and that we were doing this so that he could feel for himself the effects.

We decided on this approach only after praying and considering it deeply, then picking a time when we could explain it to him from love rather than anger. After just one week the effect was dramatic, and we never had to repeat the lesson. Later we also dropped a few of our demands. For instance, we stopped checking our boys' rooms for dishes, glasses, cans, and the like. Most of the time they bring these back themselves, but if they don't and we see them there, we simply take them to the kitchen ourselves— which is the same kindness we extend to each other.

We have come to realize that John and Jordan are not intentionally causing us extra work; they are just forgetful in the ways most kids are, especially teenagers. (See Cultural Assumption #10 in Chapter 10.) We also have noted that we ourselves are inconsistent about when we clean up. In other words, their bringing in plates and empty cans wasn't a point worth making over and over, and so we dropped it.

Regarding our son's overall insensitivity to family

needs, the tactic we tried worked—it allowed him to feel for himself the effects of insensitivity—but the other tactics we had tried before this one had failed. Furthermore, it's clear that what we did with this son would not have worked with either of our other two boys. As many parents know, you get everything figured out for one child and the next child comes along and suddenly none of the old rules quite fits. The mistake is in doggedly trying to force them to fit.

If your goal is to teach awareness and not merely to enforce an old rule or rigidly apply a new formula, eventually you will discover ways to do this that fit the situation and personality of your child. You can't expect to solve every problem that arises neatly and permanently, but anytime you work lovingly on difficult issues, there will be at least some loving effects from your efforts. You may need persistence, experimentation, and creativity to bring about real improvement, but the process itself can be healing for you, your marriage, and your child—if you keep your motive as pure and loving as you can.

A good example of two parents trying to solve a problem by increasing their child's awareness is in the story of how Jim and Ann responded to their thirteen-year-old daughter, Bonnie, when she became friends with a girl named Randi. Randi lived in the neighborhood, and it was not until the two girls became friends that Randi's association with a gang became known. At first Ann and Jim were supportive of the relationship, but as they became more aware of Randi's destructive interests, they were increasingly anxious over the possible consequences to their daughter.

Jim and Ann had very open and fear-free communication with Bonnie, in part because they had made it a priority ever since she had been little and in part because they were lucky to have a daughter who didn't withdraw when she hit puberty. They didn't want to do anything that would cause Bonnie suddenly to become secretive, yet at the same time, they knew that they could not ignore the kinds of activities that she was being introduced to. Bonnie was now occasionally drinking alcohol and smoking on the weekends, and she had been present when Randi had physically hurt girls she didn't like.

Their suggesting that Bonnie should back away from this friendship didn't work, and wisely they stopped using this approach. Each time they brought the subject up, they noted that Bonnie would become angry and, for a time at least, would stop telling them what she and Randi did together. Ann and Jim had decided that if at any time they thought their daughter was using hard drugs or seemed ready to join a gang, they would take her out of school and move to another part of town, even though this would cause them a considerable financial hardship. In the meantime, they tried to help Bonnie become more aware of her deeper feelings about what was happening. Every time she told them about something destructive that had happened, they tried to focus her mind on how she had felt. For example, how she felt when she smoked and after she smoked; how she felt when another girl was hurt or humiliated.

They did not order her to stop participating in these things because they knew that Bonnie had not seen through their new approach and would have simply started lying about what she was doing. For this same reason they also didn't try to make her feel guilty, ashamed, or afraid. **Observant parents learn not to *add* to their children's feelings but to help them become more aware of the ones they already have.** Healing takes place from the inside out; it can't be imposed through disapproval and irritation, which tend to harden the behaviors.

Jim and Ann continued this approach for over a year before they saw a change in Bonnie. In fact, they had almost given up and decided to move the family when the change occurred.

Shortly before Christmas vacation, Bonnie came home one day and told them that she and Randi had gone to the mall and had broken off hood ornaments and slashed tires. Once again they asked her how this made her feel. She said, "I pictured this family coming out of the mall with their arms full of presents. When they got to the car and saw what had happened, Christmas was ruined. They were poor and didn't have the money for new tires. They had to take their presents back."

Her parents said, "Did you tell Randi about this thought?" "No," their daughter said. "She would have just laughed. I decided not to see Randi again."

Because she had arrived at it herself, that decision turned out to be permanent.

INTERPRETING CHILDREN'S MOTIVES

Although the previous story is an obvious exception, we often have noticed that children are less likely to misread the motives of other children than are adults. John and Jordan are usually quicker to see the innocence of little kids' antics and jump to their defense than we are. They also have a better instinct for how to meet the play needs of these little kids, especially those of boys. And many girls, especially between the ages of eight and thirteen, are highly intuitive about the needs of babies and small children. However, most adults read their own motives into what they see kids do.

Among the most remarkable victims of these misinterpretations are two- and three-year-old children. Just think of what it would be like to have lived for only a couple dozen *months*! Unfortunately, most of us have lost those memories. Nevertheless, one would think that no adult would seriously believe that a normal child of that age would be capable of malice, yet one of the most widely read nonreligious children's authorities states that not only are they capable of malice, they *often* are motivated by revenge! Many religious writers go even further and teach that children start out basically evil.

Unless little children have genetic damage, unusual brain damage, or have been horrendously abused, it is impossible for them to be motivated by an evil intent. Even if their motivation springs from damage, it is not truly evil. It is confused, chaotic, or crazy. Evil intentions require a focused mind, and damaged kids are usually very unfocused.

It is nonetheless true that most two- and three-year-olds behave in a wide variety of ways that are misunderstood by adults. They may be unresponsive when spoken to; talk to themselves incessantly; give away family secrets; tell tall tales; issue commands to adults and children alike; boast and exaggerate; push, poke, or punch other kids; break things to find out what is inside; stare and ask "rude" questions; and do many other things that would take on an entirely different meaning if done by an adult. For example, most kids are deeply honest and yet may lie easily as a practical means of solving an immediate problem. This is quite different from the basic deceitfulness that can develop in an older child or adult.

The older children become, the more likely parents are to read adult motivation into what they do. When parents assume that there is a negative reason for a child's behavior, their censure of their child—not their decision to intervene—damages communication and destroys the sense of oneness between them.

Tim and Jason were over playing with Jordan when Jordan suddenly remembered that he had bought several incense candles the week before. He asked us if he could light them in his room, and we said, "Sure."

Later Hugh went in Jordan's room and saw that the boys had melted one of the candles into a glass bowl, had stuck several matches in it, and had a pretty good flame going. Hugh said he didn't think that was such a good idea because the bowl was sitting on top of a dresser and the heat could damage the finish. He also pointed out that someone swinging in the hammock chair could knock the bowl over. So Hugh took the bowl away, leaving the matches and the other candles.

Later Gayle went in the room and saw that the boys had done the same thing, only this time they had put the melted wax in a thick plastic bowl that conducted less heat and had moved it out of the way of the hammock chair. Gayle said that she didn't want them to make a flame that big and she put it out.

Later Gayle told Hugh that the boys had once again made a big flame even though they had been told not to do this by both parents. So Hugh went to the room and said, "Jason and Tim, I'm going to take you both home now. You know why, don't you?" They both nodded and said it was "getting late anyway." Hugh kept himself from smiling at this adult turn of phrase.

While driving them home, Hugh asked both boys what had been so interesting about the fire. He also asked Jordan the same question when he got back home.

All three boys said about the same thing. They had noticed the colors that formed at different heights of the flame and had gotten in a discussion about which color represented the highest temperature. They knew we were anxious about their little experiment, but each time we said something, they had taken steps to make things safer. Nevertheless, all three boys had understood that we probably didn't want them making the flames no matter how safe.

Neither of us had gotten upset, but we had intervened when it became clear that the boys were probably going to continue thwarting us. But this was not malice on their part. We have a great affection for Tim and Jason and know that they are not and never have been in a power struggle with us. Their and Jordan's interests were merely different from ours, and they pursued those interests as far as they could.

Afterward, the boys didn't feel unfairly treated and we didn't feel deceived and manipulated—but that definitely would have been the outcome if this same situation had arisen ten or fifteen years ago. Then we would have jumped to conclusions about "defiance" and "willfulness" that would have been misinterpretations on our part. Now, without our giving anyone a lecture, all three boys knew that from that day on they could not do fire experiments in Jordan's room, and the issue has never come up again.

RHYTHMS OF CHILDREN'S GROWTH

Contrary to the assumption that many parents are acting on today, they have remarkably little power to make their kids permanently thinner, more outgoing, more intelligent, more coordinated, more expressive, more beautiful, more ambitious, more talented, more financially adept. Just as children teethe in their own time, they also tend to crawl, creep, pull themselves up, and walk—both physically and spiritually— all within their own individual rhythms. For example, regardless of how soon parents begin "training" children to play pat-a-cake, climb up stairs, or be toilet trained, the untrained kids will master the ability at about the same time as the "trained" ones. And this pattern holds true throughout most of a child's inner and outer development.

Our friend David Wilkinson told us that when he was four, his family lived in a rural community. His mother often packed him a lunch that he would take with him when he went exploring the countryside for the day. His parents' only rule was that he was to go nowhere near the neighbor's bull. Once he had seen this prize stud bull when he and his father went visiting. The huge animal, which was notoriously dangerous, was locked inside an iron cage and rammed his horns against the bars whenever anyone came close. However, David recognized that the bull was scared, not angry, and he had absolutely no fear of it from the first time he saw it; in fact, he felt an immediate bond.

Without telling anyone, David frequently visited the bull; he stuck his head through the slats of its holding pen, petted it, talked to it, and sat down near it to have his picnic lunch. David remembers the bull as one of his best childhood friends.

Like David, you probably can look back and see that you have always been yourself, that you were not unaware— even at a very early age—of people's unsuccessful attempts to change you, and that you have tended to become more and more yourself regardless of the influences around you. At most, these influences may have temporarily diverted you or delayed you, but they did not alter your basic identity. You know who you are; you have always known who you are. And this fact is equally true of your children, regardless of all else they do not know, how high-pitched or in transition their voices are, how tiny or tall and gangly they may be, or how naive they are about touching stoves, driving fast, or not having insurance.

Surrounding this consistent core of consciousness and identity, within each child there are the normal physical and emotional developments, a rhythm of change that can be typical or unique, depending on the individual child. Most children, perhaps all, will have at least one area of development that is outside the usual pattern and yet not at all a reason for worry.

About midterm last year we were called in for one of the regularly scheduled teacher-parent conferences. Tracy Bright, Jordan's fifth-grade teacher, said, "I realize Jordan's not making straight A's, but I want you to know that he is as intelligent and motivated as any child in my class. It just so happens that at this time his interest is athletics, at which he works very hard and is very good. He's not interested in

schoolwork and only does enough to get by. I understand
this and it's just fine. Someday he'll get interested in using
his mind in an academic way, and when he does he'll probably excel in whatever direction that takes him. In the meantime all his extra effort is going into sports. I want you to
know that I'm not worried about Jordan and I don't want
you to be."

Her refreshing attitude was based on the same same broad
understanding of what children truly need from adults as
was that of a doctor, Andrew Weil, who saw Jordan when
he was nine. At the time Jordan was having mild allergic
reactions to a surprisingly wide variety of foods and en-
vironments. We had tried many different approaches
prescribed by various authorities before we made the appointment with Dr. Weil. After he had examined Jordan,
taken his history, and made several suggestions, he concluded by saying "None of this may eliminate the problem
entirely. The most important thing is that you not make
Jordan's life miserable in your attempt to help him. If he
becomes very resistant to some approach, for example, the
elimination of dairy products from his diet, then don't be
rigid. It's better that he have a few symptoms than be in a
battle with you. He may outgrow all these reactions in time
anyway, but whether he does or not, what you want is for
him to have a happy childhood."[2]

Of course, there are more serious concerns than average or low grades in school or mild allergic reactions. For
example, your child may show signs of developmental ab-
normality such as an overall unresponsiveness, a slow
growth rate of some organ or limb, deteriorating eyesight, a
dangerous reaction to certain chemicals or foods, or other
extreme conditions to which you may have to respond
quickly and radically. But such problems do not occur as
often as many people believe within our present atmosphere
of hyperanxiety about almost everything. Most children
develop intellectually and physically just fine. Yet many par-

ents, and even some pediatricians and psychologists, fearfully read disaster into every little sign of uniqueness.

KNOW YOUR CHILD

Shortly after she began the fourth grade, the daughter of a couple we know started showing an interest in sex that far exceeded any shown by the other nine-year-olds in her class. One day her teacher happened to laugh about this in the faculty lounge, and the school counselor overheard him. "That isn't anything to joke about," she said. "An inordinate interest in sex is a sign of sexual abuse. I think we should make an appointment for her to see me."

By the end of that school year, the girl's parents, having by then had several conferences with the counselor, had ordered their daughter to have no more contact with her best friend (because they suspected that she might be the source of their daughter's sexual interests), had transferred her to another school, and had come close to getting a divorce because the counselor had intimated that perhaps the girl's father had secretly abused her. Fortunately, the counselor at the new school pointed out to the parents that one symptom by itself has no meaning and that, in her opinion, little else about the girl's behavior indicated sexual abuse. In the girl's new class was a boy who had what might be described as an inordinate interest in astronomy and a girl who was more consumed with the cello than any child the counselor had ever known, yet no one thought either of these interests had any sinister connotation.

We were so impressed with the calming effect that the counselor had on our friends that we interviewed her for this book. She told us of another time that a couple became overly concerned with signs of attention deficit disorder in their daughter and took her to three different neurologists, all of whom prescribed drugs to treat the condition and also recommended that she be transferred into a nearby private school that was set up to deal with this kind of problem. Because the three doctors had disagreed on which drugs to give the girl and because this family did not have the money to send her to the private school, they went to the counselor for advice. She told them that in the twenty-three years that she had been working with children, both as a teacher and counselor, she had seen several children as "hyper" as their little girl and all of them had grown out of it. She told them that regardless of the test scores, she thought their daughter was within the broad range of normal and that all they needed to do was to love her exactly the way she was. As a result of this conversation, their daughter's life was not disrupted. Just last year she graduated in the top third of her class, of which she had also been elected vice president.

Naturally, if you are concerned about any aspect of your child's development, you should take whatever steps you need to inform yourself about what is going on. We have interviewed many parents who intuitively knew that their child had cancer or some other life-threatening condition well before it was diagnosed, and continued to know it even after receiving a misdiagnosis. We also have talked to many parents who knew that their child was just fine despite fears raised by a therapist, doctor, or other authority and were eventually proven right. Your intuition is not infallible, but often it is signaling you to look closely and calmly at something that is occurring in your child's mind, body, or relationships. More mistakes have been made by parents who ignored their quiet knowing than have been made by those who overinterpreted it.

No set of rules can safeguard you against all parental mistakes, and if you seek a professional opinion about your child, naturally you should listen to it very carefully. However, it has been our experience that those parents who consistently try to know their children deeply eliminate many false starts. Rather than personally misdiagnosing your child's development or allowing yourself to be panicked by an outside opinion, the mistake you are far more likely to make is permitting anxiety to interfere with your *relationship* with your child. Genuine intuition is never experienced as an anxiety—although anxiety can certainly be added to it—and fear or judgment is never a component of love.

Parents exercise their capacity to be true guardians through deeply seeing and deeply accepting their child. **The cardinal rule of spiritual parenting is: Know your child.** Knowing calms you. Knowing comes from listening and watching, not from deciding, classifying, and categorizing. Knowing is an open, ongoing process that is able to see change as it occurs, whereas making a decision about your child's character or personality type can blind you to what is happening *now.*

Instead of seeing clearly and then acting, parents try to analyze and assign blame. Instead of consulting their own hearts, they stir themselves up with other people's opinions and points of view. Instead of using their mind to attain a calm vision, they use it to try out one angle of interpretation after another. They endlessly discuss quite ordinary home-life events, attempting to reach some permanent meaning. And they assign layer upon layer of conflicting significance to everything they do to their child and that their child does to them.

A GROWING PREJUDICE AGAINST BOYS

In our culture, to be born a girl is still far more of a handicap than to be born a boy. Within our own country, and more openly in many other parts of the world, female children are routinely and ritualistically murdered, mutilated, raped, and sold into prostitution and slavery. While the historical and worldwide injustice against the female sex has been well documented, unfortunately this knowledge seems to have fueled a growing indifference to the needs of boys in our homes and especially in our schools. Any boy being born today shoulders part of the shame of all the men who have come before him. This does no one's cause any good, and as parents, it must become as intolerable as the unjust treatment of girls.

At one of the weekly worship services we give, a single mother recently got up during the prayer-request segment and asked for prayers for her daughter. On the verge of tears, she explained that just a few days before, her three-year-old girl had said that she wanted to be a boy.

That parents become upset by something so common as little boys saying they want to be girls or dressing up as girls, or little girls saying they want to be boys or acting like "tomboys," merely indicates how often parents fail to observe for themselves how children think and play. It wouldn't be unusual for kids around that age to say they want to be a bird, to be invisible, to grow up and be a wrestler, a rap singer, a NASCAR driver, or a sniper on a SWAT team. However, within our culture's climate of growing prejudice against males, we wonder if this mother would have been equally upset if this had been her little boy saying he wanted to be a girl.

When we got home from the service, we told John that a mother had asked for prayers because of something her little girl wanted to be.

"What was it," he asked, "a prostitute?"

"No, a boy."

"Oh," he said, "that's much worse." At sixteen he is well acquainted with the prejudice against his sex.

Even Jordan and his friends have long been commenting on the lack of tolerance for boys among most teachers. For the last four years (Jordan has just started the sixth grade), we have heard them complain about how girls are always believed above boys and how boys are always being punished or lectured for the ways they act out, whereas girls are not. Several times we have seen girls who kicked or hit boys given, at most, a mild verbal reprimand, whereas a boy who once pushed a girl away, despite the fact that she had just bloodied his leg, was dealt with quite harshly by the school.

Unquestionably most boys do tend to be rough, loudmouthed, disruptive, and even obnoxious. They squirm, shove, swagger, brag, fight, and fib. They think burps, profanities, farting noises, and impolite behavior are funny. But they also can be very brave and very loyal to their friends in the face of authority, and can persist at an activity despite extreme adversity. They learn by taking things apart and (hopefully) putting them back together. They learn by taking risks, often unreasonable ones. They learn by direct experience, preferring not to wait—not to be shown or *taught*—but to dive in and do it themselves.

Obviously many girls have these qualities also, but as a group, boys don't fit well within our present elementary and secondary school approaches. In our culture most adults have failed to respect children and to see them clearly. And now, in the name of fairness and equality, we have added to this insensitivity the *ideal* that we are not supposed to acknowledge any differences in children based on sex.

The public school emphasis on "staying on task" is quickly shrinking "break" (play period) into insignificance and is even starting to cut deeply into the time allotted sheer physical activity during PE.[3] These activity periods, when kids can run around, play basketball and other games, or just "hang out" together, are like lifeblood to many girls and to almost all boys. This unfortunate shift in how school time is used illustrates the enormous gap between what adults decide that children need versus what simple observation would tell them they need.

Instead of saying "boys will be boys," as we once did, we are pathologizing many ordinary male behaviors. For example, ADHD (attention deficit hyperactive disorder) is now the most frequently diagnosed behavior disorder among children, and boys are about four times more likely to be so diagnosed than girls. The *New York Times* reports that the American production of Ritalin-like drugs, used in the treatment of ADHD, has jumped 250 percent since 1991. Clearly, some of these kids have a serious organic disorder requiring medical treatment, but most of the boys so diagnosed with whom we have had personal contact would have been called "boisterous" or "rambunctious" in an earlier era. Nothing pathological would have been read into their restlessness in class or their competitiveness on the playground.

HOW KIDS LEARN RESPECT

When most of us think about our early days in school, we remember how we felt rather than what we learned. It's whether certain teachers liked or disliked us, not what they taught us. It's how we felt during tests, not what they were about. And when we think back to the times we got in trouble at home, it's the emotions we had while being disciplined, and not the misbehavior that we were being disciplined about, that we remember best.

As we shepherd these little ones in our care out into the world, our duty is to give them the awareness they will need. But we can't help our children see their effect on others if we ourselves are insensitive to them. Respect cannot be faked. The power to influence children lies in our attitudes, not our words. Kids are very aware of adults' moods and quickly learn to read this level of reality, because it, more than what parents say, indicates what is going to happen to them. This is why they are keenly aware of whether they are being appreciated, dismissed, or looked down on. **Telling your kids that you respect them is nearly meaningless. You must know and feel the grounds for this respect yourself or else it will not be communicated.**

One common area in which children are not respected is the attitude of most parents toward their child's possessions or collections—especially if they are monetarily worthless, or old, or dirty. They usually throw out or give away these things without asking the child's permission.

Kids often collect quite odd things—old bottle caps; cutouts of pictures, ads, or illustrations; pieces of rusted metal; personal notes or scraps of paper from school; insect carcasses. *The act of acquiring and possessing is more important to them than the objects themselves—just as it is for many adults.* Look at how many things most of us have that we don't need, don't use, and don't even particularly want, but if our children even *use* some of these without our permission, we can become very upset. If they went to the extreme we do, and just tossed them out, we might think they were mentally unstable.

We once made the mistake of throwing away an old, dirty beer bottle that had recently appeared in John's room. Because we didn't first ask, we hadn't realized that he and a friend had started collecting these. He instantly noticed that it was gone when he came back from school and complained loudly. Later that week, after seeing what he had fixed himself for a snack, we said, "Please don't open expensive jars of food without asking us first. Those stuffed olives were a gift." His answer was "I didn't know they were expensive. All I did was *eat* some of your expensive olives—I didn't throw the jar away."

In talking about this later, we realized that we had a belief that we needed to rethink. We viewed certain foods as too good to be used for a kid's snack. They could be used only as hors d'oeuvres or "party snacks" on special *adult* occasions, especially if the adults were ones we didn't know well and didn't love as much as our children! One outcome of this discussion was that we set aside three shelves in the pantry, one for us and one each for John and Jordan. On these we put the special foods that no one could have without that person's permission, and we made it a point to buy at least one or two things for each boy's shelf whenever we went shopping. They both seemed pleased with this small acknowledgment of them as equal members of the family, and it had the unexpected effect on us of making us more aware of their likes and dislikes when we went shopping.

Another related way that many parents are insensitive to children occurs when they take a small child into a grocery store. Parents pick out anything they want and put it in the cart, whereas often the child is not allowed to pick out even one item. This creates a running battle that can be heard during peak hours in many large supermarkets.

We know one mother who gives her four-year-old daughter three dollars to spend however she wants, the only exception being that she is not allowed to put something in the cart that could harm her. The mother never tries to dissuade her daughter and never gives her a lecture on how impractical any choice is. This practice has not only made shopping with her daughter less stressful but has also allowed her little girl to gain an early sense of arithmetic and of what things cost.

DO ADULTS KNOW BEST WHAT KIDS SHOULD FEEL?

Gayle was attending the "Anne Frank in the World" exhibit, which passed through Tucson recently, when the auditorium began to fill with eight- to ten-year-olds. They were being bused in from Phoenix schools.

The teachers who were with the children—probably eight hundred kids in all—were making a mistake that we have seen adults often make when talking to children who are in grief from a loss or who have a parent who is dying. They were trying to feed the children what they felt to be the appropriate emotional response. And they were becoming increasingly distressed because the children were not showing the right emotions in their faces and didn't have the right feeling tone to their voices.

The kids were all "well behaved," but they were merely looking at the photographs and exhibits with quiet interest and mild curiosity. The teachers kept directing their attention to the saddest and most shocking features of Anne Frank's story. Their tone of voice said, "Here you are in the face of tragedy. React accordingly!" But of course the kids reacted like kids, not like adults.

From having worked with many children whose lives had become very tragic, we know that they can feel loss extremely deeply, but until they are much older (often past the teen years), they don't know and are not very interested in the affect that adults think is proper. Their feelings are their own, and letting others know how they feel has not yet become a priority.

Jordan's friend Jason (age eleven at the time) stayed with us for five days while his mother was in the hospital with a recurrence of a very serious illness that Jason knew she had almost died from a few months before. At no time during his stay was there anything unusual about his demeanor. He was the same happy, gentle boy he always is when he is over here. However, once every day, usually in the afternoon or early evening, he would ask to be taken to see his mother and would persist in this request until we could juggle our schedule to accommodate him.

Jason is a very undemanding child, yet his concern for his mother overrode his usual personality. But this concern was never expressed in adult ways, and we have found that most children will not respond "appropriately" to even sudden and horrible tragedy. Adults wrongly assume that they are either in denial or that they are "very resilient."

With few exceptions, young children handle emotion more through thoughts and fantasies than through outward display, but they definitely need love, support, and understanding from the adults around them. It is not helpful for adults to *pressure* them in any way to "act out" or "talk out" what they are feeling.

The obvious mistake that the previous generation of parents made was they forced their children to *appear* thoughtful and considerate without providing a spiritual sense of why this is a happier approach to life. True kindness has little to do with mere appearances. The parent must lead with a strong *inner* model. Manners, for instance, are meaningless if not motivated by love. Yet sensitivity to the effect of manners on another person and the willingness to do the little things that make that individual happy can definitely be an expression of kindness. For example, many adult children have learned what topics their parents can talk about comfortably and out of love for them do not stray from those subjects.

Although parents and adults of this generation may place less emphasis on formal manners (the appearance of having the proper emotions), a general lack of respect for children's moods and feelings still prevails. Hugh once took Jordan to a restaurant after his baseball game and the waitress who came over to their table immediately said to him, "What an unhappy face. Let me see a big smile." Jordan, age ten, did not accommodate. He had had this kind of thing happen before. After she left he said, "Why do strangers talk that way to children? She never would have said that to you."

Jordan, like many children, does not like to be cajoled. Adults assume they have the *right* to change children's moods, to tickle them, to make faces at them, to ask them endless questions, and to give them unsolicited advice about their attitudes. Another example of this assumption can be seen in the approach to kids' emotions often used by coaches of teams in Little League, Pop Warner, basketball leagues, and soccer leagues. Many of these coaches—but certainly not all—yell at their kids to "put on their game faces" or to "suck up the pain." They think nothing of humiliating them in front of their parents and teammates during a game, and then, especially in Little League games, they make them yell "Who do we appreciate" of the team members who just beat them—and then line up to give them all "high fives"!

Very few professional athletes would put up with any of this, and very few adults would take this kind of treatment from a friend or even a boss. This type of arrogance directed toward one's spouse could bring on a divorce. And yet many parents, teachers, coaches, and the like, assure one another that these entrenched ways of disrespecting kids' emotions actually "build character." We personally don't think that most parents who say this actually believe it, but perhaps unconsciously they do recognize that a *consensus* of disrespect must be maintained if they are to continue having free rein to exercise it at home. At home, a dad's and mom's right to override their kids' emotions is what keeps their kids out of their hair. But merely making child care convenient is not the aim of spiritual parenting, and it is not the key to enjoying children.

You are not without considerable experience and insight into parenting, regardless of what books or articles you have failed to read or what degrees you fail to possess. The quality of the parenting and the strength of the home life that we have observed in many "disadvantaged" families has been equal to and in some instances far greater than in families that have had many advantages. Love has nothing to do with income, position, or education. Everyone's link to God is the same.

Within your family's basic goal of oneness, you are both teacher and student to your children as well as your spouse. Herein lies your greatest reward and source of wisdom. Knowing when to step in and when to step back is the art of spiritual parenting and will be an outgrowth of your attunement to your own personal compassion and intuition. Do not be afraid to actively exemplify your understanding of the importance of awareness and sensitivity. Likewise, don't be afraid to treat your kids with more respect than our culture thinks is normal. Most important, don't be afraid to receive fully the rich presence of reality that your child brought into the world. Children are a shortcut to happiness.

Part II

—

TEENS, TWEENS, AND "PROBLEM CHILDREN"

Note to the Reader

There is some evidence that puberty is starting at an earlier age for many children than it was even a few decades ago. Certainly what most people think of as "adolescent behavior" is beginning sooner, although this may be, in part, the mere projection of a society that has become more judgmental of this kind of behavior. In this chapter we use the term "tweens" for children who are roughly between the ages of ten and twelve and the terms "teens" or "teenagers" for kids who are about thirteen to twenty. We use the term "adolescent" to refer to the span of years between the first signs of puberty and physical maturity or adulthood. Most of what we say here applies to all kids between ten and twenty.

7

ARE KIDS MANIPULATIVE?

LABELS ARE ALWAYS JUDGMENTAL

It's clear from attitudes found in early child-rearing texts and sprinkled throughout much of American literature that we always have been judgmental of our offspring. Today, however, kids from infancy on are being tagged with psychological and medical labels that parents feel helpless to combat. Of these the label "manipulative" is so harmful to children and to the parent-child relationship that although we have mentioned it previously, we feel that it needs to be singled out and given careful attention.

Ask most parents or teachers today to describe any kid they know who is a "problem child," and almost always they will mention the characteristic of manipulativeness. But we have been surprised to discover how widespread is the thought that even babies are manipulative. In the 1940s, parents were told that "babies are always looking for ways to get you under their thumbs." Now, it seems, we take more responsibility for our part in how babies are and speak of "spoiling" or "creating unreasonable needs" in infants. Yet many authorities also point out that it's almost impossible for parents to avoid doing this. So whether babies try to control you right from the start or whether you unavoidably make them that way yourself, the result is the same: Babies are demanding, overly needy, and manipulative—and it is up to you to rein them in.

How does labeling our children so early in life affect them and our attitude toward them? The label could be anything—"hyperactive," "a late bloomer," or "a good baby" (meaning she eats, sleeps, and wants to play when it's convenient for *us*). But let's say the label is merely "colicky." Instead of thinking, "This evening my baby is colicky; what can I do about this now?"—and noticing with equal ease when she is *not* colicky—we are told by a friend, a relative, or perhaps a doctor, "You have a colicky baby." The jump from "My baby is colicky this evening, and has been colicky most evenings for several weeks" to "I have a colicky baby" is enormous. One is an observation; the other is a label. One is a way to start studying a problem that occurs off and on (no baby has colic unremittingly); the other is the beginning of a judgment or decision about your baby.

As with all labels, it isn't the word or phrase ("a well-behaved baby," "a colicky baby") that causes the problem but the *decision* about the child that is behind it. For example, this little colicky label first might lead to a suspicion that your child has a weak or improperly functioning digestive system. And perhaps there is some evidence that this is so *now*—but no evidence that this is or must be a permanent characteristic of your child. Next comes the thought that maybe your kid is constitutionally weak or unhealthy (has a disturbed metabolism, a poor immune system, too high or too low an energy level, and so forth). Then, inevitably, into your mind come the behaviors and dependencies that are believed to flow from early bad health—and are even warned against in many books.

The baby appears irritable when he has colic. He doesn't seem to appreciate your efforts to comfort him. In fact, he may appear to get angrier the harder you try to relieve his pain. Now the *questions* start bubbling up: "Does this child have a basically unpleasant personality? Or is he too needy? When this fretfulness starts, at first I feel sad, then I feel inadequate, then I start to get mad. Am I becoming codependent? Maybe I should do nothing and just let him cry himself out."

When children are labeled "sickly" ("weak," "not healthy," "allergic," and the like), it is often assumed that they also have become too reliant or dependent on other people. Unquestionably **a child or adult of any age can get used to a certain level of attention or a certain way that things are done and resist this being altered.** This means, of course, that children can get used to being cared for in a particular way when they are sick, just as any adult can. Large companies that change ownership often provide seminars for the old employees to explain how and why things will be different and provide aids to help in the transition.

The officers of a corporation would not say, "We've instituted this new policy, but all the old employees have become manipulative. It's time they learn responsibility." More likely they would say, "There are a lot of new procedures to learn and given the amount of resistance we are meeting from the old employees, perhaps we should move a little more slowly." Yet when children are asked to take orders from a new stepparent, to enter a new school, or to move into a new home and stepfamily, we don't necessarily say that they are "having trouble adjusting" or they are "resisting doing things a new way." Instead we jump to the conclusion that their reaction to change means that they are becoming overly needy and manipulative.

In the first months of infancy, your child may need to be burped often; to be held or rocked because the movement and the warm pressure on her stomach relieve the pain. In the evenings she may need a quiet and peaceful surrounding. And perhaps she may need certain foods fixed for her and certain medications given. With all of these measures, perhaps her health problem—colic, indigestion, diarrhea, hard stool, whatever it may be—begins to clear up. But as you modify the routine, she may start crying to get the extra attention she is used to, wake up "before it's time," hold out her arms asking to be picked up, and so on. Now you begin thinking or are told by other people that she is "too dependent," that she is manipulating you to sustain this dependency, and that you are contributing to her "problem" by "giving in" to her. Thus a story begins about why your child is the way she is, and as she grows older, everything she does tends to become part of the fabric of the tale.

Once a child is labeled, he is seen either as doing the behavior or not doing the behavior—but now everything is defined in terms of the behavior. In almost every family we see in which there are several children, a powerful story can be told about how one of the kids became manipulative. And a surprising number of these tales begin in infancy. Something happened whereby he got "too much" attention or one or more of the primary caregivers were not as strict as they "should" have been, and no one intervened to halt the permanent deterioration of his character. Now he is manipulative, we are told by family members, and although it's unfortunate, the effect of his history means that he probably always will be.

The manipulative label is so universally applied that in a number of families the parent, stepparent, or an older sibling believes that the child in question is exaggerating or faking altogether a medically diagnosed condition. Or the kid is milking it for everything it's worth. In some families even a dying child is still described as manipulative!

POSITIVE LABELS VS. APPRECIATION

Positive labels such as "genius," "good teenager," "gifted," "quiet baby," "daddy's girl," "responsible like her mother," and "great athlete" are no exception to the truth that labels are never wholly accurate and always judgmental. They inevitably backfire when children no longer seem to be living up to their earlier promise.

We are not calling here for some stilted way of saying nice things about your child. A label is not a phrase or a word; it is a thought. If you have something good to say about your child, it isn't more spiritual for you to qualify the statement. ("He's a good boy . . . uh, but sometimes he's not.") We are simply pointing out a common mind-set that we have observed in family after family.

The difference between a positive label and appreciation is that one is fixed and the other moves with the present. For example, a couple may see that their son is outgoing on most occasions but also be aware that there are times when he is bashful around strangers and other times when he needs to withdraw altogether. They also recognize that he, like everyone, has an ego and that although he is usually friendly and kind to other people, he can also be sullen and angry. They are comfortable with their own egos and they are comfortable with his.

Another dad and mom might make the mistake of *labeling* their daughter as academically gifted. They may talk about this within their circle of friends and relatives and get used to having a new achievement story to tell anyone who inquires about their daughter. Occasionally, however, the daughter does poorly on an essay test, or she gets a new teacher whom she has great difficulty following, or, as often happens, she starts losing interest in schoolwork altogether and her grades go down. This is where the trouble that positive labels cause can be seen clearly. The overall drop in grades precipitates a family crisis. Parents may assume that their daughter could do well but "just isn't trying" or that she's "running around with low achievers," or some other judgmental explanation.

In cases like this, it isn't hard to see that the parents have been putting pressure on their daughter to live up to their label—even when she was doing quite well. These expectations play themselves out in numerous families regarding grades, popularity, sports, physical beauty (which is always changing as the body changes), and numerous other areas. The parent starts identifying with the label—whether positive or negative—and stops identifying with the child.

Understanding that Love or Truth exists *now* is fundamental to approaching parenting as worship. We know God in this instant only, and only in this instant can we know a child of God. Labeling children makes it nearly impossible to see them clearly tomorrow and the next day, because the label dictates how they must be in the future. And what we can't see, we can't love.

Instead of telling yourself that your child is manipulative, try thinking, "Right now my son is trying to manipulate me with his anger" or "Today I am reacting strongly to what I think of as my daughter's manipulative whining." That is quite different from a stepdad saying, "Your son sure knows how to manipulate you." Or a stepmom saying, "Your daughter has you wrapped around her finger."

Tracy Bright, Jordan's fifth-grade teacher, demonstrated how adults can react to children's insistent demands without jumping to the conclusion that they are trying to manipulate. When Jordan started the year with her, he looked around and realized that not one of his friends had been assigned to her class. And he didn't particularly like the kids who were in it. He spoke to us about this, so we met with Mrs. Bright to see if we could get him reassigned. She told us that the school had a policy against that, but she would like an opportunity to see what she could do for Jordan.

So Mrs. Bright set about getting to know Jordan, getting to know his fears and his loves. She discovered, among other things, that he felt intimidated by the first book the class had been assigned to read and that above all he loved sports. She took him aside, gave him a different book, and told him if that one was too hard, to let her know. She also sometimes watched him play basketball and when he got back to class complimented him on a particular hook shot or said, "Twelve baskets. Not bad." Occasionally Mrs. Bright let her class participate in physical contests with other classes, and in front of Jordan she would tell us that he had won the thumb-wrestling contest or whatever it was. It wasn't long before we heard Jordan say something that we had never heard him say in his life: "I like school."

This entire experience was in marked contrast to what John had been through when he was Jordan's age. Because John was first home-schooled and then attended an unusual alternative school, when he started fifth grade in public school, he had never received a grade, had never had a classroom test, and had never taken home an assignment. As sooner or later happens with most kids, he was assigned a teacher who had favorites—and John was not one of them. Although we explained to her (we will call her Ms. Clark) that John had had no experience in writing down assignments or doing homework, Ms. Clark not only didn't give him help in how to do this, she seemed to go out of her way to make the process confusing and difficult. When we saw what was happening, we went to the school counselor, a man we had known for several years, and discussed the problem. He in turn arranged a meeting among the five of us. There Ms. Clark said she would talk to John and straighten everything out. But for two weeks nothing changed, and so we phoned her ourselves.

Again Ms. Clark said that she would meet with John and explain to him what she wanted. When another week of

homework assignments went by and still she had not met
with him, we left a message for her to call us.

When Ms. Clark returned our call, she told us irritably that she had been watching John carefully and had
concluded that he was just manipulating all of us. "Look at
how he has all of us hopping around. He has your attention,
doesn't he? And he has everyone else's. I've concluded that
he has a hidden agenda here." At this point we decided to
stop talking to anyone at the school about this and simply
began helping John with his assignments. This worked quite
well, as we discuss in the section "Abandoning Your Child
to the World" (page 258).

OUR RESPONSE TO CHILDREN'S DEMANDS

When adults feel pressured or hassled by a child, they usually label the child's behavior as manipulative. However,
seldom do they see a demanding adult in this light—even
though they feel attacked by the adult's demands. **When we
feel attacked, we want to attack back; thus it's important to
question our interpretation of what someone else is doing
to us,** especially if we think an attack is coming from a child.

The basic difference between Mrs. Bright's reaction
to a child's demand and Ms. Clark's reaction was that Ms.
Clark interpreted it as an attack and Mrs. Bright did not. As
parents we can choose to comply with or decline our kids'
demands. One behavior is not more spiritual than the other.
Perhaps we need some time to ourselves, and so we decline.
Perhaps we see that we can comply happily, and so we accept. Either response is fine. However, if we comply yet are
resentful of the time it's taking or of what it's keeping us
from doing, we will feel attacked by our child. And if we
decline yet think that our child's request was designed to
make us feel guilty or was unreasonable, we will feel attacked by our child.

Whenever adults feel attacked by children, one of

the ways they frequently retaliate is by continuing to build a case against them, especially the case that they are manipulative. In other words, **most of the time the label "manipulative" is used defensively.**

Naturally kids will try to get what they want—and so will every other life-form on Earth. Sometimes children do develop a particularly subtle way of meeting their needs and desires, but subtle does not automatically mean devious and deceitful. Clearly there are kids who are deceitful, cruel, even murderous. But on the whole children scheme less than adults and their honesty runs deeper.

One of John's good friends, whom we will call Babs, is a girl our family got to know when she and John were five and Babs lived just a few houses from us. Our boys have grown up having girls among their closest friends. They spend hours talking to girls on the phone, and frequently girls spend the day at our house playing. On more than a few occasions, each of our three sons was the only boy invited to an otherwise-all-girls party. At first Babs was just one of the many kids who played in and around our house, but soon she and John had become best friends.

Babs has two other sisters, one younger, one older, plus an older brother. Her father, Frank, is a successful lawyer who provided generously for his family. They had many outings and fun times together, including numerous skiing trips and long vacations to exotic spots. This all came to an abrupt end when Frank announced that he was divorcing Beverly, Babs's mom, and marrying his beautiful, young legal assistant. He told Babs that because her mother had gained some weight that she wouldn't take off and because they always had fights when he came home from the office he had simply "fallen out of love" with her.

Babs saw her circumstances change dramatically. Suddenly they no longer had all the nice family times together. They couldn't afford the ski trips and vacations. And soon Beverly had to sell the house and move the family into a smaller one. Meanwhile Babs's father continued to drive an expensive sports car, take nice vacations, and, with the birth of his first child with his new wife, began to spend less time with Babs and his other children.

At about this same time the nature of Frank's law practice started to change and he began taking on very questionable cases. We once asked him what he did if he suspected that his clients were lying just to get money. He said, "I tell them I don't want to hear about it and I try to get the case in and out of my office as fast as possible." Frank often bragged about the size of the settlements he was getting. This, plus having abandoned his family and deceived his wife about his affair, gave a clear message to his children.

The effect on Babs and her two sisters was quick and unmistakable. The only one who seemed untouched was Babs's older brother, who was seventeen when his father left. But the girls, who were all very pretty, started to lie and use their considerable good looks and charm to get what they wanted. In short, they started being manipulative on many occasions.

From numerous conversations we have had with Babs over the years, we know that she "learned" that love can end, that even the deepest relationships cannot be relied on, and that if she wanted the kind of life she had growing up, she was going to have to scheme to get it, just as her stepmom had done.

Beverly is an excellent mother and has done everything possible to protect her children emotionally. She intentionally has remained unmarried and has continued to bring Frank into as many decisions about their children as she can. Nevertheless, the lesson Frank taught his three daughters is more affecting than the lesson of gentleness, faithfulness, and commitment that Beverly has taught them. While Beverly's lesson is truer and is the one her children eventually will arrive at themselves, in terms of children's personality development, a parent's betrayal is often a more powerful factor than a parent's love.

Although children who are frequently or occasionally manipulative did not all become this way because of some mistake their parent or guardian made, it is vital that parents remember that **no child is manipulative at birth and no child concocts such an unhappy approach to life on his own.** You may have in your care a child who is sometimes manipulative, but at her core she is the same as us all, as innocent as her Source.

HOW TO DEAL WITH MANIPULATION

It should always be kept in mind that true manipulativeness is an extremely rare quality in children. The behavior that adults tag with this label usually occurs when kids want to do something that they are not being allowed to do. Parents attempt to distinguish it from crying, begging, whining, and nagging by attributing it to a more sinister and devious force. They think it has more intelligence behind it and that it's more disturbing when expressed than these other behaviors.

The harm in describing children as manipulative is that a suspicion is cast on everything they do, even so-called normal mistakes and behavior. They are given no leeway, no margin for error. The label often becomes so suffocating that they are forced into the mold of that single interpretation and come to think of themselves in the same way.

Therefore, no matter what behavior you are dealing with, you want to avoid labeling the child. Yet what should you do when you suspect that your child *is* trying to manipulate you in the present situation?

1. **Never attack your child in any way.** Merely because you think his behavior is manipulative, you should

not call your child manipulative or describe your child's *basic nature* to yourself or anyone else in this way.

2. **Don't say "no" too quickly.** You are not involved in a time trial here, or any trial at all. You are involved in the sacred task of guiding your child home to God.

3. **Listen without suspicion.** Listen carefully and consider deeply and kindly what your child is saying *this* time. There is no reason to be on guard against your own child.

4. **Don't respond to manipulation.** Children can't be manipulative unless they have someone who is willing to be manipulated. If, having followed the first three steps, you now truly believe that your child is trying to manipulate you, then you should not respond to the manipulation *in any way.* For example, if your kid is trying to "get on your good side" by telling on a sibling or another child, is being falsely charming or complimentary to you, is "sweet talking," "fast talking," or lying to you, or is in any other way trying to manipulate you, then you certainly don't want to teach your kid that this approach can succeed. You must, therefore, take a firm stand—and not reconsider.

5. **Do not decline the attempted manipulation angrily.** Your function is to show your child that manipulation *does not work.* Anger undermines your position because it is itself an attempted manipulation. Anger is the desire to make our children feel guilty. (See "How Parents Instill Fear" in Chapter 8.) But we don't say honestly, "I want you to feel guilty and bad about yourself." Instead we bring up a point that we believe will have this *effect,* such as, "I can never trust you. You pat my back, tell me that you love me, and say you'll be back by eleven, but you and I both know that you have no intention of keeping that promise." Thus we teach our children that we also believe in manipulation. But as Jerry Jampolsky says, "Teach only love."

8

ADOLESCENTS AND FEAR

HOW PARENTS INSTILL FEAR

The mother of one lifelong friend of ours never hit her; she kept her in line by giving her "the silent treatment." She would not only do this for several hours but on three occasions went for several days without talking to her. Sometimes a spouse will go for minutes or hours without talking to his or her partner, and so many people think they know what this feels like. But at most they know only what it feels like *as an adult*. Our friend told us that she would speak to her mother but that it had no more effect than if she were "a ghost trying to be heard." She said that those times, even the shorter ones, were the most terrifying experiences she has had in over forty years of life. As the silence continued, her fantasies would run out of control and she would become increasingly panicked about what was going to happen.

Most adults have lost the child mind and have forgotten how imaginative they once were, how real the images
that danced in their heads once seemed. In fact, some adults
who have retained a powerful imagination are considered
crazy by those who haven't. Many parents, for example,
don't realize what they are asking when they send a young
child to the back of the house to get something or demand
that their kid pick up a dead insect and throw it in the trash.
When Jordan was six, a neighborhood boy killed a bird in
our backyard with a pellet rifle. For days Jordan worried
about the bird's mate and babies. How would they feel
when he didn't fly home? We found it very difficult to comfort him, because his imagination of what a bird's life might
be was more powerful than our words.

When Scott came to live with us, the only separate
space we had for him was in a little converted trailer that
included a toilet and shower. Because he was already in his
teens, it didn't seem appropriate for us to share a bedroom
and bath with him. However, from infancy on Jordan and
John have always felt free to sleep in the same room with us
whenever they wished. We have never questioned their reasons for doing it or not doing it, and they certainly are no
more fearful or dependent than kids who have always been
made to sleep by themselves.

For instance, neither of them has ever had any desire
to tell on other kids at school. This is not a point we have
instructed them on; they simply have no interest in doing it.
Jordan recently asked us if the kids who told did so because
they needed someone to take care of them, an interesting
insight. Our experience has been that children who are
forced to "go through their fears" often are less self-
confident than those who are allowed to grow out of their
fears in their own time.

Of course, there are countless ways that parents, often unsuspectingly, engender fear in their children besides
giving them "the silent treatment," physically intimidating

them, forcing them to handle insects, or making them sleep alone. We will discuss a few more, but it should be remembered that no laundry list of parental mistakes, no matter how long and detailed, can substitute for parents studying their children. They must pause long enough and frequently enough to get a deep sense of how each of their kids actually responds to a particular style of parenting, no matter how innocuous that style may seem or how widely used and recommended by others.

When John was still too young to have any understanding of the role food played in his growth and health, we sometimes imposed the rule that he had to eat a reasonable amount of nutritious food before he could have dessert. We didn't do this often, but when we did, it usually proved an effective way of getting him to eat a more balanced meal. However, when Jordan came along, even though he had much less desire for sweets than John, sweets were more symbolic to him. Often he would eat only a part of his dessert, sometimes none at all, yet it was very important that he be offered one. His fear of loss from the "no dinner, no dessert" rule was so intense that we quickly saw that in his case this was overkill. Since he liked a wide variety of foods and had an excellent appetite, we decided simply to augment his diet with nutritional supplements and drop the issue about how much he ate before dessert.

We have seen kids in other families react far more deeply to voices being raised, promises being broken, a curfew being too rigidly enforced, pets being given up, and the like, than would be expected in most children, and yet, because the parents thought that their own behavior was reasonable, they failed to see and fully respect their child's response. Later, they always paid a price for this insensitivity, whether conscious or unconscious on their part.

One couple realized, when their daughter was about two and a half, that shutting a door between themselves and her was more traumatic than for most children. Therefore they decided to do this as little as possible. If she needed a "time-out," they would have her sit in a special chair where she could still see them. When she was a little older and could understand being sent to her room, they allowed her to leave the door open or only partially shut. By the time their daughter had reached seven, the symbolism of a shut door had lost its charge for her. They are convinced, as are we, that if they had forced her to endure closed doors, her reaction to them would have lasted longer and perhaps even carried into her adult life in some form.

We wouldn't dream of forcing our spouse to handle more spiders if she were afraid of them, nor would we set up extra shopping trips for our partner with friends and acquaintances in order to force him to work through his strong dislike of shopping. But we often make our children do something merely because they are afraid of it or dislike it. A man we know was repeatedly forced to ride a horse that would take the bit in its mouth and run, *because* he was afraid to do so. He didn't become less scared of an out-of-control horse, but he did learn not to show his fear to his father. A woman we know became the designated member of the family to bring up wood from the basement *because* she was afraid to. When her dad discovered that she was scared of the basement, he assigned her the task "to get you over this stupid fear." Many parents will let their children turn on a light to read or to go to the bathroom but will not let them turn on a light to get rid of darkness. **Insisting that children do something that increases their fear does not teach them fearlessness.** Obviously it can be helpful to lovingly encourage children to take a reasonable risk, but badgering or forcing or shaming them into doing it is always a mistake. Like most punitive approaches, these methods merely destroy trust and cause estrangement.

Unquestionably, you can use fear to control your child. It is often quick and effective as a temporary measure. However, it will increase your child's resistance to *you,* and it will teach nothing of lasting value. Finding alternative ways of guiding your child requires time, study, and experimentation. But many moms and dads don't want to be bothered. They already feel overburdened, and intimidating their kids seems like a reasonable expedient. In fact, fear is such an obviously effective tool that most parents unconsciously build a permanent state of it within their children so that they can trigger it at will. Through threats or tone of voice, they let their children know that they just "don't want to hear about it," that their kids are a burden, and that they would be happy if it weren't for their kids.

Children, especially young children, love their parents and don't want them to be unhappy. They especially don't want their parents to withdraw. **Possibly the most pervasive, long-lived, and destructive tension between parents and children is the child's desire to have more of the parents' time and the parents' desire not to be bothered.** During adolescence or shortly before, this conflict starts to come full circle. Eventually parents begin to feel what it was like for their children for all those years—as they themselves begin chasing after their adult children. Now all the jokes are directed at the needy, burdensome *parents.*

How much *should* children need their parents' participation in their lives? It is very difficult for kids to comprehend an adult's notion of what are reasonable and unreasonable needs for them to have, especially when that notion changes with the parent's mood. Consequently, the usual effect of their fear that they will make their parents withdraw is that kids communicate less about everything and feel anxious whenever they do speak to their parents. And this is exactly the effect that many parents think they want—until it's too late.

Parents often sense their kids' anxiety and use it to "contain" their kids' desire to interact with them. In our culture, children who "always want something"—to play catch, help in the kitchen, or just talk about what happened at school—often are pictured as needy or codependent. Parents correctly sense that their kids ask them to do things that they could do for themselves—simply because they want the participation, the support, the assurance of the parent: "Would you fix me something, Mom? I'm hungry." "Fix it yourself. And don't leave a mess." "I can't get this shoelace through the hole, Dad." "If you would tie your shoes, the laces wouldn't get frayed. You're just going to have to live with it."

It's a short jump from parents sighing and saying "You're driving me crazy" and "Can't I get a moment's peace around here?" to kids thinking that they have caused their mom or dad to get sick. After all, don't parents repeatedly imply that the kid is the cause of all their troubles? Although the physical distress that children fear they have caused is usually only a headache, a cold, lower-back pain, tiredness, or some other minor ailment, they don't really know what that condition will lead to and often they assume the worst.

There is no greater nightmare for young children than the possibility that their mother or father will die. It's our experience that **young children are more profoundly disturbed by the prospect of a parent's death than of their own.** Yet we have been surprised at how many adults, through direct or indirect means, *strengthen* their child's belief in their vulnerability. We have known a number of parents who encouraged their kids to believe that they were the cause of their physical difficulties, even going so far as to say "You will end up being the death of me" or some other version of that thought. They do this because their kids' concern for them becomes more apparent and therefore more gratifying and especially because they know that fearful children are easier to handle.

*   *   *

Another devastating fear, and one that has been growing over recent decades, is the fear of abandonment. Within the ongoing epidemic of divorce, of which any child of school age is aware, most kids are quite naturally afraid that what has happened to so many of their friends could happen to them: Their family could be torn apart. Consequently, arguments or obvious distance between their parents symbolizes far more to most children than the issue does to the adults.

When we moved from Patagonia, Arizona (an isolated community of 1,000 with a very low divorce rate), to Santa Cruz, California, it wasn't long before our boys were becoming upset at even the smallest disagreement between the two of us. The reason was obvious. In their new school, *every* teacher and the majority of their classmates' parents had gone through a divorce. Many of the children they knew were now in chaotic family situations, and they could see no reason why this couldn't happen to us.

In response, we began taking more care not to resolve our issues in front of them. And we explained to them over and over that we had taken a vow never to leave each other and that this commitment was sacred. We told them that it was not only our promise to them but to God. Nothing could make us divorce, and they could rely on that. Gradually their fear began to lessen and they stopped asking "Are you going to get a divorce?" every time they sensed that the mood between us wasn't good.

Children recognize that arguments are often about them, and it's reasonable for them to believe that if they didn't exist, this fight wouldn't be happening. Parents should be more honest with themselves and see clearly that turning against each other over an issue about their child is seldom motivated by loving concern for the child. Likewise, when parents encourage a kid to take sides in an argument between the two of them or when one partner openly sides with a child against the other partner, the child perceives the damage being done to the family relationship and knows that he or she is participating in it. Naturally, the child's fear and guilt grow each time this happens.

To young children and to most older ones, the family is their nest, their place of safety. **Most young kids have no stable identity apart from their family,** but within its boundaries they know who they are; they know that they belong; and they know that because they are loved, they must have value.

Adults can feel slighted and unappreciated even when a friend moves out of town! The unconscious thought is "If this person were truly my friend, she wouldn't move." And yet these same adults somehow expect children not to feel unvalued if one of their parents files for divorce. We were in the room when a mother told her little girl that she had decided to divorce Daddy. "You can't do that," her daughter said. "He's part of the family!"

The parents we are seeing today tend to inflict more psychological pain than physical pain, although a surprising number of parents still physically attack their children or intimidate them.

Even when there is no physical abuse, another form of abuse is especially prevalent in professional and middle-to upper-middle-income households: The spiritual side of the child is lost in the parents' push for excellence and achievement. They become so rigid and overcontrolling that they prune away the basic nature and individuality of their child. Of course, they can't actually produce such a radical alteration, but like badly pruning a plant, they can wound and twist the child's growth.

For example, the father of a close childhood friend of Gayle's was completely passive, refusing to have anything to do with disciplining her. Her mother, on the other hand, would swear at her and call her names. Gayle was in their house on several occasions when the mother launched one of her verbal assaults, and simply because she was a large adult, the threat of physical violence hung in the air. Gayle's friend is convinced that the names she was called as a child were as painful as if she had been struck, and stayed with her longer. Most of Gayle's other girlfriends were spanked by their mothers and only rarely by their fathers. In those days switches or hairbrushes were favorite devices. Gayle's own father also seldom spanked her, probably because her mother was the parent who was with her throughout the day.

Besides fearing physical punishment, most of Gayle's girlfriends learned to fear their mother's comparisons. If they told their mom about any problem they were having at school or with another kid, she would bring up the exemplary behavior of a sibling or another child and would ask why they couldn't be more like that person. Those who have experienced these comparisons know that this approach did not motivate them to be more like the "model" child or sibling; in fact, it often backfired, motivating them to be opposite that child. Whatever other effect it had, it inevitably made them feel bad about themselves and encouraged them to hate their own brother, sister, or whoever else the model child was.

Teachers are using a version of this same mistake when they consistently single out certain kids in class for praise or when they overemphasize grades. The children who are singled out are being done no favor. Often they learn that their popularity depends, at least in part, on *not* being well-behaved or academically outstanding.

As we have pointed out, most adults can't spank or verbally attack a child without anger—whether they first wait to cool down or not. In fact, the waiting period for the child who knows that he is going to be spanked is in effect an additional punishment that increases fear and fuels the child's violent imaginings. Most parents simply don't realize how loudly their emotions speak. They naively believe that if their voice is quiet and their body under control, their kids will think they are being struck more lovingly and thoughtfully.

Until kids reach adult size and strength—and sometimes even financial independence—they tend to react emotionally as if their safety, even their life, depended on reading their parents' moods correctly. Most kids become proficient in detecting instantly their parents' emotional state and pay much closer attention to that than to the parents' explanations. If in the end they are going to be hurt, they will pick up the signs of this in the parents' underlying attitude. **It's unrealistic for adults to think that kids follow the logic of the speech they hear prior to being punished.**

The parents we see today often used verbal reasoning as their first weapon of choice for inflicting distress. They are making their child feel guilty, just as their parents once made them feel. However, since their own attacks are couched in logic, it's more difficult for their son or daughter to recognize the unfairness of the comments. No matter how democratically framed, an argument with someone who holds the strings of your life is inherently unfair. And an abstract discussion with someone who has not yet developed the capacity for abstract thought is also unfair.

Obviously adults can outreason kids. Children's interest in the exchange of ideas comes much later than most parents and many educators seem to realize. Adults are thus in an excellent position to become verbal bullies, and unfortunately many fall into this trap. The results are that *all* discussions with adults become increasingly distasteful to children.

THE HALLMARK OF GOOD DISCIPLINE

All children are capable of feeling and receiving love from their parent—but only the love that is in the parent's heart that instant. Whenever kids are corrected out of love, the correction is more likely to last and the overall effect is a closer bonding between parent and child. **If you feel personally estranged from your children after correcting them, you can be sure that the correction was based on your belief in guilt rather than your experience of oneness.**

It's crucial that you discipline from the deepest part of your being. Don't hesitate to break from the disciplining process—by walking out of the room if necessary—as many times as you need to in order to remember how important your child is to you. Keep in mind that anger not only includes dislike but also the desire to make your child feel guilty. (See Cultural Assumption #8 in Chapter 10.) Instilling guilt always backfires sooner or later. If nothing else, you will impair the communication between you and your child.

Most adults know when they are getting angry. **Anger may be unavoidable under the circumstances, but continuing to relate to your child while you are angry is always avoidable.** Just make yourself physically pause or step away, then release the anger in some other way than by engaging your child. (See "How to Meet Your Needs" in Chapter 3.) Become once again the parent you want to be. We can tell you with certainty that you do not lose face with your child by exercising this form of self-discipline.

Proceeding in this way doesn't mean that your kids will like being corrected. Often they won't. But the increased sense of closeness between you and your child will soon become apparent—if your decision was made and carried out in love. Obviously, the children in your care may have been damaged by the time you use this approach and you may have little prospect of getting an immediate positive effect. When dealing with foster, step-, or adopted kids, you may have to confront an entire history of mistakes in almost every interaction you have with the child. In these cases you relate from love because of its purifying effect on you and for its *cumulative* effect on the child.

To center yourself in a feeling of oneness with your child before you act, to at least do the best you can in this respect, may take a moment or two. Yet you are likely to feel the urge to *pounce* on the misbehavior, as if punishing quickly were a virtue. No time can be better spent or have greater rewards than the time you use to remember what your relationship with your child means to you.

The mere affectations of love—smiles, a soft voice, and a ready willingness to say "yes"—are of no value to your child if you don't feel a bond with her at the time. Many books and articles on raising children emphasize the form rather than the content of parenting; they recommend words and actions rather than the feelings they spring from. We have seen many unconventional approaches to parenting succeed brilliantly—because the parent was making all decisions out of deep love and respect for the child.

We know one young man whose single mother encouraged him throughout his adolescence to pursue his love of full-contact kickboxing and even continued to pay for his lessons after he started his first after-school job. Today he is one of the most gentle and harmless young men we know. Clearly, the violent nature of his sport was not the determining factor. We also know two other boys who have remained bullies despite their participation in the same type of classes and matches. These children's parents do not allow the activity out of honor and understanding of their kids. They seem merely to want them out of the house.

Another family has allowed their young daughter to act in horror films, and yet, because of their love for her, the closeness of the family, and the guidelines for her protection, she has matured into a humorous and loving young woman. Once again, mere permission to participate in an activity is not the key. The tragic stories of other child actors who were not so loved and protected by their parents are well known.

*   *   *

When Jordan was nine, he invited Joe, a new friend he had made at school, to spend the night. After we had gone to sleep, they sneaked out and "papered" several houses. Our suspicions were aroused the next morning when we noticed that ours was the only home near us that didn't have toilet paper in all its trees and cacti, and they were confirmed the day after when we discovered that our supply of toilet paper was gone.

This discovery occurred when both kids were in school, so we had plenty of time to pray and think through what to do. Our initial reaction was anger and shock. We had specifically told them that under no circumstances were they to sneak out of the house that night. Now we felt that Jordan had betrayed our trust in him. We also anxiously began wondering whether this was the start of a tendency that would take a more destructive form when he became a teenager.

The rising level of violence among adolescents has given rise to increasingly strident calls for more and harsher discipline, as if most of these violent young people were the product of indulgent luxury and excessive attention. However, this message of retribution, because it can be carried out quickly and directly, can be very appealing when we think we are faced with a child who may be getting out of control.

One problem we faced was whether to tell Joe's mother. Our past experience made us think that she might break up their friendship if we told her, despite the fact that this was the only time either of them had done anything like this, together or apart. Another question was whether to have at least our own son apologize to the neighbors (by this time all the toilet paper had been removed), some of whom did not seem to be particularly friendly.

Until we prayed, we believed that the primary task before us was to decide on what form the punishment should take. However, when we did pray (stilled our minds, held Jordan and Joe in God's light, and looked deeply in our hearts for what we wanted to do), the answer we received was that our function as Jordan's parents was "not to crush him but to motivate him."

For the last several years we had begun to question whether punishment is the most *efficient* way of correcting behavior, and we had, without making a rigid rule, dropped it as a form of relating to our boys. So we decided to talk to Jordan and see how that went, before we did anything else. Prior to this talk, we set the single purpose of showing him why he did not *want* to do this again. We decided against all secondary purposes such as making him feel guilty, catching him in a lie, or scaring him into compliance.

When we sat him down, Jordan at first denied that he and Joe had left the house at night. We were already certain about what had happened. Since our goal was not to get him to confess, we overlooked his denial. We carefully explained to him all the dangers inherent in two young boys moving around in strangers' yards very late at night. We ended by saying that if anything like this happened again, Joe would not be allowed to spend the night. When Joe came over to play that afternoon, we had the same talk with him and added that the next time we would have to inform his mother.

When we use a firm and loving approach rather than a punitive one, our kids eventually feel closer to us. Jordan loves to hug anyway, but he initiated more hugs than usual for the next day or two, and even Joe was noticeably more friendly. All three of our sons have at times been unhappy with us when we have insisted that something stop or that some task be completed, but these reactions pass quickly and soon they feel nearer to us—if we dealt with them from love. **The hallmark that you have disciplined well is that the bond between you and your child is ultimately strengthened.**

As Saint John said two thousand years ago, love and

fear cannot occupy the heart at the same instant. The agent of fear and the victim of fear feel cut off from love and therefore from the source of their oneness. As parents we should aspire to as pure a relationship with our child as our Parent has with us. Fear is not the lesson we truly wish to teach, and it is not the basis of the relationship we want with our child. It may take a few moments longer to discipline without fear—either the fear of displeasing our child or the desire to spark fear within our child—but this time spent is a small sacrifice to make in return for a greater presence of Love within our homes.

PARENTS' OWN FEAR

Our culture seems to assume that the millions of parents who came before us have already thought about adolescence and that it is pointless for us to attempt to see anything new in or respond any differently to this stage. As novices, not only must we accept our culture's pronouncement that this stage is miserable but we must absorb all the instincts necessary to ensure that our experience of it remains the same as everyone else's.

Without exception, all the parents we have counseled about the problems they were having with their teenagers have had vivid memories of what it was like to go through adolescence. Even more interesting is that they also remember, just as vividly, the mistaken ways their mom or dad reacted to them at this age. But the most telling pattern of all is that most of them confessed that while dealing with their own teenager, they often caught themselves sounding and acting just like their own parents.

Why—if you've been through it yourself, you know what the problem is, and you know what does not work—would you consciously repeat the same mistake? In our experience, if you carry on some version of your own parents' pattern, you do so primarily because of fear.

Fear that you are losing your child too soon as it is and that any change you make might speed up the process. You know that other parents are going through the same things you are. Just a few years ago their families were close. Their kids talked to them, confided in them, brought problems to them, and now, just like you, they are experiencing the pain of seeing their children withdraw and turn against them. The children spend as much time away from home as they can, and even when they are home, they are always in their room or on the phone. They lie—they never would have done that before. You suspect they may have started stealing, even from you. They don't take out the trash or do the few little things you have asked—despite the fact that they know how much you have to do. They not only don't respect your opinions the way they once did, they now talk back and won't concede even an obvious point. You suspect or even know that they drink or smoke and maybe experiment with drugs—despite years of your teaching them the dangers in this. They bring home rude, alienated kids and don't seem to care what their friends' attitudes are toward you. These peers, these "bad influences," are like some modern Pied Piper leading your child away, while you stand by virtually helpless. If it hasn't happened to you yet, at least you know a parent or two whose children have run away—perhaps they came back, but one day they may not. There are pictures everywhere of kids who have disappeared.

Fear that if you try something new—or even think something new—the effect that your teenager is having on you will get worse. You are already giving more time, emotion, and energy to this than you are capable of. It's hurting your marriage. It's affecting your sleep. It's very bad on your other children. It's certainly not good for business. And it's socially embarrassing. You can't take any more. Just go by the rules. Just do what your elders did. Didn't *you* turn out all right?

Fear that if you don't have the same attitude toward adolescents that every other parent seems to have, then what you have heard them warn will happen. "Don't mess with our sacred teenage doctrine or you'll be sorry. Look what happened last year to that nice family at school. In fact, look what's happening right on your own street. Look what happened to the baby boomers. Look what happened to our national deficit. Look what happened to our country's morals. Look what the Bible says."[1]

Fear that you might end up ruining your child's life. Early pregnancy can dash all your kid's dreams. Bad grades can destroy your child's career opportunities. Bad manners can keep your son or daughter from getting hired. Drugs can fry your child's brain and lead to crime, violence, and depravity.

Fear that you might put your child's life at risk. Bad driving can get your kid killed. Drinking can get your kid killed. Hanging out with the wrong people can get your kid killed. Bad eating habits can cause cancer. Smoking can cause everything.

And these fears are anything but groundless. Having counseled many parents who had a child die, we can tell you that this can happen to any family. As we write this chapter, our local paper, *The Arizona Daily Star,* has just published some highlights from a recent (1996) Justice Department report on juveniles and crime. Among other statistics that the article discusses are the following:

- The *murder* rate among fourteen- to seventeen-year-olds has increased 165 percent in the last ten years.
- Juvenile arrests increased 117 percent from 1983 to 1992.
- Eighty-three percent of young inmates in juvenile halls say they owned guns.

❧ Thirty-five percent say, "It's okay to shoot someone if that's what it takes to get what you want."

❧ One in every five crimes is now committed by a juvenile.

❧ That figure is expected to double in fifteen years.

DOES LUCK PLAY A PART?

Obviously there are numerous external dangers to your kids that are beyond your power to control. But, also, many of the *behavioral* problems that most people think are within your control may not be. For example, just within our immediate circle of friends, three families have been affected by circumstances that could just as easily have occurred in our lives.

Jordan has a friend named Lue whose mother was killed when he was seven and whose dad has a dangerous medical condition that is very expensive to treat. If Lue's dad were to quit his job, he would lose his insurance coverage. If he were to move, he would lose his subsidized housing. Although Lue lives only seven blocks from our house, he is in a different school district. Almost every day he witnesses a fight at school. Jordan has never seen a fight. Three of Lue's other friends take hard drugs. Jordan has never known a boy who takes hard drugs. Once or twice a month Lue is approached by a pusher. Jordan has never seen a pusher.

Another family we know has three girls, one of whom is a sixteen-year-old named Betty who has considerable musical ability. She is also very funny, kind, an excellent student, and has never had a behavior problem of any consequence. We know of no couple who have done a better job of raising their kids than Betty's parents.

Since she was twelve, Betty has been attending a

prestigious music camp for gifted children. The most famous teacher there, for whom she had an almost worshipful admiration, fell in love with Betty last year. Betty's parents had gotten to know him well over the years, and he had stayed in their home on several occasions. They considered him a trusted friend, but that didn't stop him from telling Betty that the two of them were soul mates and that his "guidance" was that they should live together for the rest of their lives. He told her that other people wouldn't understand a love like theirs and that she shouldn't talk about it. He was evidently as sincere about his feelings as he was mistaken.

Betty was very flattered and confused by all of this, and she did in fact leave town with him. Her parents found out about it almost immediately. They located her and physically brought her back home. She was furious with them, but for three weeks they kept her in the house, talking to her almost day and night. Among other appeals they made to her, they kept returning to the point that this teacher had a wife and child and could not possibly be doing this out of love, regardless of how deeply he had deceived himself. They also contacted the teacher and got his promise never to speak to Betty again.

Two months later, Betty's parents had to attend a medical conference out of town, and while they were away the teacher came to their house, got down on his knees, and begged Betty to run off with him. Although she did not relent, they told us that this crisis may not be over.

A third family we know had three kids—two boys and a girl. The family was deeply religious and very active in helping the needy and unfortunate in their mountain community. Their oldest boy and his sister were both excellent and well-trained rock climbers. They had never been injured. Perhaps their parents should not have allowed them to participate in this dangerous sport, but that didn't matter, because one day, after school, while they were merely taking a short hike together down a well-traveled path, the side of the mountain gave way and both were killed. Many people from the town used to take walks down this path. There was simply no way of knowing that it was dangerous.

TEENAGE MISTAKES AND CRIMES

Our family has had its difficulties, but we are well aware that we have been lucky in ways that these three families and a million families like them have not been. No one is in a position to judge another family's problems. We simply don't know and could never know all that has fed into the circumstances in which other people find themselves. Likewise, you are not in a position to judge your child. As we pointed out earlier, no child is helped by being judged. And yet condemning teenagers has become a favorite national pastime, whether they're teen mothers, teen gang members, teen drivers, teens who use bad language, teens who are sexually promiscuous, teens who don't try in school, or the small fraction of teens who are involved in a growing percentage of our cities' crimes. As would be expected with any ego-driven attitude, the more that adults bash teens, the less obliged they feel to encourage them in positive directions or to acknowledge their successes.

In a letter to the editor, one parent recently asked a local newspaper to reconsider its decision to stop publishing the names of high school students participating in sports meets other than football (swimming, cross-country, golf, volleyball, etc.). She wrote:

> I am not asking that you decrease the attention you give to high school football, or even that you cease to focus on every negative thing done by every teenager in this city, but only that you assume some responsibility for supporting those young people in your community who are al-

ready motivated to do well; who are proud of their athletic efforts; who despite the time their sport requires of them, maintain remarkably high grade-point averages; but who are also human enough to be encouraged when a newspaper acknowledges their efforts with a few small lines of print.

It is obviously beyond the scope of this book for us to deal with the specific problems that arise for individual "juveniles" who have committed themselves to lives of violence and crime. But this much we can say: As a parent your function is to reflect your Mother-Father God's commitment to you. This means that *your* children cannot do anything—anything—that could make you stop loving them. Regardless of the individual's age, someone who is a proven danger to other people obviously should be taken off the streets and should not be put back on the streets by a failed parole or release system. But if your child falls into this category, you must not turn against her in your heart and you must not lessen your prayers for him or dampen your other spiritual efforts to bring about a breakthrough.

If your religious tradition is Christian, remember that Paul's transformation came soon after he had participated in the stoning death of Saint Stephen. And remember also that not only did Jesus fail to judge Paul for his helping murder one of Jesus' own followers, he didn't even mention it. This was hardly an oversight, because as we pointed out earlier, in Jesus' parable of the prodigal son, the father also fails to mention his sons' sins and mistakes. He merely makes his home theirs. Jesus does not indulge in shaming and attacking Paul. He merely corrects his direction and shows him the way home. That takes care of everything.

A miracle or breakthrough is always a possibility. The mistakes of a lifetime can be brushed away in an instant, and this has certainly happened more than once. Your job as a parent is to work toward that end. It is to make sure—as best you can—that every word you speak and every thought you think helps lift your child's ego into the light of God, so that it can gently evaporate like mist before a warm sun.

Naturally this doesn't mean that you must use the word "God" in talking to your children. It doesn't even mean that you must visit, write, or speak to an older daughter or son. But it does mean that if everyone else on this earth has forgotten, you alone must remember that your child's core is one with God. And remember, too, that as for all of us, your child's spirit, the self that God created, will be returned Home. That promise cannot be broken.

9

HOW TO LIVE WITH KIDS
WHO AREN'T AFRAID OF YOU

THE ALTERNATIVE TO FEAR

A few years back, Hugh and Jordan were doing a little male bonding. In other words, they were on the couch watching TV. Hugh was continuing his ongoing instruction of Jordan in one of the basic lessons of being a man: how to channel surf. They happened upon a fight that was being broadcast from Mexico, and one of the boxers was Julio Cesar Chavez. This caught their attention because *Sports Illustrated* had just declared him, pound for pound, one of the greatest fighters who ever lived.

After watching a couple of rounds, Jordan turned to Hugh and said, "Dad, there isn't a fighter alive who couldn't beat you up."

Hugh said, "You're probably right."

Jordan was ten at the time and Hugh was fifty-three,

but even if Hugh had been twenty-three, Jordan's statement still would have been accurate. Against a professional fighter, most untrained adults would have no chance.

Nevertheless, Hugh was secretly shocked to hear a thought from his son that never would have occurred to him about his own father, and if it had, he wouldn't have dared suggest it out loud.

It was probably only a month later that Hugh said to Jordan, "Guess what, I've lost ten pounds!"

Jordan thought about that for a moment, then answered, "Dad, you could lose a whole lot more weight and no one would notice."

Again Hugh said, "You're probably right."

If an adult made remarks like these, most people would think they were being insulted, but Hugh knew that Jordan was merely voicing his honest observations. Unlike either of us, he had grown up unafraid of being open. There have always been things he has not been allowed to do, but honestly showing his feelings and revealing his thoughts to his parents and to his two older brothers has never been among them.

Children's openness with a parent grows out of trust, the deep recognition that no matter what mistake they make, there always remains this one person who is forever committed to them, that nothing they can do will end the love of their mother, their father, or whoever it is who assumed the role of guardian in their lives. Thus a parent models God's love and provides evidence of oneness within a world that pictures only separation.

All of the world's images of commitment and love are fleeting. By one means or another they all must end. Romance dies; friends all too often drift apart; the wonderfully intimate conversations between parent and child frequently stop at adolescence; and toward the end of their life the brain of one's relative or lifelong friend may deteriorate to the point where this person no longer recognizes anyone.

If nothing else cuts short the picture of oneness, death will do the job. We will see everyone we know die, or they will see us die.

Yet there is another reality, an unshakable and lasting truth. And it is possible for the memory of that truth to remain with children throughout their lives. If their parents never lost sight of their innocence, no matter what adolescent span of rebellion they are passing into or what adult stage of case-making against their upbringing they may be "working through," whether in the process of divorcing or at the height of fame, whether in illness or even in death, at least one connection to truth remains in their awareness. Perhaps nothing else happened in their life that pointed to truth, but if during their childhood they glimpsed the nature of eternal love, then an echo of that love can still be heard, no matter what their circumstances. Although there are many other ways it can happen, parents can awaken in their children the memory of God. But to do this, it is crucial that parents learn that, as the apostle John said, "there is no fear in love."

Fear is a wellspring of separation, alienation, and loneliness and thus reinforces the primary images of the world. It blocks access to intuition and empathy. It throws off timing, making one hurry or hold back. It agitates. It depresses. It leads to inappropriate action or inaction. It contributes to countless illnesses and accidents. It fuels aggression. It promotes hopelessness. It is the base of anger. And in its grip one feels forsaken, even by God.

It is never necessary to teach your child fear. **Every duty you will ever have as a parent can be carried out effectively without once using fear.**

KIDS AND SPANKING

Spanking is perhaps the most common use of fear in parenting. Our oldest son, Scott, lived with his mother, who had custody of him until he was fourteen, at which time he came to live with us. We never considered spanking him, because we both thought he was "too old" to be spanked. At the time it didn't occur to us to question this strange value: that the bigger and more physically able to absorb a beating that children become, and the more experienced and versed in adult logic they are, the more "inappropriate" it is to beat them. Ironically, *little* children find being hit incomprehensible and, because of their small mass and the fragility of their bones and organs, they are the ones most likely to be injured. Yet as a culture we believe deeply in using violence with smaller children. As late as 1988 a federal study found that almost 90 percent of parents had spanked their three- to six-year-olds one to five times in the past *week*. More recent estimates confirm that there has been little change in this practice. Probably fewer than 5 percent of parents use no form of corporal punishment at all.

Many older children won't tolerate being hit—they will either hit back or run away—and this fact probably has more to do with why parents stop spanking them than the rationale that they are now "too mature" for childish forms of discipline.

Our decision not to spank our other two boys came early in their lives. When John was four he got down some matches and set a fire in the kitchen. Hugh discovered it and, after quickly extinguishing it, gave him three hard swats on the butt. John had never been spanked and, not knowing what to do about the pain, turned around and said between sobs, "Daddy, would you kiss it and make it well?"

Hugh was jolted by this request. Should he immediately try to take away the pain? Shouldn't he let John remain in discomfort as a lesson? Instantly he saw his mistake. His function as a father was to heal, not hurt. So he kissed John, explained about fires, put the matches out of his reach, and never spanked him again.

KIDS AND CURSING

When Jordan was nine we realized that we needed to start teaching him the complex rules of "guarding his tongue" when talking to adults outside his own family. Earlier in the year he had been punished at school for using the word "damn," quite a different reaction from the one he had gotten to that word six weeks before when we were vacationing in California. A camera crew and producer for the *Arsenio Hall Show,* which at that time was still on TV, were out on the sidewalks interviewing children about songs, when Jordan and his two brothers happened to walk by. The man with the mike stopped Jordan and asked him if there were any he didn't like. He answered, "I hate that damn Barney song." Everyone broke up laughing and the producer told him his comment would be on the show for sure. About three months later, it was. If he hadn't used the word "damn," it clearly wouldn't have made the show—and if he hadn't used the word "damn" in class, he wouldn't have been punished. That is an insane distinction to try to teach a child.

About a month after Jordan was on TV, he and a friend were in the friend's backyard building tunnels in the dirt. The friend's mother walked up behind them and overheard them both using the word "fuck," a word we have heard many kids their age use. The mother's reaction was to stand both of them up and slap them hard in the face.

When Jordan came home he was visibly upset, but when we asked him why, he said forcefully that nothing had happened. It took us over an hour to gently assure him that it was safe to talk to us about it, whatever it was. When the story finally came out, we were both surprised by the degree of shame he exhibited. He believed he must have done something very evil for another boy's mother to slap him, but he didn't know what it was. At first he simply couldn't believe that anyone would react that violently to a word. We told him that the world was not a logical place and that in several instances drivers had shot at other drivers merely for giving them the finger. We told him that if one's purpose was to know God and to feel God's presence (a concept he was very familiar with), what his friend's mother had done was a greater mistake than what he and his friend had done. Violence is not a path to the peace of God. Violence is not even an effective way of solving an issue between two people, whether it's between two adults or between an adult and a child.

In talking to him, we realized that he could see for himself that **getting attacked doesn't make someone feel like being a better human being.** On an emotional level, he first wanted to attack himself (shame), then, after he got angry, he wanted to attack the mother. He said bitterly, "If her husband said 'fuck,' I bet she wouldn't slap him in the face." He could see the double standard that most adults use when dealing with children, and understandably he didn't like it. We assured him that he had no reason to be ashamed and that he certainly didn't want to make the same mistake she had made by now thinking up ways to attack her back.

We told Jordan that the time had come for him to begin learning some of the things that could set adults off. For at least another hour we tried to explain adults' varying reactions to certain words, words he had heard professional baseball and basketball players use during games he had attended, had heard their coaches use, had heard famous actors use in movies, had heard adult entertainers use in stand-up comedy and rap music, and had heard teachers use the day he took a test in the teachers' lounge. We finally realized that a reasonable explanation of what this mother had done was impossible because her behavior was not reasonable. Instead, we simply impressed upon him that when children said certain words, they opened themselves up to the *possibility* of extreme reactions from adults and that this is merely the nature of our society. We also carefully went over the words and gestures that could produce these reactions.

We did not try to teach Jordan a philosophical framework for determining good and bad words, because we realized that we ourselves were inconsistent in this regard. For example, neither of us like the word "goddamn" and yet we occasionally say "Oh, shit!" In our home we have outlawed the first swearword simply on the grounds that it's jolting to us personally. Our children respect this in the same way that we respect the fact that two of our three boys like to be kidded and one definitely does not.

Our first impulse in response to what had happened was to confront the mother and tell her that she was never again to use corporal punishment with our child. Since we were certain that this would cause her to break up the boys' friendship, we waited until the next day to decide. In a calmer atmosphere, we reviewed the fact that this woman had always treated Jordan very well and that only recently her marriage had begun to break up. We also took into consideration that our family was new to Tucson and that, at the time, this boy was one of Jordan's few friends. We decided to wait and monitor each visit carefully. For the next several months we questioned Jordan about what had happened whenever he returned from his friend's house. That was three years ago and there has been no further incident.

FORBIDDEN ACTIVITIES

Both John and Jordan led a very secluded life until we moved to California. At that time Jordan was four and John, seven. Before the move, we lived in the mountains several miles from a very small town and both boys were home-schooled. Within days of moving to California they discovered swearing, video games, sweets, and TV. With the exception of a few—very few—foods, shows, and games that we thought were especially damaging to children, and the one swearword that we just mentioned, we allowed them to indulge themselves as fully as they wished in all four areas.

They both got bored with video games, TV, and sweets and lost their sudden addiction to all three within a few months. Now these are an occasional interest of theirs but have never again been an obsession.

This outcome is in sharp contrast to the one experienced by those parents who have strictly forbidden any or all of these foods and activities for children their age. As we have watched these kids grow and mature, we have noticed that most of them have retained an inordinate fascination for whatever their friends and classmates have been permitted but they have not.

On one occasion we had a birthday party for John at a roller rink. Several of his friends who were not allowed sweets had been invited. After eating some of the birthday treats, all the kids left to skate, except for the children who had grown up in homes where sweets were forbidden. These kids—five different children from four different families—stayed at the table eating cake and ice cream as if they were starved, assuring us all the while that their parents said birthdays were an exception to the no-sweets rule. Then, we soon discovered, they took the money we had given them to skate and spent it at the snack bar on candy.

John went through a period of intense swearing for a few months and then lost interest completely. We can't remember his having said any swearword for two or three years now. Jordan, however, retained a gradually weakening interest in swearing for several years before there was a substantial change. He and Hugh were talking several months ago when suddenly Jordan got down on the floor and started doing sit-ups. Hugh said, "What're you doing?" Jordan answered, "I just said 'shit' and I'm training myself not to curse." "Why?" asked Hugh, who had heard Jordan say that word so many times that he hadn't even noticed. "Because it's beginning to cause me problems at school. When I play basketball sometimes I curse and don't know it and a teacher hears me. They always say something that gets me off my game."

It's worth noting that being slapped by his friend's mother did not change Jordan's *interest* in swearing. Perhaps his decision is not yet permanent, but we find it remarkable that we have not heard him swear since he arrived at the decision himself.

Naturally, there are many activities that are too dangerous to allow kids the freedom to experience for themselves, but generally speaking, even though letting children learn in their own time takes longer, the lesson is rooted more deeply. Equally important, it reduces stress on the friendship between parent and child. **Your child's relationship with you can tolerate less and less strain the older your child becomes.** This sad and easily observable fact often becomes undeniable when your children reach adolescence.

SIGNS OF THE LESSON VIOLENCE TEACHES

In interviewing kids who are living or have lived in a home where they were struck by an adult and in interviewing adults who grew up being struck by their parents, we have been impressed by how often these kids have fantasies of striking back at, or doing worse to, their own mother or father. Also, frequently they go through a stage of bullying other kids and later in life often have urges to solve their marital problems through striking.

Parents who use violence demonstrate that they personally believe in violence, and, of course, the child internalizes this belief. One of the earliest signs of this often is seen in the way kids treat their toys. Children who are spanked, struck, cuffed, shaken, or angrily picked up and put down often are physically abusive in their fantasy games in very similar ways. Gayle, for example, who was spanked with a brush or switch almost daily, can remember repeatedly spanking her dolls. Hugh, who was belted and slugged, can remember the times when he would suddenly decide that he no longer liked some possession and would angrily smash it. He also remembers breaking the toys of kids he didn't like.

As we pointed out before, parents who spank their children don't like their children *at the moment* they are spanking them. In our work with batterers (of a child or partner), we have seen that their urge to hurt is healed more quickly when batterers are taught how to increase their love for their spouse or their child than when their attention is directed at stopping their own behavior through remorse and self-criticism or through willpower alone.

We motivate ourselves by remembering the times we love, not the times we forget to love. And we motivate our children by loving them, not by acting out our momentary dislike of them. When we love, like, appreciate, enjoy our kids, they see in themselves what we see. This counters the general disrespect for children that our kids must wade through when they are not around us.

When we began teaching batterers how to heal themselves, we found that if they worked hard at training their minds to focus on their spiritual accomplishments, rather than their failures, they eventually reached a time when they cherished their children or spouse too much to want ever to hurt them again. Now they were no longer fighting "themselves," because they had glimpsed a deeper, more compelling self.

Theoretically, it is possible to hit someone and like that individual simultaneously, but we have never worked with parents who claimed that to be true in their relationship with their own children. Most kids who are spanked learn that when you think someone is difficult, it is only natural to want to hurt them. This is what Mom and Dad do, so this is what everyone must do. The lesson remains implanted in the child's psyche regardless of what the parents call the violence, what verbal preamble they give before they are violent, what books condone the particular form of violence they use, or how deliberate and controlled they think they are while being violent.

FEAR DISTORTS PERCEPTION

On the block where Hugh grew up were five other boys his age, and like him, all were afraid of their fathers, and one or two were also afraid of his mother. Fear was certainly not the only emotion they felt toward these parents, but it unquestionably colored all aspects of their relationships with them.

This was also true of school friends whom Hugh knew well enough to visit at their homes. To them, their dad was that large, shadowy figure with whom they came into contact only when he would whip off his belt to "teach you a lesson," or when he was instructing them in those tasks or sports he had decided they needed to learn. To get their cooperation, all their mother had to say was, "I'll tell your father" and they did what she said.

Accompanying this fear of their dads was an unrealistic view of their fathers' abilities. Although Hugh can't remember any friend saying "My dad can beat up your dad," some thought similar to that was present in all of them. My father is stronger or richer or smarter or never wrong . . . something that made their primary source of pain superior to other mortals'. They each secretly believed that their dad was a little god, and he was often as moody and arbitrary as any worshiped by the Greeks and Romans.

That's why Jordan's comment about Hugh not being able to beat any boxer came as a surprise. No boy Hugh knew growing up would have allowed himself such a thought. Gayle believed that her dad, who was a banker, was probably the smartest man alive, and most of her friends thought that their dads were superior in some special way.

Fear of our parents distorts our perception of them. Because of the particular set of values prevalent in the 1940s and 1950s, that distortion tended to be aggrandizement. For many years we both believed that "honoring" one's parents through this form of misperception was natural, mentally healthy, and virtuous, but our boys have demonstrated how mistaken our assumption was. Their sense of themselves, their ability to see the world as it is, and their level of happiness are far greater than ours were at their age. Yet those few parents who know our approach tend to look at John and Jordan with suspicion. They usually don't object to their behavior—both boys are reasonably polite, "well behaved," and make good grades—but the high percentage of our time and income that we spend on them, and the fact that we don't spank or shame them, by definition make them "spoiled" in those parents' eyes.

Today fear still causes a distorted perception of one's parents, but now the distortion is overly negative rather than overly positive. One senses at times a subtle competition among adults as to which one had the most dysfunctional childhood. Tweens and teens trade complaints about their moms and dads, and any of them can tell you in what specific ways each of their friends' parents are unreasonable and unfair. This way of looking at one's family may seem more honest, but because it blocks vision of the deeper nature, it is equally a hindrance to the perception of oneness, which is the core of spiritual development. Unless we are willing to look at our parents' egos with calm, undistorted honesty—even parents who have repeatedly struck us—we simply can't see past their small, separated self to their larger self with which we are already joined.

FEARFUL KIDS OFTEN "BEHAVE"
AROUND ADULTS

In their presence, the children of parents who use physical or psychological intimidation are generally more "respectful" and less demanding of their attention than the children of parents who refuse to use fear to control behavior. And, until they begin approaching the teenage years, their children—when mentally capable of doing so—often perform better academically, especially for those teachers who value predictable performance and precise results over discovery, creativity, and the joy of learning.

Thus for several years, the parents who use fear as a motivator often will appear to be on the right track. Usually it's not until their kids approach puberty that the hidden effects of fear begin to surface.

In our general neighborhood, there are four couples who frequently spank, hit, and yell at their kids. Three of the boys and one of the girls (none from the same family) are now old enough that the effects of this approach are becoming apparent. One boy (eight) tortures and kills birds and hurts children who are weaker than he. A second boy (nine), although he doesn't first torture anything, also kills neighborhood wildlife, picks on weaker kids, and compulsively tells on his classmates, even though this makes him unpopular. The third boy (twelve) will tell on someone only when he himself has been accused, then he will lie to shift the blame; he also kills wildlife, punches kids who are weaker, "keys" cars, damages mailboxes, and occasionally destroys other children's possessions if he thinks he can do so undetected. The girl (also twelve) is not physically violent toward other kids and doesn't kill wildlife but does work quite hard and effectively to turn her friends against kids she doesn't like and even against one another.

All four of these children are very polite to adults; in fact, they have developed that type of social skill well beyond their age, and certainly beyond most of the kids we know who have loving and fear-free relationships with their parents. When they reach the teen years, some of them may choose to stop acting respectfully toward adults, may even become contemptuous of adults. This outward change, although it may lessen the feelings of intimidation they once had, will not undo the damage their upbringing caused. Many of them will heal only by learning to become loving parents themselves, as was true with Hugh.

Within the stepfamilies Hugh shuttled between, he was spanked, hit, and saw his mother repeatedly beaten. He remembers well the anger he felt for children and animals weaker than he was. A long hunting-and-bullying stage began to end when he first felt the presence of God during his teenage years and stopped entirely when we got married.

No given outcome inevitably flows from a fear-based parent-child relationship. We have known fear-free kids with advanced social skills as well as children who have been physically intimidated, some very severely, who were remarkably gentle in nature and honorable toward their peers. In general, however, kids will tend to treat other kids the way they themselves are treated at home. If they are not valued and respected, usually they will see little value in respecting others. If they are attacked for their weaknesses and mistakes, usually they will attack the same in themselves and others.

This is certainly not logical. You would think that those who have experienced the effects of being hit would never wish to hit anyone themselves, that having felt how miserable it is to live with people who are unpredictable and unfair, they would be motivated to be consistently kind. But egos are not logical, even those of children, and a concerned mother must see with her own eyes the effects that her anger and impatience have on her kids; a devoted father must observe for himself the effects of intimidating his child.

STUDY YOUR CHILD'S REACTIONS

In our work with families we have been amazed at how often parents assume that their approach to disciplining impacts their child the same way it would impact another adult or the way it's supposed to affect them according to the latest child-rearing theory—without ever observing for themselves if this is true for *their* son or daughter. Consequently, they never develop a good instinct for each of their kids' distinct ways of reacting and often are unaware of the fear they are generating in one or all of their children. They are also insensitive to the difficulties that a particular approach may cause not only within their own future relationship with the child but within the other relationships the child will have as an adult.

From a spiritual standpoint, following the guidance of your heart is a higher approach—and in our opinion a far more practical one—than blindly following a strategy that you may hear of or read about. Children see through formulas surprisingly quickly. They sense manipulation faster than adults. Even very young kids detect when their parents are insincere, when they lack understanding or belief in what they are attempting.

Your kids may behave the way the technique is supposed to make them behave, but making a habit of relying on formulas can cause unforeseen problems. For example, repeatedly saying "If you don't eat your vegetables, you'll stop growing" may make your child anxious about his appearance. Thumping a one- or two-year-old's chin every time she reaches for the salt may make her more stubborn. Saying things you don't mean such as "If you don't stop throwing sand, I'll never take you to a park again as long as you live" can teach a child to doubt *all* your assertions. Children yearn for a real relationship with real people, one in which actions are an outcome of the heart, not of calculation or mood.

Techniques in and of themselves are not a mistake. But using a technique as a substitution for vision is. For example, parents frequently get into a battle of wills with their two- or three-year-old. But young children are able to concentrate better on what they want than adults. They also have less going on in their lives to distract them from pursuing their purpose. Consequently, they can outendure an adult and win the battle of wills—unless the adult resorts to hitting, shaking, or shouting, which is always a mistake. Here is where increased vision or awareness can be an effective tool. Your purpose is not to win but to *see* your child's interests and needs clearly and to work with them rather than against them.

For example, Terrianne Jacobson has a vast repertoire of techniques that she uses freely, but she doesn't use them manipulatively. Her goal is much deeper and broader than a change in behavior. Mark and Kolby, Terrianne's three- and four-year-old boys, now have great enthusiasm for picking up anything they are finished playing with. Naturally, they didn't begin life this way. Other parents marvel at their attitude. Yet it was their *attitude* toward picking up and not the behavior itself that has been the focus of Terrianne's efforts. "I always try to teach, never to boss. I ask myself, 'What am I trying to teach in this situation?' With cleaning up what I wanted was a lifelong enjoyment of order, enjoyment of both the results *and* the process. So the first thing I did when they were very small was to get down on the floor and start picking up the things they were through with myself, and making a great game of this. They would see what fun I was having and usually they would join me. As we worked together, I would praise each little accomplishment. 'Oh, look, you've picked up all the red ones!' When they got bored, I would not make them feel bad for 'quitting'; I would simply finish the job myself—because my goal was for them to learn enjoyment."

Most parents know that when a small child decides to help you clean, cook, fold clothes, and the like, the job takes longer to complete. When parents repeatedly become irritated with this kind of delay, they teach children that getting something over with is the important thing, even more important than their kids. Obviously there are situations in which delay is not feasible and the child must be removed so that the job can be done. However, most situations are not urgent and parents become impatient merely because they don't want to be bothered. They have forgotten that the decision to have a child *is* the decision to be bothered. We invited the child into our lives because on some level we recognized that **our willingness to be inconvenienced is the door to a deeper, more permanent happiness.**

As they got older, Terrianne was able to suggest games for Kolby and Mark to do on their own. "I'll start counting to ten and I just bet you can't get all of that picked up before I finish." Or "Now we get to clean up!" (and maybe she would start singing the Barney song "Clean up! Clean up!"). Or "I'm going to go make up the bed in my room and *you* can clean up the floor in *this* room. Do you think you can do that?"

If either of the boys didn't want to clean up, or stopped too soon, perhaps she would use the technique of giving him an alternative in order to get him started. "Which blocks do you want to pick up first, the big ones or the little ones?" If this and nothing else worked, she would never get into a power struggle. She would simply finish the task herself. However, the next time there was a mess, she would again initiate cleanup time. She would not ask them if they wanted to and thereby set up their egos to oppose her; she would simply announce that cleanup was starting now.

As a consequence of her goal to teach *enjoying* doing

this task, both her boys have virtually no negative associations with picking up and putting away, and now they do it automatically.

In our experience, all "problem children" are scared children. Eliminate fear and, unless there is genetic damage or some other highly unusual condition, any child, including teenagers, will begin to settle into a gentler attitude and approach to life. The earlier parents stop using fear as a disciplinary tool, the shorter the journey back to Oneness or Family will be for both parent and child. Enjoying your child can't start too soon. It can even begin while you are picking up a mess, cleaning up vomit, or changing a diaper. And Love is there to give you an attitude adjustment whenever you need one.

You may be feeling resistance about, even distaste for, what you are doing for your child, but that is never *all* you are feeling. To simply remember God turns your mind toward your source of peace. Remembering is a gentle act that requires no expertise or noticeable effort. When you are discontent, angry, depressed, sad, lonely, or fearful, you can still remember God. You never have to get rid of an emotion or change it into another emotion to remember God. You just remember.

10

CULTURAL ASSUMPTIONS ABOUT ADOLESCENTS' NEEDS

YOUR TEENAGER IS YOUR CHILD

A mother told us that about a year ago she "woke up in her kitchen" just as she was starting irritably to clean up the crumbs that her teenager had left on the counter. "He cleans up pretty well, but never as well as I want him to. I was about to wipe up these little seeds that come off the top of rolls when suddenly I thought, 'What if he were no longer here? What if he were dead?' Then every day I would *long* to see these seeds on the counter just one more time." This mother told us that she hasn't used the words "clean up" to her son since that day.

In their lectures and workshops, Diane Cirincione and Jerry Jampolsky often tell the story of a mother who for many months had a battle with her teenager over the issue of whether he could wear the same T-shirt day after day.[1]

The mother was neat and well dressed at all times, and when she would take her son to events and places where dressing "improperly" was looked down on, their arguments over this favorite T-shirt would become particularly heated. The war with her son ended when, at age sixteen, he was killed in a car accident. After his death she said that she wished he were alive long enough that she could tell him that he could wear whatever he wanted to. When this mother buried her son, she dressed him in his favorite T-shirt.

We have heard this kind of story from many grieving parents. When it's too late, they finally realize what was important—and what was not—in their relationship with their child. Please contrast this gentle way of looking at teenagers to what we edited out (and slightly rephrased) from columns and articles that appeared in newspapers published *just this morning.* Over half this list comes from one widely read syndicated pediatrician:

> You are not your adolescent's friend, rescuer, short-order cook, entertainer, banker, or employer of last resort.
>
> Your child came into your life, not you into his.
>
> You never need to explain why you are telling your adolescent to do something—simply say, "Because I said so."
>
> You are not a servant. Your kids should be able to get themselves up and fix their own breakfast from age four on. [We're not making this stuff up!]
>
> You are not obliged to take a forgotten book or assignment to school, even if your child phones pleading for you to do so.
>
> You are not obliged to referee your kids' fights.
>
> You are not obliged to give your teenager gas money or to pay for car maintenance and repair.
>
> You are not obliged to put up with your adolescent's rude friends.
>
> Your teenager should occupy herself reading,

not endlessly watching TV and playing loud music. Try making her run laps around the house if she disturbs your peace.

Assign your children their "share" of the household chores that *you* want done.

When you have guests over, it's reasonable for you to expect your child to dress presentably, to be polite, and, afterwards, to help you clean up.

Make the penalty fit the crime: Teens who don't follow car safety rules should lose their driving privileges. Teens who can't speak respectfully should not be answered. Teens who use money in ways you have forbidden should have their allowance cut. Teens who fail to do their chores should be given additional ones. But for major violations [drinking and driving was the example given] the penalties [unspecified] should be more severe and painful.

Putting aside the punishments for a moment, and putting aside also the question of whether any of these suggestions is reasonable or unreasonable, if you simply take this list as a whole, its underlying tone reflects our culture's attitude toward adolescents almost perfectly: It says to parents, "You are not your child's keeper." This of course is an outgrowth of the broader philosophy of our times, "I am not my brother's keeper."

Are you your brother's keeper? No, you are far more than that. You are your brother.

Many parents experience their oneness with their infant quite strongly. And as long as she is completely subservient and they can pick her up and put her down as they please, they remain open to that experience. They say, "My baby is a gift from God." And indeed they mean it. Yet no one who rides the wave of current opinion has any chance of one day feeling "My teenager is a gift from God."

One columnist said, "You're not raising children; you're raising future adults." And that's exactly what this approach does. It skips childhood and goes directly to the modern adult's bottom line: "What's in it for me?" It says to young people, "I don't exist for you; I exist to serve my pleasures and needs. I have the power and this is how I use it. When you become an adult, you can be selfish, but for now, I set the selfishness level."

Most of the things that adults now are being told that they don't need to bother doing for their child, they willingly, happily, and automatically do for their second spouse, or their current lover, or even for a good friend. If the one we loved needed a break from chores, we would take over. If the one we loved wanted a special meal, we would fix it gladly. If the one we loved left behind important paperwork, we would take it to them—without even thinking of delivering a lecture and penalty along with it. The fact is that for the one we love we are *frequently* a "rescuer, short-order cook, entertainer, banker," and sometimes an "employer of last resort." And we are certainly a "friend." As counselors who have been called to the homes of many families, we are sadly aware that the basic reason parents don't do these little things for their adolescent is *not* that she is irresponsible, but that she is no longer the one they love.

"No. No. No," says the psychology of our times, "you're missing the point. An adult cannot and should not treat a child as an equal. You are the one with life experience, maturity, and seasoned judgment. You alone are responsible for feeding, sheltering, and guiding this adolescent. You earn the money, pay the rent, bring home the groceries, and keep things repaired and running. It's your household—your kid doesn't even own his own room. It's your role as parent to take charge and make the hard decisions."

Certainly it's true that on the basis of bodily age and ego maturity, you and your child are not equal. And indeed you must make clear and thoughtful decisions concerning many aspects of your child's life. But merely because parents have a role in their children's lives does not mean that their children have no role in theirs. Spiritually, you and your adolescent are not only equal, you are one. Spiritually, there is no place where your child's interests end and yours begin. You must make all decisions with your child—not with her democratic vote or her ego advice—but with her heart held tightly to yours. Only when you look at the choices before you through both of your eyes—which spiritually are the same eyes—have you become a whole parent.

We simply can't teach fairness without being fair, or generosity without being generous, or consideration of others without being considerate. If one moment we say, "You must *help* me baby-sit your siblings, be *responsible* and write down the message when someone calls me, maintain the *quietness* level I want, and *share* the chores I decide must be done—but I'm not going to lift a finger for you" (or, to paraphrase one of the columnists, "Once you've met your kids' basic needs, you're done with them"), then we teach nothing but hypocrisy.

The present attitude doesn't teach self-dependence, it *forces* self-dependence. It teaches the mere *appearance* of "helping," "responsibility," "quietness," and "sharing." And if we add "Let's get this straight; I'm the adult—you're the child," we inevitably reap the chaotic, blame-filled relationships with our adolescents that most of us now have.

YOUR ADOLESCENT HAS ADOLESCENT NEEDS

Adolescence was not the most feared and isolated age group until recent decades. Certainly there has always been *some* fear and jealousy of the youthful. In most forms of life this is the stage when the younger generation begins to assume the power held by the older generation. Among humans, power comes in many forms: earning potential, health and energy, physical attractiveness, ambition and aggressiveness, men-

tal acuity, and bodily strength. Although this is the age when
the child enters womanhood or manhood, and becomes a
threat to those in whom the vitality of youth is fading, in
more structured times and within more formal cultures, this
has also been the age when young people begin mastering
a trade, acquiring the skills of social intercourse, or training to be a warrior, all of which entail a time-consuming
process.[2]

However, today there are shortcuts to getting
money, power, and "respect." Violence is a door open to
any young person willing to walk through it. If you own a
gun or push drugs, for example, you have access to instant
power and earnings potential. Although most adolescents
don't choose a violent way of obtaining money or dominat-
ing others, all of them know that it's available to them, and
the way our culture now looks upon and treats this age
group is pushing an ever-growing percentage of them in
that direction. On one hand, we provide no mentorship; on
the other hand, we set the wrong example. In fact, in those
areas where young people have their greatest strengths and
are most willing to excel, we set a horrifying example.

The youth of this country are entering a society that
has an annual violence and crime rate of about 25,000 murders; 30,000 suicides; 100,000 rapes; 600,000 robberies; and
over a million aggravated assaults and now contains two
thirds of the world's serial killers. At present, our chosen
way of dealing with those adolescents who respond to their
country's call to violence is to become even more violent
toward them than we have been.

As individual families, there is much over which we
have no control, and the trend of the culture around us is
one area we are not going to change quickly. But the key to
successfully parenting an adolescent is to do what we can do
within our homes. Perhaps the place to begin is to question
our culture's basic assumptions about this age group so that
we don't mindlessly take them on ourselves. The way our

culture is now handling the teenager's entry into adult society is clearly a failure, but we can assure you from our experience as counselors and parents that you don't have to adopt any aspect of this mistake, regardless of what your kid's school, the parents around you, and your community are doing.

In earlier times, many societies, including our own, valued the basic *qualities* of adolescence and provided ways of honoring and utilizing them. The teenagers' capacity for hard physical labor was welcomed on the farm or frontier; their passion, fearlessness, and love of danger made them good hunters or warriors; and being nearer in age to their siblings than were their parents and grandparents suited them well for the care and teaching of younger children. By tradition their parents, relatives, or designated mentors took responsibility for initiating them into the society of women or men, and the people of the town, village, or tribe formally and consciously acknowledged their new standing as adults. Even within our generation and certainly within our parents', there were echoes of this celebration of young manhood and womanhood. "Look at you!" relatives and friends of the family would say. "You're becoming a real woman! It won't be long before you have children of your own!" Or "What a fine young man you're growing up to be. I bet you're going to be taller than your dad!"

Now there is no community of people who have seen the sons and daughters of this family grow up, who recognize and acknowledge the stages of each child's growth. These kids have already had to move twice by the time they reached thirteen, and there is a 50 percent chance that they no longer live in an intact family. Stable communities are virtually nonexistent and even immediate neighbors come and go so frequently that many families no longer bother getting acquainted with the people on their block. Thus this last little vestige of outward acknowledgment—just walking among people who have seen you grow up—has vanished.

The teenager is more isolated now than he has been at any other time in history. He is a stranger, and all that we can see is that he is a teenager—someone to prey on or someone who will prey upon us.

On the whole, adolescents have been left to fend for themselves because within our diverse and chaotic society a widespread structure for acknowledging and guiding them no longer exists. Having no other real alternative, they have turned to one another for guidance—and teenagers are not particularly good leaders of other teenagers. A lack of balance and perspective is definitely one of the weaknesses of adolescence. No matter how often parents say, "You are now eighteen and should act responsibly," and no matter how many duties they pile on or how often they punish signs of immaturity, they will not succeed in abolishing this necessary growth stage. But they *can* make teenagers very angry, which is just what most parents and what society as a whole are doing.

Any group that feels judged will attack back, and teenagers, even though they are still children, are not an exception. This is the heroic age, and if these kids are not given a good cause, they will take up a bad one. **Society has changed toward adolescents but the basic characteristics of adolescence have not changed.** Not only have we failed to provide mentorship, we have gone to the other extreme of isolating and vilifying them. This minority, which has very little economic clout and no political influence, has become one of the principal lightning rods for our blame of what's wrong with society. Not only do most couples blame many if not all of the difficulties between them on the teenager who is under their roof, but most of the ills of society now are being systematically laid at the feet of these kids. The media, politicians, educators, religious leaders, and ordinary parents continually point out these children's weaknesses and spend very little energy highlighting their strengths. This unremitting attack is not just "human nature." It's in sharp contrast to the more balanced view we have of many other groups—farmers, veterans, small business owners, senior citizens, and so on—groups who actually *are* capable of taking greater responsibility for their actions.

Yet our society has gone way beyond just vilifying teenagers. As a people we are deeply troubled and spiritually sick. It's a clear sign that a society has lost its way when it begins to feed its children to the wolves. And this we have begun to do. We have fed them by the thousands to pointless wars of our own making and we have abandoned them to street wars, drugs, crime, early pregnancies, and homelessness. Once we were the protectors of children. Now we are their enemy. And teenagers know it.

Don't let this sickness into your home. Adolescents can do very little to change the basic forces that drive them at this age, but as parents we can do a great deal to see our tweens and teens more clearly and to adopt an approach that will help them get what they need from this transitional period.

If parents recognize that **teenagers need to be active, need to take risks, need to test their abilities and come up against their limitations,** they will encourage them to take part in reasonable activities that permit this. Parents who give up on their kids and let them do anything regardless of the risks involved or those parents who have to control every detail of their kids' lives both fail to fulfill the role of mentor. We need a thoughtful, intuitive, and *balanced* approach that is based on our adolescents' individual needs and abilities.

We were recently faced with a decision about John that demanded this kind of balance and perspective. It also demanded that we free ourselves from a strong prejudice we shared. In working with grieving parents, we have encountered more than one story of a family who lost a child to rock climbing. The son of a woman we were very close to when we lived in Santa Fe died from a rock-climbing accident, and Scott, our oldest boy, fell from a mountain while climbing and lived only because he landed in the branches of a tree. Added to this were two close calls Hugh had while climbing when he was in his twenties. So when John, at age sixteen, asked us if he could go rock climbing with a group of his friends, our first impulse was to say no. He had done some rappelling at a camp he had attended when he was younger and more recently had taken a semester of rock climbing at his high school, but none of that had occurred on the sides of mountains.

First we informed ourselves about the experience level of the other members of the group, the quality of the equipment they would use, and the degree of difficulty of the slope. Then we sat down, closed our eyes, and worked to release our minds from the bias we had against this activity. We didn't try to ignore its dangers or to deceive ourselves that because we were praying we were somehow giving John special protection, but rather we tried to look at the dangers calmly in relation to teenagers' love of physical challenges and their strong need to extend themselves.

We decided that although we personally disliked and distrusted this activity, in many ways this was an ideal outlet for John. He would be striving to complete a difficult physical task; facing and mastering some of his fears; and most important, *cooperating with other teenagers in a positive goal* of mutual assistance and protection.

He and the other kids—about six boys and two girls—have now had several successful climbs. Because of his own fall, Scott had stopped climbing and originally was against John trying this sport. After he saw the positive effects John's climbs had on him, he bought John the safest climbing equipment available and gave it to him this Christmas and also invited John to attend a climbing camp with him this coming summer.

There are numerous positive challenges that adolescents can take and will take if their parents are understanding of their needs. Some kids love striving to master a musical instrument, or taking on the mental challenge of chess, or learning to weld or sculpt. You can expect many false starts before a principal interest takes over, but **even a series of short-lived interests can adequately meet the heroic need of your adolescent.**

Sports—whether team sports, competitive ice-skating, jumping horses, modern dance, deep-sea diving, or running marathons—offer boys and girls perhaps the most diverse set of opportunities for meeting adolescents' need to strive, toil, and test themselves. Yet these endeavors often are perverted by adult coaches and supervisors who cheat or attack their athletes or strive to win at all costs. Parents must become advocates for true sportsmanship. Also, **parents must try not to impose ideals that are wholly inappropriate to adolescence, such as doing away with competition or eliminating all possible risks.** Adolescents are *going* to compete and take risks. That is their stage of life. Our job is to make this enriching, fulfilling, and self-affirming. **When your adolescent shows interest in any reasonable challenge, you must encourage it and support it with whatever means are available to you.**

YOUR ADOLESCENT NEEDS SYMBOLS

To parent your adolescent effectively, you must be conscious of the powerful effect of symbols at this age. **When you support the symbols of your child's yearning to be her own person, you support your child.** Many parents ask themselves the wrong question when deciding whether to allow their adolescents to buy and play adolescent music, to dress and wear their hair like other adolescents, to speak in adolescent jargon, to watch adolescent movies and TV shows, to stay up unreasonably late, to talk on the phone unreasonably long, and the like. Parents usually look at the activity and ask whether it is inherently good. For example, is it good to start every third sentence with the word "like"? Is it good to rebel against society's neatness norm within your own room? Is it good to eat pizza two meals out of every three?

The more appropriate questions are: "Is this activity a symbol of my child's drive to be independent of parental figures and free of his childhood personality? And if I think it is, do I really believe it threatens his life or basic health?" For example, many parents look at TV programs that depict youth rebelling against adult authority and assume that these shows fan their children's cruel and violent emotions. But this is not the basic appeal these programs have for *adolescents*. They are simply one of the few aspects of our culture that kids can look to that affirm their need to break from the past and become their own person. If parents would merely observe the effects for themselves, and not read "studies" about the effects, they would see that *most* adolescents are not more violent, war prone, or criminally minded after seeing one of these shows. They are *not* more likely to take on a gang single-handedly, to beat up other kids at school, or to smoke and swear.

Admittedly, there *could* be better ways to affirm the adolescent's need to leave the nest, but until there are, you should not deny your child programs and movies of this sort *out of hand*. If you are concerned about a particular movie or show, you should watch it yourself and make up your own mind about just how dangerous this is for *your* child.

Adolescence is a growth process in which the child takes a series of steps to go from immaturity to maturity. Although this is a natural progression, it can be disrupted, and parents who know their children well are alert to the things that support this process and the things that don't. When Gayle was fifteen, she started to smoke. Smoking was socially acceptable for adults—both of Gayle's parents smoked—but it wasn't for adolescents. At that time, our culture's objection to children smoking was based not so much on addiction and health as on social propriety, and Gayle's parents were deeply desirous of always appearing proper. Thus they angrily opposed Gayle's doing this. They screamed at her, grounded her, and called her names. Gayle and her mother believed that Gayle's father might have inherited a family proclivity for early death, and so her mother brought out the ultimate weapon. She repeatedly said, "If you keep this up, it's going to kill your father."

Gayle, however, had the challenges that most adolescents have, one of which is trying to fit into a desirable group of kids at school. Gayle didn't want to be a cheerleader. She wasn't able to be a beautiful, popular flirt. There were no team sports for girls at her school, and so she couldn't be an athlete, which would have been her first choice. She didn't want to be what today would be called an academic nerd. And above all she didn't want to be a nobody; few adolescents do. But by smoking she was able to fit into a group of girls she liked and, it turned out, remained friends with most of her life.

No matter what Gayle's parents said or did to her, never once did it occur to her to quit smoking. The three-year battle they waged resulted only in destroying their relationship with her and motivating her to leave home permanently at age seventeen. Gayle is convinced that this battle slowed her maturing process by forcing her to react to her parents instead of thinking for herself. Their efforts were pointless in all ways because in her early twenties, when she finally began to think for herself, she gave up smoking on her own. She would have given it up sooner if her parents had not made it the greatest issue of her childhood.

You must never make a decision quickly, lightly, or righteously when you are considering any aspect of the world to which your child is strongly attracted. Again, don't focus on the nature of the activity itself but on what it represents to your child. Naturally, there are dangers so extreme that they are exceptions.

An old friend of ours, a teacher named Roy, raised his son and two daughters by himself. The boy, Ted, now is a junior in college; the younger girl, Lillian, is a freshman; and the older girl has just graduated. Roy had to confront his son's love of handguns when he was eleven. Month after month Ted used his small allowance to buy gun magazines and used-gun books. He well knew that his dad's position on handguns was that they should be banned; nevertheless, he felt very close to his dad and would show him pictures of guns and discuss their various features. Roy saw little harm in all of this until Ted asked him if he would buy him a pistol for his twelfth birthday, then take him to a range and let him shoot it.

Roy agonized over his decision for several days. He was deeply disturbed by the rapidly increasing percentage of Americans who carry handguns, and yet he had always been quick to recognize and meet his children's stronger needs. For example, he put his daughter in an ongoing group horseback-riding class when she was ten and desperately wanted a horse (which he couldn't afford), and he consistently refused to take away her weekend riding privileges as a form of punishment, even though other class parents told him how powerfully effective that punishment was.

Roy recognized that just as many girls love horses, many boys go through a strong warrior stage. He himself had grown up in a small town in Texas where rifles and shotguns played an important part in his and most of his friends' youth and were one of the few interests he had shared with his dad. He also had seen some disturbing evidence that parents who dismiss or rigidly oppose gender-oriented urges can create unnecessary problems for themselves. Recently a local newspaper had run a story about six fourteen-year-old boys who had taken a gun into the desert. One of them had badly injured his leg while trying to "quick draw." Roy didn't know the injured boy, but he did know that no one with any training would ever try to quick-draw a loaded revolver or autopistol.

Two of the boys in the desert had been in Roy's eighth-grade class the year before. He called one of their parents and discovered that none of the parents of the six boys had allowed their sons to have contact with guns. This information finalized his decision to allow Ted to meet his need in a safe environment. He bought Ted a 9mm and a membership in a nearby indoor handgun range and enrolled them in a father-and-son gun-safety class.

To this day Roy believes that his decision about Ted's interest in guns did more to deepen his bond with his son than any other single decision he made during Ted's childhood. However, when we interviewed Ted, he said that he saw nothing unusual about his dad's support on this issue; he had always supported him in the things that really mattered to him.

A few years later, Roy was faced with an equally difficult choice when his daughter, at age twelve, asked him if she could have her nose pierced. He instantly thought of permanent disfigurement. But he wisely waited a day before he gave her his answer. As a schoolteacher who taught the elementary grades before he was assigned to middle school, Roy had long been distressed to see how many girls lost their self-confidence at the onset of puberty, when suddenly they were judged by a new and decidedly more superficial standard. The only group that seemed immune to this loss were the better girl athletes.

Unfortunately, Lillian had little athletic ability. But in talking to her about why she wanted her nose pierced, he sensed that this was her way of holding on to her integrity and independence. Once he saw this, he realized that there was another group of girls who usually remained strong well into puberty: the girls who dressed in what he had always thought of as a defiant manner, and often these girls were not athletes. He wondered if they would have kept their strong sense of themselves if their parents or the school had not allowed them to dress this way. He didn't know the answer, but he decided he did not want to risk finding out by going against Lillian's strong desire to do something that plastic surgery could undo a few years later if she so desired.

Lillian still wears a nose ring as a freshman in college. She may continue to wear it, even when the day comes that she has to find employment. But in this regard our family was fascinated to discover recently that the new doctor we have all started going to has a nurse-receptionist with a nose ring!

It's important that we see our culture's present stance on adolescence clearly and contrast it consciously and deliberately with what we feel in our hearts. In our research for this chapter we have tried to isolate the basic assumptions behind the opinions that we have read and heard expressed most frequently by authorities on children, and especially by parents. We believe that the following "cultural assumptions" are the primary ones that undermine parents' actions and attitudes toward their tweens and teens. Clearly, these ideas can be found in our schools, but usually parents rather than professionals are the ones who state them bluntly.

Here, then, are ten assumptions that most parents make about what causes the problems between themselves and their adolescents, what they believe are the best ways to deal with those problems, and how these same difficulties can be approached within the spiritual parenting guidelines we have been discussing in this book.

TEN ASSUMPTIONS OUR CULTURE MAKES
ABOUT ADOLESCENTS

1. *"They're just seeing how much they can get away with; the more you give in, the more out of control they'll become."*

In the life of all kids, a time comes for them to try out their wings, to take risks, to start the process of leaving the nest. Most little birds have a few bad landings before they get the hang of it, and so do most kids. **Adolescence is a child's time to make mistakes,** and the wise parent consciously decides to step aside and allow this to happen. But this isn't easy—because our kids will make decisions we wouldn't make and do things we wouldn't do.

They may be secretive, or sullen, or dress faddishly, or speak in coded language, or have odd tastes in music, or crazy pleasures, or all of the above. Whatever it is at the moment, experienced parents work hard not to get caught up in all of that. Instead, they recognize the kinds of antics an adolescent is likely to indulge in, and why. And *they come up with reliable ways to maintain their perspective.*

For example, perhaps you can try writing letters to yourself or to your partner, gentle reminders of what your child is going through and what kind of parent you want to be. These you can take out and review when things get crazy. Or you may want to schedule regular breaks for yourself, times when you can step back and look at things more calmly. Or you might reread certain books or holy scriptures that you know will bring you back to your senses. Or maybe you can find another parent or friend to talk to who sees the innocence of children, and who can laugh easily.

A little bit of craziness characterizes most periods of transition, even for adults. The teenage child is becoming his own person. To accomplish this he has to try things out—different ways of talking, acting, and looking at life.

Even different beliefs, faiths, and personality types may be tried on and discarded until the child finally finds a persona and an approach to life that feel comfortable. **It is very difficult for parents to stand by and watch their kids make wrong choices,** and certainly parents must intervene if they think something poses a real danger.

Two months ago we had to tell John that we would not allow him to drive from Arizona to his California cross-country–running camp on just two and a half hours of sleep. He had already made plans to have two other boys meet him at our house at three in the morning to begin the trip. But he had not gotten to bed the night before until after midnight, and since the other boys were too young or inexperienced to help with the driving, we told him that he couldn't leave until he had at least six hours of sleep.

Our stand made John very angry. He had already talked to his friends. They had cleared the trip with their parents. He believed he knew what he was capable of. And he didn't want to have to tell his friends that his parents had intervened.

But we explained to him that his safety and the safety of the other two boys were our responsibility and we were sorry but we were not going to change our minds. We have taken very few rigid stands with our boys, but they know when they are up against one, and so John stopped arguing, called his friends, and slept in until ten o'clock.

As we have said, it's not within the scope of this book to address the special problems that accompany extreme forms of misbehavior such as drug addiction, criminal activity, and violence. However, *most* parents of adolescents will see their children at least flirt with some of these things. Many kids will not allow themselves to become deeply destructive, but parents can't rely on their teenagers' self-restraint. They must be alert to signs of danger and step in unequivocally. The problem, of course, is knowing when to do this. Parents who jump in too soon and too often undermine their child's self-confidence and close down channels of communication that need to stay open.

There is no magic rule about when to intervene. Your knowledge of your child, your intuition, and the guidance you receive from prayer are your essential tools during these times. Once you have felt a sense of peace about what to do, then act with assurance and do not reconsider. On one occasion we moved residences to get John away from the influence of some particularly destructive boys he was friends with. As we knew it would when we made it, this decision caused a financial hardship for all of us that we felt for several years. Looking back, we see that this was a small price to pay for the changes in John that it helped facilitate. On another occasion, when Jordan's hatred of school had become alarmingly strong, we took him out in the middle of the year and home-schooled him. We had to radically alter our routine and give up most of our free time, but seeing Jordan's hatred dissolve made it well worthwhile. In the seventh and eighth grades, when Hugh was getting into increasing trouble at school and becoming destructive to himself and others, he asked his father to send him to boarding school and persisted in this request until his father agreed. Hugh's instinct was right. His life turned around dramatically in the new environment.

You must never make anything more important than your child. If the decision is between a loss of income and your child, a loss of time and your child, or a loss of friends and your child, the decision you face is a "no-brainer." In fact, you have no choice. To lay down your life for your child is your duty and your salvation. And this is our promise to you: If you will live in this simple, straightforward way, the inner gains you will receive will be so enormous that your sacrifices will eventually become meaningless in your eyes.

*   *   *

Behind this first cultural belief about teenagers is an even older and more basic belief that children are naturally bad. In the West we have a long history of religious, educational, and psychiatric pronouncements about the devious, willful, vengeful, and even satanic nature of kids. Hence the concept of "beating the devil out" of children and of "breaking their will." But some surveys also indicate that many educators and even psychologists think that children "need" to be spanked because of their basic natures.

Little wonder that so many parents say "no" to their kids automatically. "No" *should* be the automatic response if their children's *basic* desires were for the wrong things. But just as most little kids are better human beings than the adults who surround them, our experience is that the instincts of most teenagers are at least as sane as their parents' and in many instances they are patently saner. Dads or moms who assume that they always "know best" are usually arrogant. Naturally, parents are the ones who have to make the decisions, but it doesn't follow that they therefore have the most goodness with which to make them. Hugh recently addressed a group of parents about their teenagers and made the following statement:

> I think I am a good human being. I've worked hard to become one. I think I am a moral, devoted husband and a committed and attentive dad. I think I am finally a pretty good friend to those who are in Gayle's and my circle of acquaintances, and I know I am a moral and devoted minister. But we have one teenager living in our home—so far just one—and he is a better human being than I am. I can sense this when he talks about how he should treat his girlfriend, how he should handle another girl's sexual advances, how he should respond to a friend's prejudice against gays, how he should react to another friend's breaking of a promise. What I sense is that my decency, honesty, and honor are recent achievements, and they are still based in part on ideas and philosophy. That means

they are still a little shaky, whereas John's are instinctive. He never lost them, and it would be nearly impossible for him to lose them. He may come to me for advice on how best to express his goodness, but his goodness is never in question—where there are times I still have to battle for mine. He's old money; I'm nouveau riche—in the currency of God.

As to the last part of cultural myth number one— that teenagers want their needs satisfied more than is good for them—surely even to say such a thought out loud exposes it as absurd. Children's needs do not operate differently from adults' needs. On one level we all keep wanting more and more, but we also reach plateaus of relative satisfaction. Human needs are human needs, whether they are within a five-year-old, a fifteen-year-old, or a fifty-year-old. Parents who let their kids use their car Saturday night do not start them on a car addiction. Parents who let their kids miss a day of school are not hit the following day with a demand that they be allowed to drop out permanently.

Don't be afraid to see your child's needs and meet them. Don't hesitate to be the mom or dad your kid wants and needs. Of course there are limits, but let them come from your heart, not from our culture's fear of teenagers.

2. "Teenagers are rebelling against their parents."

In dealing with a "problem child," the principle is very simple: **The core effect of any corrective technique you use will be of no higher quality than the core motivation you have for using it.** Until your child's sense of identity becomes separate and autonomous—a change that is usually completed in late adolescence or early adulthood— you must grow spiritually before your child can grow spiritually. Clearly there can be other influences on kids besides their parents, and these may or may not help them become more aware of God's presence. But keep in mind that parents can affect their children only in the moment, and they can't give what they don't have now.

When you question this or any other cultural assumption, you swim against the tide of our times. We know what you are up against because we have almost never spanked, punished, or scolded our three boys, and the extremely few times we came close to doing anything like that we quickly apologized to them. If most of the adults with whom we come in contact knew our approach, they would think it was nothing but dumb blind luck that ours have turned out to be good kids. However, most of them don't know because we have learned not to talk about it. We try not to make our children's way harder in the world, and as we have pointed out, kids of parents who are known not to punish are invariably tagged as spoiled.

Obviously, not punishing is a very small part of spiritual parenting—and **it is even possible to punish out of love**—but trying to be punitive and loving at the same time has proven to be so difficult for us personally that we have opted for using alternative ways of guiding our children. The result is that we are a very close family; our kids still talk to us about even the most intimate aspects of their lives; and perhaps most significant of all, our boys are very good with younger children—they like them and they are quite effective in teaching and coaching them.

Can we take credit for this? Only in part. We have counseled a number of families in which the mom and dad love each other deeply and have stayed together; they are devoted to their kids; their approach to parenting shows a good balance between firmness and flexibility; their kids are genetically normal and chemically balanced; there are no unusually bad influences in their children's circle of friends; and there has been no sexual abuse or other traumas early in their kids' lives. And yet they had or are having very bad problems with one or more of their children.

As we said earlier, we know that to some degree we

have simply been lucky. But we also know that our boys' happiness, kindness, insightfulness, and ability to cope well with the world are at least in part a legacy of our having tried to have a single priority as parents: enjoying our kids. We have deliberately made this consideration more important than our desire for our kids to be popular, to make good grades, to be good athletes, to stay clean and be neat, to be obedient to us, to be polite to adults, to use "clean" language, or to "stay on task."

For example, "staying on task" is one of the "reform" movements now sweeping public school systems, and in various forms it has become one of many conflicting priorities for parents. As with most loveless priorities, adults are once again applying a different standard to kids than to themselves—and kids know it.

This evening a fourth-grade teacher told us that he had just come from a daylong seminar on how to mentor new teachers. He said that only about 10 percent of the time was spent on the relationship and rapport between student and teacher, whereas between 70 and 80 percent was spent on how to train new teachers to stay "on task" from the minute they stepped into the classroom; on how they in turn could keep their students on task; on how to evaluate new teachers according to how well they and their class stayed on task; and in listening to audio- and videotapes that emphasized staying on task.

We asked him if he had liked the seminar, and he said it was quite enjoyable. The audience was composed of mentor teachers and some resident (new) teachers, the entire group had snacked and laughed and talked to one another throughout the day, and occasionally someone would make a funny comment about what had just been said by the facilitator, who also had a good sense of humor. "In other words," he said, "we all had a good time and learned a few things as well, because not one person in that room stayed on task."

Most people—including children—function more efficiently in an atmosphere of flexibility than in one of rigidity. In almost every office it is common to see people talking by the water cooler, taking a coffee break, chatting with a coworker in the hall, or joking with someone at a nearby desk or workspace. Many people think better when they get up and walk around a little. John frequently watches TV, listens to loud music, talks on the phone, and does his homework—*all at the same time.* On the one occasion we brought this subject up, he smiled and said, "When I stop making straight A's I'll be happy to hear your suggestions." That was the end of the conversation, because *we* were both made to "stay on task" when we were in school and neither of us made A's until our junior and senior years in college—when the atmosphere was very flexible.

As we write this section we are having a small therapy pool installed in back of our house. This is not a large project, but it entails several stages. The company doing the work has two crews of three men each, all in their twenties. We'll call them Crew F (Flexible) and Crew O (On task). Both crews do essentially the same work and whichever crew is available is the one that comes.

We have a basketball hoop over our garage and the foreman of Crew F always takes a few minutes before and after the job to play a little basketball with his men, and if they are here long enough, they take a basketball break. Crew F not only has more fun, they are also happier when they are working than Crew O, which goes straight to work, takes no breaks, and leaves when the job is over. Crew O is significantly more on task than Crew F—but they are twice as slow! They also aren't as nice to their customers or as pleasant to be around. If we owned a business that had to make a profit and we had these two crews to choose from, we would hire the one that gets off task.

It's true that when teens are punished they sometimes begin to "walk the line," or at least pretend to. But do they identify more lovingly with their own body or with other living things as a result of the loss of a privilege? In fact, when parents administer punishment angrily or disrespectfully, an increase in anger and disrespect is the *only* inner change they can expect in their child. There is really little mystery why most teens become more secretive, sullen, and distant with each attempt their parents make to correct them. **Adolescents are not rebelling against their parents, they are rebelling against their parents' rigidity.**

3. "If parents don't intervene, adolescents will act that way for the rest of their lives."

Please close your eyes and take a moment to remember how you were as a teenager. Perhaps write down a few of the ways you dressed and behaved. (You can tear the list up as soon as you finish!) List what music you liked. What kind of person you were attracted to. What your attitude toward school was. How concerned you were about your future prospects or any other prospects. Remember the other kids you knew and how they treated or mistreated you. Remember how you looked physically and whether *your* parents could afford to or were willing to let you dress as you thought you needed to in order to fit in. And while you are on the subject of your parents, what dead-certain road of destruction and infamy did they or other relatives tell you you were headed down? But were you? Did any of your antics last more than a few years?

If ever it was going to last, the way young people dressed, wore their hair, and sought their pleasure in the 1960s would have lasted. Supposedly these trends had their origins in how Thoreau lived at Walden Pond and symbolized compassion for the masses as well as high ideals about war. And yet very few people who were caught up in all of that—some good trends, some not so good—are still acting that way today. And we say that as two people who left

Texas in the sixties and moved to the Bay Area to become hippies. We lasted one and a half years before we copped out and went to work for the establishment. Yet all the while we were in Berkeley, several of our relatives obviously thought that we were throwing away our lives.

Society's disapproval today is aimed more at the TV programs, movies, and music our kids are drawn to than at their hairstyles and political views. We now look past the sixties and see in the 1950s a *picture* we think we like. There we see churchgoing and patriotism, nuclear families, and obedient kids. The trouble those kids got into, we tell ourselves, were just "pranks," and the music they liked had lyrics that may have been silly but at least were about a culture we were comfortable with.

Now along come rap, violent video games, R-rated movies, unbridled computer conversations, cable TV filled with sex and profanity, and talk shows on which people advocate every known and unknown depravity. Our kids steep themselves in these things the way we once addictively listened to the Beatles.

And so what is our response? We attack rap music because its words shatter the picture. We attack TV and technology because they paint an entirely new picture. And we attack the weak, dependent, and "different" segments of our society because they have been rudely brought to our attention—and we don't like the real picture any better than the computer-generated one.

In place of all of this we are attempting to "reform"—not the hearts and souls of our young people but the picture they present. We are trying to intervene, yet all our efforts are directed at mere appearances. We don't like the way the world looks right now, so we tell small children not to watch cartoons; we tell young kids to save the earth from pollution; we tell tweens not to play "anti-social" videos; we tell adolescents not to have sex; and we tell teenagers to get a job before they marry. But we never tell any of

our children about the wisdom of their hearts and the goodness of their spirits. We never tell them how wonderfully
they laugh, how brightly their eyes shine, how quickly they
forgive, and how wisely they stay in the present. We just
want them to stand still for one Kodak moment, so we can
all relax. Because finally the picture will be just fine.

The problem with this third cultural myth is not that parents actually believe that when their son is forty he will still
be wearing his underwear above his pants line and their
daughter will be trying to get a job wearing black lipstick
and purple hair. The problem is that parents *act* as if they
believe it. Why? Because that's the way parents are supposed to act? Because now they know what's best? Because
their teenager is embarrassing to them? Because they just
can't give up controlling every detail of their kids' lives?
Because that's the way their parents reacted, and their parents, and their parents . . . going back to hieroglyphic in-
scriptions that express essentially the same general concerns
about the younger generation? Whatever the reason, it's insane. **Never make a parental decision out of fear of what**
might happen in the future. This means you can safely lose
your faith in Cultural Assumption number 3. It will make
life easier on your adolescent. And it will allow you to get
back to the only thing that is important: enjoying your child.
You can't enjoy *anyone* you disapprove of.

4. "Adolescents are overly dramatic. Their problems
couldn't be that bad—they have their whole life ahead of
them."

"Stop being adolescent," we might say to another
adult. But wouldn't it also be true to form if we said to
adolescents "Stop being adult"? We faithfully watch soap
operas, carefully follow sensational trials, give the highest
ratings to abusive radio, send the revenues of violent films
through the roof, fan the flames of discontent in our friends'

marriages, insist that our TV broadcasts give us one political crisis after another, buy the magazines whose covers
promise the most scandal, and repeat the same mistakes in
our personal lives over and over. And yet, with a straight
face, we say that *adolescents* are the ones who are addicted
to drama.

A few weeks ago we were having lunch at a large local restaurant. We had been seated in a room that held about a
dozen tables, most of which were filled. It seemed to be a
safe, stable environment to bring an elderly relative—
Gayle's aunt from Montana—and all was going well until
about halfway through our meal.

Suddenly a waiter pushed two large tables together
next to us and about twelve girls, ages fourteen to sixteen,
sat down.

We instantly looked pleased, because we were still
working on the section on adolescents for this book. Gayle's
aunt instantly looked displeased, because that's the proper
attitude toward teenagers.

Soon five teenage boys were seated at a smaller table
at the other end of the room. Now the adults were surrounded. It was evident that they were aware of this, and it
was equally evident that the teenagers were not aware of a
single adult.

The girls' table was only four or five feet from us and
although it wasn't at all noisy, Gayle's aunt kept saying that
it was. What we finally realized—because her comments
always came after the girls laughed—was that it was the
girls' happiness that annoyed her.

The same waiter served their table and ours, a very
nice, good-humored man, but one who had too large an
area to cover. We could hear what the girls were talking
about, and they complained often to one another that the
waiter was late in bringing one thing or another. They never
said anything to the waiter himself because, being an adult,

he didn't exist to them as a person. Here were a dozen teenage girls, but not one of them noticed that the waiter had too many tables. And not one of them acknowledged with even a glance how interested the adults in the room were in them. They were in a world of their own, and only a visit from one of the teenage boys at the other end of the room could break into that world.

The blunt truth is that most teenagers are not particularly interested in a relationship with Mom or Dad anymore. It is beginning to dawn on them that they are going to have to make it in the world on their own. Someday they will see the importance of earning a living, but for now their world is a world of relationships, and it is very unstable. Sadly, many of them realize that they can't rely on family relationships, and appeals to them such as "Why don't you spend more time at home?" or "You're never a part of family activities anymore" fall on deaf ears. If you want a real relationship with your teenager—and not just the forced appearance of one—*you* are going to have to do most of the work. And that will not be easy if you are resentful about all you have done for your kid in the past with little or no acknowledgment.

Most of these girls were coming into the height of their physical beauty. That plus the obvious fun they were having could create envy in those around them. Although teenagers are in many ways locked into their own world, to many adults that world seems filled with desirable potentials that they know they themselves will never have again.

Adolescents can't be expected to see that they have their whole life ahead of them; or to see how much of their behavior comes from peer pressure; or to see that their bodies "will probably turn out just fine"; or to see that romances at this age often don't have the depth of commitment that relationships will have in a few years; or to see that not making the team, or first chair in band, or winning the treasurer's election, is not the end of the world. In a sense, all these potential disasters *are* the end of your child's world today. And most adolescents can't see very well past today. Thus it is up to *adults* to see. And to apply what they know wisely— not just use it to spice up a lecture or a scolding.

Never discount your children's sense of catastrophe or argue against it. You, personally, want to be their harbor in the storm, their true friend, their reliable supporter. Because you take their pain seriously, you are an alternative to pain. Naturally, taking it seriously doesn't mean that you get caught up in the same emotions yourself and lose *your* perspective. A sense of proportion is one of the strengths you possess, and you don't want to discard it under the mistaken assumption that oneness with your child means oneness with his or her impaired perspective. You merely wish to be the one who listens instead of lectures, who understands instead of judges, who offers endless comfort instead of endless advice.

Some friends of ours have a daughter, Cindy, whose boyfriend, Allan, tried to commit suicide shortly before the two of them met and started going out. Despite the fact that he had to have his stomach pumped and was hospitalized for three days, his parents did not take the attempt seriously. The boy, fourteen, tried to explain his actions to his parents by saying that he didn't have any friends at school. "Of course you don't have friends," they said. "We just moved here and you're a freshman at a new high school. You'll make friends—although it may take a little longer now that you pulled this stunt." Actually, it was the "stunt" that got Cindy interested in Allan. One day at lunch she sat beside him and asked him if he had really had his stomach pumped. "Yes," Allan said tentatively. "Did it hurt? Didn't the tube make you want to throw up?" "I've had better times," Allan said. And that was the start of their friendship.

As Allan began to share more of his feelings with Cindy, she discovered that he had had an experience that perhaps happens to girls more frequently than to boys. He had been sexually abused when he was eleven and his mother, whom he told about it, decided that he had misinterpreted the advance that her brother, Allan's uncle, had made. Because he was embarrassed, he had not told her the complete story. When he came back later and angrily added what else had happened, his mother told him that he was lying and to never say something like that again.

Most children are sexually approached by an adult before they reach maturity, and a surprising number of them feel either that they can't talk to their parents about it or do talk to them and are rejected in some way. One of Gayle's best friends was molested by a prominent psychiatrist she used to work for after school, but at the time she couldn't get *any* adult to believe her. This caused her a number of problems later in life, as might be expected. Hugh has a cousin who went to her mother over and over about the jokes her father was making about her large breasts, but her mother never thought it was serious enough to have a "family fight" over. Consequently, she lost faith in her parents and never again trusted either of them with a confidence.

Allan's parents should have put him into long-term therapy immediately after his suicide attempt. His mother should have demanded that her brother never speak to or have any further association with her son. The family and adult acquaintances of Gayle's friend should have gotten her immediate help and then should have gone as a group to the psychiatrist and demanded that he never again have contact with young girls. And the mother of Hugh's cousin should have insisted that her husband stop all jokes about his daughter's sexual development and apologize to her sincerely.

Parenting is a job. It can be a pleasant job, and it should be. Yet when some of its necessary functions are unpleasant, we still must carry them out. If we can keep from yelling at our boss, we certainly can keep from yelling at our teenager. If we can keep from making sexual jokes about our supervisor, we certainly can keep from making them about our own child. We may not like attending the annual company picnic, but we attend it. We may not like going to graduation, or every track meet, or the school awards ceremony, but we go to them nonetheless.

Claiming that we have some duty that is higher than our duty as a parent is *truly* "overly dramatic." It is also dishonest. We behave dishonestly when we don't confront our mate, or brother-in-law, or school principal, or lifelong friend, when they are doing something damaging to our child. This does not mean we have to "fly off the handle," "shoot from the hip," or "go ballistic." If you aren't sure what the facts are, find out. But never discount what your own child tells you. Never *assume* that she or he is overinterpreting. Just as you would investigate a wisp of smoke coming from the kitchen, and not assume that it was just something cooking, you must take what your child says seriously and look into it thoroughly.

5. *"Teens are more mature than tweens and are capable of shouldering greater responsibility."*

We have watched with interest and considerable sorrow the downward course of one of John's oldest friends. John has known Robert since the fourth grade. When he first started coming over to our house, Robert was an exceptionally happy, bright, and loving child. He was an excellent reader, devouring the classics and popular novels with equal enthusiasm, and the songs he composed, even at that young age, were funny and highly imaginative. He was a good athlete, quite popular at school, and a straight-A student. He got into his share of trouble, but his behavior was not destructive or cruel and was well within the bounds of what most boys his age did.

Robert's life continued on a healthy course until puberty. By then he was tall for his age, intellectually ahead of his peers, and when he turned thirteen his parents suddenly started treating him as if he were capable of taking on greater responsibility than he had been at, say, nine or ten. They increased his chores and they began grounding him for even small infractions of family rules.

Currently "grounding" is a commonly recommended way for parents to "modify" a teenager's behavior. It has largely replaced spanking and other harsher punishments and perhaps in that respect does not harden the teenager's ego quite as much and creates a little less alienation between parent and child. However, like Robert's parents, most moms and dads don't ask themselves what they are really trying to accomplish by grounding. When we ask parents that question, they usually say, "We're teaching responsibility." They see a behavior they don't like and apply the formula—without deciding for themselves what actual effect this has on their particular child.

Perhaps parents could ground routinely out of a deeper understanding of their child's needs, but we have yet to see this approach used regularly *and* lovingly in any family that we have counseled or known intimately. Parents may use it thoughtfully a few times, but the temptation for them to rely on the punishment instead of their attitude eventually becomes too great.

Certainly teenagers sometimes stop doing what will get them grounded. More often, however, they just become more clever about how they break the rule. Almost never do they gain a deeper understanding of how to approach life, nor do they increase their love or appreciation of the grounding parent. This has been dramatically true in Robert's case.

If he failed to turn in a homework assignment on time, he was grounded. If he was late in taking out the trash, he was grounded. If he "spoke back" to either parent, he was grounded. Soon John stopped seeing him on the weekends, because Robert was always confined to his house. As his grades began to slip and as he started getting into more trouble at school, his parents increased the duration of his confinements, once grounding him for two months because he was caught smoking.

At this writing, Robert has failed his last two years of high school; he takes a variety of drugs when out of sight of his parents; and his mom has moved out of the house because, she says, her son is "a case." Recently Robert's father attempted suicide.

Despite all of this, his parents' practice of grounding Robert goes unquestioned. His last period of confinement was for the entire summer.

Because of the overwhelming number of physical, social, and sexual changes occurring in teenagers' lives, and because their egos have reached the stage of independence and individuation and they feel a powerful urge to complete this process, teenagers are more scattered and preoccupied than when they were only a few months or years younger. They are therefore far *less* capable of shouldering responsibility than they were as tweens. **Parents who are alert to teenagers' impaired mental and emotional states decrease their chores, relax the rules, and concentrate on keeping them safe—and on being their friend and advocate.**

6. *"There is a right or best punishment to use."*

Most adults believe they can begin a punishment (or "consequence") in anger or indifference—and the punishment *itself* will do the work. For example, when teens get caught driving too fast or too recklessly, parents often take away their driving privileges for several days or weeks. They believe that with the passing of each day, "the lesson sinks in" more deeply. But what is the lesson? As each day passes, do these kids grow in their desire to be protective of children or pets running across the road? of pedestrians and other drivers in their path? or of their own body and possessions? If teenagers don't sense their parents' loving concern behind this particular punishment on this particular occasion—not be told there is loving concern, but *feel* it for themselves—nothing has been added to their life that could possibly lead them toward love.

If one partner in a marriage tries to punish the other partner, or if one friend tries to punish another friend, or if one relative tries to punish another relative, it backfires. In fact, it does more than that. It damages, perhaps destroys, the relationship. What would be the effect if you took away your husband's "right" to watch TV? What would be the effect if you confined your wife to her room? What would be the effect if you scolded, lectured, and shamed a relative? What would be the effect if you spanked your business partner?

At the turn of the century, when women were in many ways thought of as children and men were considered the primary parent, the "father figure," the "head of the household," some husbands did in fact take away their wives' driving privileges for "driving misconduct." Could there be any doubt as to the effect that had on their wives? Did they feel God's sustaining love more strongly? Did they grow in love themselves? Is there any possibility that the punishment made even one woman feel more protective of others?

Although punishment obviously would backfire with our friends and relatives, somehow it is supposed to have the opposite effect on children. How often has it been said that the reason baby boomers turned out the way they did is that their parents weren't strict enough with them? How often has it been said that the reason so many teenagers are now committing crimes is that their parents are too lax in disciplining them? Although we are now calling it consequences instead of punishment, as a culture we not only believe in the effectiveness of a punitive approach to parenting, we really think it's the *only* way. It's the commonsense way, the biblically correct way, the American way.

And it works! Or at least it often appears to, temporarily. So, *is* the effect magically the desired outcome? Not long term. Being well over the half-century mark, as the two of us are, doesn't have many advantages in our culture, but in counseling it has one priceless advantage: You get to see how certain loveless approaches play themselves out in family after family that you follow over the years. It's true that the effect of a punitive approach on children is not what you would expect it to be on most adults, but it *is* similar to how, say, players respond to a cruel and highly feared coach when they desperately want to remain on that team. Or how employees respond to a cruel and highly feared boss when they desperately need to keep that job.

Taking the more common circumstance of employees abused by a boss, in the short run the abuse seems to get results, but what are the long-term effects? Incidents of stealing, lying, and sabotage go up. Division among employees increases. And—through seemingly unrelated events such as sickness, accidents, the unexpected breakdown of equipment, and a higher turnover of personnel—production efficiency begins to fall off.

Anyone who feels unfairly treated will attack back in some way, and this includes children. In our experience, adolescents almost always feel unfairly treated when their parents use punishment to control them.

As we mentioned earlier, our oldest son, Scott, didn't come to live with us until he was almost fourteen. And he did not come willingly. He had been encouraged to leave by his mother and new stepfather, and once he left, he was told that he could never come back. We had not yet had John and Jordan when Scott arrived, and we were not mature parents.

Scott was angry and destructive, as any child would be who had just been betrayed and abandoned by his own mother and stepfather, and at first Hugh dealt with him the way Hugh's father had dealt with him.

Scott, when asked about those first few months, said that he remembers the first (and only) time Hugh handled him roughly. Hugh grabbed him and swung him around and yelled in his face about some issue that neither of them can now remember. To Scott this felt just like the beatings he had frequently received from his mother. He told Hugh recently: "I remember that our relationship changed at that point. It was as if something clicked in my mind and I lost all trust in you. And it was years before I started to feel that I could trust you again."

Scott came to us an adolescent, but parents usually have to dispense punishments for many years before they stamp out the trust their children have in them. Often it's not until the tween or teen years that kids are first able to admit to themselves that they no longer trust their parents. This doesn't mean that they don't still love them. Most kids continue to love their parents long after they have stopped trusting them, as is shown by the number of adult children who seek out parents from whom they were taken away after physical or sexual abuse. In these cases, clearly it is not revenge that draws them back, but the yearning to experience again the oneness with their mom or dad that they once felt—and, if they are able to turn deeply enough to God, can still feel.

7. "Misbehavior is the problem—setting limits and teaching consequences is the answer."

When children do something that adults don't like, they are "misbehaving," "being bad," "being a challenge," or "being disruptive." Or their behavior is "unacceptable," "inappropriate," or "out of place." Or they are "wild," "unmanageable," or "out of control." But when adults explain their own behavior, they are having "a bad day" or a "crisis." Or they are going through a "transition" or a "passage." Or they are "in a selfish period" or need some "me time." Or they are being "driven crazy" or "pushed to their limits." Or they've had their "space invaded" or their "boundaries crossed." Or they simply aren't "getting their needs met."

A teacher might explain why she had an affair by saying "I wasn't getting my needs met at home," but she would not explain why a child in her class keeps squirming and getting out of his seat by saying "He isn't getting his needs met in my class." A dad might explain why he sent his daughter to her room after her birthday party by saying "She was misbehaving." But he would not say that he got angry at his wife at the potluck dinner because *she* was "misbehaving" (or "being bad" or "being a challenge" or "being disruptive").

In other words, **we think that we behave the way we do for a good reason but that children do not.** Ironically, even though we don't believe children are well motivated, in this culture our emphasis is on changing their behavior, not on changing their motivation. We seem to believe that if we can just get our kids' behavior straight, the order and appropriateness of their actions somehow will seep into their hearts and they will *want* to do what's right.

Your children act the way they do because of how they use their minds. Thought precedes action. It may be confused thought or preoccupied thought or misdirected thought, but behavior always flows from some state of mind. This is why you don't want to undercut your children's awareness of this connection. When you discipline without full recognition of what *you* are thinking, your kids definitely sense this, and the lesson they learn is that it's not important to be conscious; it's only important to win.

Merely getting our kids under control does not increase their awareness of their core—which is the part of them that yearns to do and be good—because it doesn't increase access to their own mind. Focusing on changing behavior is like telling little kids which direction the bumper cars are supposed to circle but not how to drive one. First you have to "put them in the driver's seat." So you set them behind the steering wheel and place their little hands on it and move it around for them. Then you show them where the accelerator pedal is and let them push it up and down a few times. Then you must go one step further and make them conscious of why they *want* to go in the direction that the person running the ride says they must go.

When the body "behaves," it acts out a thought. It can act out a thought of fear or one of understanding, but **no child "acts without thinking," and no child "learns to behave" without thinking.**

You want your children to understand the importance of their own mental processes because you can't always be there to "make them behave." Your kids will soon be more out of your sight than under your scrutiny, if they are not already. And of course the day will come when they will be completely on their own with only their minds to guide them. Therefore, you don't want to relate to your kids in such a way that they discount the function of mind. And yet, if *you* discount their mind, they will enter adulthood either looking for someone else to tell them what to do or acting out of unconscious motivation.

One parent whose son recently confessed to a highly publicized series of violent crimes told a reporter that she just didn't understand how this could have happened. "We didn't bring him up to act that way," she said. This is a common reaction. Parents frequently make statements like this when told of some crime their adolescent or adult child has committed. But usually the evidence that rules and punishment are not sufficient to guide children becomes obvious long before adolescence. Many parents have been surprised to discover that their kids behave more destructively than they would have guessed once they start school. Now out of sight of the authority they fear the most, they feel free to do the kinds of things they were *told* not to do but were never allowed to learn why they didn't *want* to.

The mere fact that some children behave destructively at school or even commit violent crimes as they grow older does not necessarily mean that their parents made mistakes in the way they brought them up or even that these parents were not deeply spiritual individuals committed to their children's well-being. Because kids are subjected to powerful influences and dangerous circumstances today, even very good kids from loving families can get caught up in bad situations. This may happen so quickly that parents are caught off guard and the damage is done before they can respond.

However, as parents we should try to be as alert as we can to the circumstances in which our kids find themselves. To do this effectively we must admit to ourselves how we are personally participating in the problems they face. One very common way that parents participate is by seeing an injustice, perhaps even complaining about it, but doing nothing. For example, a school bully is the problem of every parent in the school, not just the parents of the bully's victims.

When we lived in California, John once had as his "core teacher" (the teacher with whom he had the most classes) a woman who was so overcontrolling and had such a strong prejudice against boys that most of the boys in her sixth-grade class began acting out in ways that were very unlike their past behavior. She referred to five close friends as "the bad boys," and John was a member of this group. She was especially harsh in her treatment of these five, and she also tried to poison other teachers against them.

The effect this had on the boys' popularity with the kids in the school was dramatic. Their exploits were exaggerated and became legendary and it seemed that every girl in school was in love with them. John was not only resigned to being tagged a bad boy but was beginning to relish his reputation and to act and think in ways that were very disturbing to us.

Fortunately, although we were unable to convince the principal of what was going on in this teacher's classroom, most of the boys' parents were acutely aware of the situation. We joined another family in organizing the parents of the boys. Several of us set up a schedule whereby at least one parent was visiting this class at all times. Our agreed-on function was not to challenge this teacher in front of the students or to get her fired, but simply to be present so that she could not be unfair to these five kids. The parents of each of the boys also talked to him at home about how he really felt. Did he want to be controlled by an unfair teacher, and if he didn't, could he see that breaking rules was a reaction to her and therefore merely another way of being controlled by her?

The effect on both the boys and the teacher was very positive. By the end of the school year all of "the bad boys" had returned to their normal patterns of behavior. If that had not occurred, and if John had had the same teacher the following year, we were prepared to move into another school district or to take him out and start home schooling again.

Several school counselors have told us that they can pick out the kids who are treated the most harshly or unfairly at home simply by the type of destructive behavior they display at school. Most kids will get in their share of trouble in the classroom and on the playground, but children who are treated with respect and affection at home will seldom consistently hurt other kids at school.

It doesn't matter how we make our children act if we don't also teach them to respect their own reading of the choices before them and apply the innate values of their heart. Because the heart is connected to God, to that which is lasting, **values are not actually "taught," they are awakened.** Children feel their own desire to walk in gentleness and peace. So often parents try to teach gentleness harshly. But over and over the wise parent has encouraged the child to look to the stillness and peace of the heart and now the child has a resource that he or she can call on even in the most confusing of circumstances.

If the situations our children will face as teenagers and young adults were the same ones we had instructed them how to respond to when they were younger, then perhaps "teaching them how to behave" would make sense. But there are very few behavioral rules that we can set forth that will neatly fit the actual situations our children will encounter throughout their lives. The circumstances will seem unfamiliar to them. This time the decision will appear to be an exception. So what do children who have not learned to respect their own mind turn to? They consult their ego emotions and act from their moods, just as they have seen their parents do all their lives.

Ego-driven emotions are *not* the guide you wish your children to consult. Yet unless you have taught them to think well of their own ability to make decisions, and to appreciate the values that flow from God into their heart, that is the only guide you have left them with.

When we speak of encouraging kids to use their mind, we don't mean saying things like "Think, girl, think!" or "Use your head, son!" or "Look at what's in front of your nose." We are not talking here of trying to teach kids that the world is logical and that by being more logical themselves, their lives will work out. The world is not logical and it does not work. The key to life is to see the nature of the world honestly and then choose a path of peace through the chaos. Our mind can enter the kingdom of God merely by choosing to do so this instant, but it will never solve the ancient problem of how to build securely on shifting sands.

8. *"Anger is the only way to get through to them."*

In counseling families over the years, we often have noted that parents' anger toward their child is almost always a desire to make the child feel guilty. It is, therefore, an attack and the reverse of spiritual parenting. It is also an act of arrogance because it assumes that parents are in a position to judge their own child. If God, in whom we trust, does not attack us and make us feel guilty, are we in a position to decide that our child deserves attack? Obviously not. But we think we are.

As we said before, any duty you need to carry out as a parent can be accomplished without using judgment and disapproval. Certainly you don't want to fall into the *habit* of getting angry at your child, because this can indeed end up destroying all communication between the two of you. Anger is a side road that you want to take as infrequently as possible. It plays no positive role in your walk home to God.

Parents tend to think of anger as a deep and important emotion. Dads often believe it is an essential part of manliness and strength of character, that it even teaches these qualities. Thus coaches, drill sergeants, and the like think that displays of anger are good for the young people under their control. They believe these "build character" and make "men out of boys." Many mothers, especially today, believe that anger is a form of self-affirmation, a way of honoring and standing up for themselves. They think it's good to model anger, especially to their daughters.

At the same time that we believe that anger is positive—even to the point of encouraging one another to "get angry" during group counseling sessions—we are also afraid of it. Many men are now very reluctant to show anger or irritation, especially in the presence of their wives, who often are quick to read the worst possible interpretations into their husbands' outbursts. And their husbands, in a mistaken attempt to defend themselves, won't even acknowledge that they are angry. Unacknowledged, the anger is not released in some alternate and less destructive way, and so naturally it builds up.

Anger plays an equally prominent role in the media. It is the rock star of emotions. The angriest call-in shows get the highest ratings. The angriest passages in speeches are the ones quoted. On television, the comment and opinion segments and even the movie reviews now are often presented in the popular angry-confrontive format. And if the President or any other prominent domestic or world leader gets angry, the anger of itself is a big story.

Yet anger is not a deep emotion, certainly not as deep, for example, as fear, and in comparison to even the simplest of spiritual qualities, it clearly is not an important one. It is merely a mistake. But if you let it go unchecked year after year, it can cost you your relationship with your child. Because anger lacks depth, it is possible for you to release it quickly. To do so you must be willing to look closely at it, admit to yourself when you feel it, and observe how it enters your mind, toward whom it is really directed, and how it leaves your mind.

A nice illustration of a learning-based approach versus an anger-based approach is in the story of how our friends Amanda and Bob handled a bit of "crazy teenage behavior." When we first met them the police had just detained their son Justin (fifteen) and his best friend, Rico (fifteen), for vandalism. These two boys had been friends since the fifth grade and Rico, because his single dad was almost never home, spent so much time at Bob and Amanda's house that they thought of him as a son.

Two nights before, the boys had walked across the roof of an elderly couple's home. One of them had stepped through a soft spot, gone partly into the ceiling, and broken a skylight as he stumbled forward. When the couple called 911, the boys ran off but were quickly caught by the police.

They were taken to the police station and a few hours later were released to Bob.

When he received the first call from the police station, Bob was dumbfounded, and all he wanted was an explanation. The next morning, as he heard the boys tell the full story, he became furious. On a dare they had tried to break the record set by one of their friends, who had run across the roofs of three separate houses in one night. They were trying for five.

Knowing he was too angry to make a good decision, Bob left the two boys in Justin's room and went straight to talk to Amanda. He told her that the boys had been so reckless with their own bodies and other people's property that there should be immediate and severe consequences. As he made his case against them, he paced up and down and yelled. He pointed out that the boys could also have easily been mistaken for thieves and shot.

Finally Amanda said, "Bob, what we both want is for them to learn why they don't want to do this *kind* of thing—not just to stop them from walking on people's roofs, which I doubt they'll ever do again." Bob saw that she was right and told Amanda he had an idea. After making a few phone calls and telling the boys to stay in the room until he got back, he drove to the elderly couple's house.

When the husband, Mr. Chance, opened the door, Bob explained that he was the father of one of the boys who had damaged the roof and that he would pay for any needed repairs. However, Bob said the main purpose of his visit was to ask if he could bring the boys over to talk to them and if they could tell Justin and Rico how this had made them feel and in what ways it had disturbed their lives. He said that he also would like the boys to come back the next day and begin yard work or do any other jobs that needed doing for at least a week. He said he was suggesting this so the boys could get to know the people they had attacked, whether they had intended it as an attack or not.

Bob was very lucky. The Chances were an extremely kind couple who had already refused to press charges when they discovered that children were involved. They said that they thought Bob's plan was excellent and to bring the boys over.

When they arrived, Mrs. Chance took Rico and Justin through the house, showed them where the pieces of broken glass had fallen, and even showed them the chair where she had been sitting when she heard footsteps on her roof. She helped them understand what it was like to be old and not know what was happening or who was doing it.

Mr. Chance then showed the boys how he was repairing the roof to keep the rain and cold out and explained to them the risk he was taking at his age climbing ladders and crawling over a roof. He also listed everywhere he had gone that day to get the materials he needed.

Later that week Bob also took Justin and Rico to meet a parole officer who told them several stories about adolescents who had started out disregarding laws in a very minor way. Each had "graduated" to the adult prison system with all its horrors. He spared no details.

Justin and Rico are adults now. When talking to Justin about this incident, the love he has for his parents is obvious. He looks back on all they had to do in lieu of punishment with great affection and humor, and he told us that the lesson had definitely sunk in. He and Rico simply had not thought at all about the individuals below the roofs they were running across. If they had received only an angry lecture and a punishment, Justin says, they never would have.

We are assuming, of course, that over the years anger has been as much of a problem for you as it has been for us and most other parents and that you already have seen the disrupting effects even a small degree of it can have on your relationship with your child. Anger is so destructive to the experience of oneness that even people in their forties, fifties, and sixties who still have a parent living can feel deeply affected by an angry comment or a disapproving mood from their father or mother.

Gayle was in a supermarket recently when she heard a woman's angry words coming from the next aisle. She knew immediately that this had to be a mother talking to a child because adults don't speak to one another in that righteous and scolding tone of voice, especially in public. As best she could determine, the woman was reminding ("for the hundredth time") someone that he or she could not go over to another person's house "because of what happened last time."

Knowing that some of our best examples of how parents treat children come from supermarkets, Gayle walked over to investigate. As she got nearer she heard the mom say to her young teenager, "Listen, young lady, if you don't start looking at me when I'm talking to you, I'm going to get very upset." The girl anxiously started looking around to see who had heard this, which was not what the mom wanted. After a few more words, her mother gripped her upper arm and started walking her out of the store. The girl took one more frantic look around and then angrily jerked her arm free. They walked out of the store physically and emotionally apart.

The anger on both the mother's and daughter's part came on the heels of other emotions. Anger is always an afterthought. The mother chose anger as her way of dealing with *frustration*. The daughter's emotions followed a similar sequence. First she felt embarrassment, then anger.

The first emotion we feel is self-contained and therefore manageable. But when we get angry, we focus more on other people than on ourselves. Anger is the desire to involve, encounter, attack, or blame others. We think that we will get rid of the discomfort of the first emotion by going

to the second. Instead of feeling embarrassed, we will embarrass. Instead of feeling controlled (frustrated), we will
control.

But it doesn't work out that way. All we really accomplish by involving someone else is to take the *solution*
out of our own hands. Now other egos are involved and the
problem begins to take on a life of its own. All this happens
because we assume that our child's behavior not only justifies but requires our anger.

But please note that the same behavior that makes
you angry one day may only irritate you on another occasion, or it may strike you as funny or pass by unacknowledged. From this fact alone, it should be obvious that your
kid's *behavior* is not what makes you angry. If it were, it
would always have this effect. The same behavior strikes us
differently on different occasions because of what is already
in our minds when the striking occurs. This is analogous to
how certain foods strike the stomach. The same food can
cause nausea, indigestion, or no reaction at all depending
on what we have eaten previously. For anger to occur, the
mind must first be primed for it. If this is not a cause-and-
effect connection of which you are already aware, you might
try doing an exercise we prescribe for anger-prone parents,
which includes most of us.

THE NEXT TIME YOU ARE ANGRY OR THINK YOU ARE GET-
TING ANGRY, FIRST PAUSE AND FREEZE THE CONTENTS OF YOUR
MIND. In other words, interrupt all of your thoughts—just
don't complete them—and mentally step back for an instant to take a look at what is going on in you.

ASK YOURSELF WHAT THOUGHTS ARE IN YOUR MIND THAT
JUSTIFY YOUR PRESENT IRRITATION OR ANGER. ("He's cursing at
his younger brother." "Once again she's got her stereo
turned up too loud." "I don't like being talked to in that
tone of voice.")

TAKE A MOMENT TO RECALL TIMES YOU DID NOT REACT WITH ANGER TO SIMILAR BEHAVIORS.

NEXT, LOOK FOR THE DEEPER EMOTION FROM WHICH YOUR ANGER IS TRYING TO ESCAPE. In the same way that you perhaps have noticed that anger *follows* fear when another driver cuts you off, you want to see clearly what your first emotion is in this particular encounter with your child. It will always be some version of fear—fear of embarrassment, fear of being burdened or inconvenienced, fear of being controlled or frustrated, fear of being disappointed or not getting what you deserve.

FINALLY, GO AS DEEPLY INTO THIS FEAR AS YOU CAN. You might close your eyes so that you can get as far below the anger as possible. As best you can you want to identify your core fear. ("I am losing my daughter." "My son has no respect for me anymore—as I've always known, I'm worthless." "If this keeps happening it's going to break up my marriage and I'll end up alone." "I'm always the one who has to do everything and this is just going to cost me more time and money.")

Once you have seen the core fear behind several episodes of anger, you will know with certainty that **you are never angry at your child for what your child just did.** While the behavior itself may require your immediate attention and correction, now you will be able to carry out the correction more efficiently because you will be guiding rather than attacking your child.

9. *"Adolescents have no mind of their own; they're all hormones, emotions, and peer pressure."*
        Some parents try to force their will on their children. They try to overpower their kids' ego with their ego. Other parents abandon their children to the world and give them

free rein to do anything. Still others try to trick their kids into behaving differently by manipulating their emotions. These three stock approaches to parenting—overpowering, abandoning, and manipulating—teach children to discount their own inner guidance, their own ability to hear the callings of Love. They have this effect because the parents are reacting to their child's behavior and not to the mind-set behind the behavior. Thus they teach the wrong lesson. As we have been discussing in this chapter and throughout this book, unless parents encourage their children to recognize their own core and trust their own resources, they are not helping them find a way out of the world and into God. In fact they are actively hindering their children's walk home.

ABANDONING YOUR CHILD TO THE WORLD. In the area where we lived a few years ago, there was a couple who imposed no restraints on their son's or daughter's activities outside the house. Having been around this family from the time the kids were eight and ten, we know what these two children would also have to know: that their mom and dad basically don't care what happens to them.

Unless there is some other important adult figure in their life who does care, the fact that they are of no concern to their parents has a shattering effect on young children. Most of the kids we have seen who had to live with this knowledge eventually developed a personality disturbance of some kind. These children are like rudderless little boats, blown by the winds, bumping against whatever is in their path, and eventually they devise their own unhappy defense.

For many years both of these kids have acted in quite destructive ways—setting fires, stealing tools from neighbors' yards, destroying property, bullying weaker kids. Their behavior repeatedly puts them in danger because of the potential reactions from older siblings, the adults, and police with whom they come in contact under inflammatory circumstances. They are both quite intelligent and usually are not caught, but when they are, they tell their parents that they didn't do it, often covering for each other, or they blame another kid for what happened. Their parents always angrily defend their side of the story and, afterward, again release them to do whatever they want.

Parents who believe that their children can do no wrong are not being "loyal" to their kids, because it isn't a kindness to encourage anyone to continue in a mistake. Yet this is what inevitably happens if we become an advocate of *all* our children's attitudes and behaviors. Although devoted parents can make this mistake, more often this kind of blind absolution is used by uncommitted parents to be rid of their kids' difficulties.

In the case of the boy and girl we have been discussing, their parents kept them outside when they were younger (now they both live more in their cars than in their home). The only rule was that nothing around the house was to be harmed. In a sense they did leave their children's mind and inner guidance alone, but did not honor them. If as a child your parents don't value your thoughts, you aren't likely to value them either. Your only lesson is disinterest and disregard. Therefore you let your mind take you in almost any direction that occurs to you, because, after all, your life doesn't really matter.

The lack of love and concern, not the *permissiveness* of the parents, is the undermining factor in these cases. We know several parents who are extremely permissive but whose children are spiritually quite strong. Because these parents love their kids, they take steps to protect them from the dangers of the world. However, only rarely do these entail restraints on their behavior; instead, they keep the world itself at bay. For example, they might go to lengths few parents would even consider to make their house a completely safe environment—yet within that environment their young child can do virtually anything he wishes. Or if she is a teenager, they might spend more money on her care than on their own in order to put her in the safest possible car during the time kids are most likely to have accidents. The cost of the car might be driven even higher by "permitting" their child expensive options that make it more desirable in her eyes, under the assumption that she will take better care of a car she likes, and drive it more carefully, than one she doesn't like.

Extremes of any kind tend to create problems and this holds true for extreme permissiveness, especially if it comes from a philosophy rather than from a parent's quiet wisdom. If there are siblings or if another child comes over to play, a common dilemma for the radically permissive parent is how to protect the children from each other while still allowing freedom of behavior. Loving and committed parents simply will not allow one child to harm another, regardless of their child-rearing philosophy.

Another common dilemma occurs when children experiment with a destructive impulse, which every kid will do from time to time. One very permissive mother we knew would not stop her eighteen-month-old son from pulling her hair, scratching her face, or hitting her. We remember vividly when this behavior started. The mother would be at our house; her son would want to leave; and he would go for her eyes or hair when she would continue chatting. She unquestionably loved her son but did not believe in restraining him. All she would do is protect herself by turning her head or holding up her arms. As the months went by, the boy grew angrier and more deliberate in his attacks. At about two and a half, he stopped behaving in this way on his own, but by that time his ego had grown quite strong and he became depressed and sullen and remained that way into adolescence.

The mistake this mother made was failing to heed her intuitive sense of the nature of her son's motivation. She knew his actions were stemming from anger—that was unmistakable—but instead of guiding him in a more peaceful direction, she consulted her *beliefs* about child rearing, which she frequently enumerated. It was not truly loving, nor did it truly set him free, for her to allow her son to travel down the path of intentionally hurting other people.

Parents of *teenagers* usually should *not* intervene when their kids try out ego approaches to life—unless, of course, they are endangering themselves or hurting others. However, many of the issues that parents have with their tweens and teens do not arise because of their kids' ego-dominated behavior. During adolescence children are not trying out destructive approaches to life per se. They are simply trying out everything. Realizing this fact and how preoccupied adolescents are with all they suddenly have to deal with, parents can take a few gentle initiatives that will eliminate some of their children's difficulties and head off many issues that can arise between themselves and their kids.

For example, because phone conversations with their friends are so vitally important to tweens and teens, you can get them their own phone line. (Most families would not truly be hurt by this expense.) Provide them with good lighting and a good place to do schoolwork. Hang up a small bulletin board and calendar in their room and write down important appointments for them. Get them an alarm clock (or two or three if necessary!). Hide a key for them or give them one to carry. Buy them their own laundry hamper (and laundry supplies if necessary). Keep them supplied with a dry bath mat and clean towels. Write out all the phone numbers they might need, including their friends' numbers. Give them as much money as the family can afford to buy well-made shoes and clothes that are in style. And be sensitive to their feelings by never going into the bathroom when they are in it; by not walking into their room without knocking and by telling siblings not to go in at all without permission; by not even asking for kisses, hugs, or I-love-yous in public; by not correcting them (including their grammar or their "facts") in front of other people—including siblings; by reminding them often about upcoming appointments and family events that could affect their plans; and by helping them with their homework when necessary.

This last suggestion is somewhat controversial. It falls into a long list of things that parents are not supposed to do no matter what the age of their children. Other examples are: getting them "too many birthday presents"; occasionally letting them skip a day of school; not making bedwetting an issue; rewarding good grades with money; giving them the option of sleeping in your bedroom; spending more money on them than on yourself; chauffeuring their friends to and from your home more than their friends' parents; and so on. **Please do not decline a kindness to your child merely because other parents or authorities tell you "it isn't good for them."** Although it's always possible to cite exceptions, you take very little risk of harming your child when you try something merely to see for yourself what the effect on him or her *actually* is.

For example, we home-schooled John for his first and second grades. That worked fine until he began to develop social needs that clearly were not getting met. At that point we enrolled him in an alternative school with a gentle but somewhat dogmatic philosophy. John did well there for two years but then began to yearn for a more formal academic approach and especially for an opportunity to play team sports, which the school's philosophy did not allow for. We then switched him to public school.

When John started the fifth grade, we helped him extensively with all of his homework, and we continued helping him into the eighth grade. We also began treating schoolwork as his job and rewarding him for good grades. During those four years he gradually became more confident of his abilities. By his freshman year in high school, he was doing his homework without help.

This coming year John will be a senior in the same academically tough high school he has been attending for the last three years. From the time he entered public school, there has never been a grade period that he did not make the honor roll, and in high school he has maintained a four-point average throughout. Even though it cut deeply into his study time, during the last three years he also has played three separate sports (soccer, baseball, and cross-country), lettered and made the varsity teams in all three, and won the athlete-of-the-year award his freshman year. In his junior year, he made National Honor Society. Clearly, our switching schools when he needed and wanted to be switched did not "spoil" him; our paying him for the job of schoolwork did not "undermine his values"; and our helping him with assignments when he was younger did not keep him from "learning to use his mind," "learning responsibility," or just plain learning.

OVERPOWERING YOUR CHILD. Although some mothers make this mistake also, dads often fall into the age-old pattern of trying to overpower their children, especially their sons. The inevitable effect is that these kids either attack back or attack themselves, and their egos, rather than their sense of oneness, grow larger.

Some parents spank, shame, shake, deprive, or punish their kids into submission. Again and again they *impose* behavior, each time strengthening their child's belief in ego dominance—until the time comes when the child is strong enough to impose his will on the parent.

Two months ago a father we know walked unannounced into his fifteen-year-old's room and caught him smoking dope. He knew immediately what it was because of all the times he had smoked it around the same age. He yelled, "Get out of this house. You may not smoke that stuff in our home."

His boy got up and brushed past him. As he walked outside his father yelled, "And don't come back until you can swear to me you will not do this again."

Until that moment the father's attempts to over-power his son appeared to have been more or less success-ful. But now his son suddenly stopped, turned around, and walked back into the house. He shoved his father up against the wall and glared at him, daring him to do anything about it. Then he went to his room, grabbed a few of his things, and left, possibly never to return.

Usually the effects of forcing change on our children are not seen this quickly and dramatically, but sooner or later they will become apparent. Attempts to dominate backfire because even though our kids' behavior may crumble, their resolve to gain this kind of power for themselves builds.

You can't prevent this consequence by lecturing your child. When you try to "explain" your reasons for dis-ciplining in this way, you merely insult your child's intelli-gence and compound the problem. Unless your child views a punishment as sufficiently harsh, the desired change in behavior will not result. The ever-escalating curve of harsh-ness is obvious to most teenagers, and it explains why they don't buy into their parents' argument that it's merely out of respect for them that they are being treated disrespectfully. We can all remember times from our childhood when we knew that our parents were being unfairly harsh. Our own children are no less intelligent.

The word "discipline," even "self-discipline," sug-gests war, albeit good war, war worth winning, some would say. To discipline means to train, to mold, to shape, to per-fect. And this entails opposing forces: one person trying to control, tame, correct another person. A battle of wills. A battle of entrenched positions. Or it indicates the mind attempting to develop, reform, or improve the body—which always seems to have a mind of its own about such things. Or it indicates one side of the mind imposing order on another side of the mind. But it does not indicate thinking out or thinking through. It doesn't indicate discretion, choice, intuition, freedom, flexibility, or openness. It indicates a closed mind, a mind that has stopped seeing, learning, listening.

Once Gayle was talking to a mom at a cross-country meet who had told her daughter—who had a diagnosed learning disability—that if she made just one more D on anything—test, pop quiz, homework assignment, project, term paper—she would have to quit her job as illustrator on the school newspaper, which was the one activity she excelled at and loved unequivocally.

The mother said that since setting this penalty, by staying up late her daughter had brought up all her grades. Unfortunately, her work on the newspaper was also a graded activity, and her daughter had forgotten to turn in her work schedule and had gotten a D on her interim evaluation. Although this was just a report for the students' information and had no effect on final grades, the mother proudly declared to the other parents standing around that she was taking her child off the paper "because that's what I said I would do."

Once most parents make a pronouncement or start a punishment (taking away a "privilege," forbidding a relationship, grounding, reducing or eliminating an allowance, adding chores punitively, and so on), they think it's a virtue not to get sidetracked by their child's distress, entreaties, or reassurances. At all costs they must see the discipline through to the end or else the child will "never believe you again," or "always think they can get away with it," or "will never learn responsibility."

This is highly hypocritical and the child knows it. How many times have all of us failed to see things through? Our last diet; our last budget; our last exercise program; our last resolution to quit smoking; our last promise to our child; our last marriage. And always we explain to ourselves—and anyone else who's interested—that there was a "reason" for each of these failures.

Of course, there are times when as parents we must take a firm stand and stick with it. (See "How to Deal with Manipulation" in Chapter 7.) But what of the times we realize that what we are trying to accomplish with our child isn't working, or what if we see that we should never have taken this stand in the first place? What about admitting mistakes? What about teaching our kids how to start over? Those lessons are equally important as learning when to be consistent. And of all the stands that least require our consistency, our determination to see that our children receive every last ounce of punishment "they have coming to them" should be at the top of the list.

Does this mean you will never get mad, never scream, never lose your patience? If that were possible, you would be ready to ascend. When we get angry at our boys, we simply apologize to them. We have always done this and it has not "weakened our position." How can parents teach their kids to admit their errors quickly and move on if they try to justify their own lapses?

Many authorities recommend that we explain to our children that it isn't them we are upset with, it's their behavior. If that were true, if we were so spiritually advanced that within our own mind we could completely separate our child's bodily behavior from our child, we would never become angry. We become angry because, emotionally, we have *not* made this distinction.

The ego does not get mad at behavior; it gets mad at other egos. Even children can sense this—or we should say *especially* children can sense this, since their freedom, happiness, and very survival depend on their being sensitive. For us to tell our kids that we aren't angry at them, when they can *feel* that we are, is to ask them to doubt their own experience and to devalue their own minds.

During adolescence, kids look more closely at our words and actions and decide for themselves how congruent we are. And in most homes, they don't like what they see. From our experience of counseling parents and their teenagers, we long ago concluded that most teens still possess more basic honesty than the average adult—even though they may steal or lie. There are unquestionably many exceptions, but most adolescents have not yet formed as thick a layer of deceit, especially self-deceit, as their parents. You can read them fairly easily. Often they can lie quite well to get what they want or escape what they don't want, but they don't lie easily about what they believe is important and fundamental about life. If you get to the level of teens' basic perceptions of the world, their instinct is to be straight with you, and it takes an effort for them to be dishonest. Not so with many adults, who have simply lost contact with what they personally feel and believe. They have in large part become their egos, a store of memories, voices, and opinions from the past and from other people.

Imagine going down a street some Sunday morning where there are churches of several different denominations holding services. You step inside each one in turn and stay long enough to get a feel for what the minister is saying and how the congregation is reacting. Unless these are very unusual churches, in each one you enter you hear the congregation respond to their minister with unanimity—even though each minister is preaching a slightly or radically different set of beliefs.

Presumably adults' convictions about their God and about how they want to live their lives represent their most profound and deeply considered thoughts. So isn't it curious that in each house of worship that you go into, everyone has the same set of beliefs held by the rest of that congregation—everything from what is the source of healing power to whether it is moral to toast with champagne?

Now, can you imagine these same churches filled with only teenagers? Would you agree that you would probably not find the same lock step uniformity of belief? Not that many teens aren't capable of conformity—adults frequently throw in teens' faces the fact that they are so influenced by their peers. And of course they are. But note that with teenagers conformity is often more superficial—dress, language, humor, mannerisms, taste in music—than it is with adults. On the level of how in touch they are with their integrity and their personal sense of right and wrong, wouldn't you give teenagers slightly higher marks? Based on our counseling experience, we definitely would.

Although there are many individual exceptions to this generalization, we urge you to take as deep a look at your tween, your teenage son, your adolescent daughter as you possibly can, to listen deeply to what they say and don't say, to notice the ideal behind what upsets them, the sense of justice and injustice that they refer to. Then ask yourself, "What is my kid trying to tell me here?" In all likelihood, any parent who does this will hear and see far more than the effects of hormones, emotions, and peer pressure.

MANIPULATING YOUR CHILD. Fostering guilt is a powerful means of controlling another's behavior, and most parents don't often resist the temptation to use it. It seems to kids that their mom and dad are always pointing out the weaknesses in their character and implying that the kids themselves are not fully aware of them. When parents repeatedly succeed in making them feel guilty, their kids naturally begin to wonder just how deep is the darkness within them. Most adults have clear memories of being shamed as children. Many also recall their fear that maybe they really

were out of control and would never be able to stop themselves from lying, cheating, stealing, being selfish, being insensitive, being cruel, or whatever the major issue was
between themselves and their parents. Thus it should be
obvious that **parents who try to motivate through guilt,
fear, embarrassment, or other manipulative emotions are
teaching their kids to use their minds to attack themselves.**
This is not helpful to the child—or to the parent—in the
long run.

Obviously moms and dads don't tell themselves, or
even necessarily suspect, that they are strengthening self-
doubt in their children when they try to make their kids feel
embarrassed, anxious, and so on. They think that their kids
are guilty, and they are simply informing them of this fact.
Or they think of guilt as no more than an effective motivator
that does little harm.

We had just started this section when Hugh caught himself
trying to manipulate Jordan. He said, "Have you taken your
puppy out yet?" Then he realized that the only time he referred to Chocolate Mousse Pie as "your puppy" and the
only time he used the word "yet" was when he wanted *Jordan* to take her out. So he immediately added, "It would be
a big help to me if you'd take Mousse out this time." Jordan
said, "Okay." He probably would have said okay anyway,
but now he was responding to a direct request rather than
the indirect implication that he was neglecting his own dog.

Jordan is very attentive to our family's pets. In fact,
he spends so much time playing with them that we have all
come to think of them as his. He sometimes forgets to keep
the cat's water filled or to take out Mousse, but this is really
a lapse in memory, not a lapse in love. Yet even if the animals were exclusively his and if he were truly neglectful,
we would want to be straight with him about this and not
just pull out the concept of duty when we were trying to get

him to do something. Hugh's was a minor use of guilt, but even to use a little guilt, fear, or embarrassment is an ugly practice.

Take, for example, the common parental practice of making direct or indirect comparisons between one child and another or between one sibling and another. Gayle's mom used to say "Why can't you be more like Tricia Nixon?" Meaning "Why can't you look like Tricia? Why can't you be popular like Tricia? Why can't you be a credit to me?" This was a very direct attack but not necessarily any less difficult to handle than the more indirect attacks Hugh got from his dad. Hugh was an only child for the first ten years of his life. During this time he often heard his dad say in one form or another, "See how you behave? Your mother wouldn't have left you if you weren't so bad." Hugh was not being compared to an actual child but to an ideal child: "Your mother wouldn't have left a good boy. Why can't you be a good boy?" (Both Hugh and his dad have come a long way since those days. Now his dad would be incapable of such a tactic, and Hugh is finally a good boy!)

Parents don't make comparisons out of the blue. You are not in the car minding your own business when suddenly your mom says "Why can't you be more like your sister?" Comparisons usually come on the heels of some behavior of which the parent disapproves and wants the child to change. Like all manipulations, they discourage children from using their minds, from using their own evaluations, perceptions, and discretions. If you aren't even the *person* you should be, then certainly you better not rely on the mind you shouldn't have.

And like all manipulations, comparisons are cruel. They misuse children's desire for love and approval from their parent. The message is clear: "If you don't become more like your sister, I'll never love you as much as I do her." **The primary emotion that most parents gen-**

erate within their adolescents is the feeling of rejection. They are constantly being held to a standard they can't live up to.

"What is it now!" Kids in most families hear this angry question, or something like it, often. Few adults would say this to anyone but their own child, and if they did, it would be a sign of disrespect. It says to children: "Because of you I never have any time to myself. All this extra work is caused by your selfish demands. If it weren't for you I could fulfill myself. If it weren't for you I would be happy."

Over the last fifteen years we have talked to several children whose parents were dying or who had died, as well as to several professional caregivers who work with children in those circumstances. In all the cases we are familiar with, the child felt responsible for the death to some degree.

Most parents unwittingly plant in their children's minds the thought that the children can't trust themselves to have a good effect on other people, that they don't understand what makes other people happy, that they lack the inner resources to comfort.

We interviewed a minister named Daniel who remembers his father as a moral, consistent, and courageous individual, a man who was devoted to his congregation and who led an impeccably pure life. And yet, every time Daniel resisted doing something his father wanted him to do, his father would yell angrily, "You're killing your mother." The mother had terminal cancer and the father's rationale was that by being uncooperative, Daniel was causing a scene that was stressful and debilitating to the mother.

Clearly, Daniel did not manufacture the exchanges between him and his father in order to harm his mother, and the father certainly could have come up with ways to deal with his son out of earshot of the mother. Nevertheless, when she finally died, Daniel remembers vividly that, at the time, he had no doubt that he personally had caused his mother's death and no doubt that he would burn in Hell for it. As an adult, he now sees that this was one of several factors that for many years made him deeply afraid of himself—his mind, his motives, his reliability—and fed his belief that he was morally incapable of taking steps to deal with his own alcoholism.

One woman we recently counseled, whose father was still alive at ninety-three, remembers him periodically announcing throughout her childhood that he "had a feeling" he would only live five more years, or "not see another Christmas," or "not be around for you and your sister's graduations." He held this thought like a sword over his family's heads, and everyone was supposed to tiptoe around him even though he had no serious health problems. He had discovered one of the ultimate tools of manipulation: fear. Perhaps only continually beating his kids would have been a more effective way of keeping them in a state of anxious compliance.

We should never encourage our children to believe that their basic nature is so destructive that they would intentionally cause us to be tired, to be sick, to break up our marriage, to be overburdened, or to have a miserable life. That simply is not the basic will of any young child and is not what is behind their demands. Yet all children can be convinced that they are capable of malice, especially by their own mother or father. **The attitudes we pass along to our kids are far more life-affecting than the money and possessions we leave them in our wills.** No matter what change in behavior we bring about by using guilt or another ego emotion to manipulate them, it is never worth the price our children will pay for our having planted a suspicion about their basic nature.

10. "First your teenager must get his or her behavior under control, then you can think about bonding. The key to a well-functioning family is cooperation, not trust."

Assuming that you, like most of us, had parents who used a punitive, judgmental approach to getting you "under control," how would you have answered the following questions when you were a teenager, and, perhaps more important, how do you think your teen or tween would answer them now? If you wish to ask your child these questions, do so one-on-one with no other children present. If you go down this list with two or more tweens or young teens, they will often get into a rhythm of answers in which they all seem to agree—which is fine as the basis of a class discussion but may not be particularly enlightening if you sincerely want to discover what your child feels about his or her relationship with you.

- Do your mom and dad trust you?
- Do they talk to you as if you were younger than you are?
- Do they lecture you?
- Do they keep repeating themselves when you already understand?
- Do they interrupt you when you try to answer?
- Do your parents know your abilities and the things you are potentially capable of doing?
- Do they watch over you to see if you are doing it right?
- When you have finished, do they criticize you no matter how hard you tried?
- Do your parents consider how you feel when they make plans that affect you?
- Can you give your mom or dad your opinion about the decisions they make?
- Do they understand what you are trying to tell them?
- Do they get angry if you disagree with them?

❧ If you are sad, or depressed, or angry about something that happened at school or away from home, can you talk to your parents about it?

❧ Are there things you would like to ask your parents about but you're afraid they'll misunderstand why you are asking?

❧ If you do talk to them about something that happened to you, do they use this opportunity to give you a lecture?

❧ Do they try to cheer you up?

❧ Even if you are very upset, do they try to convince you it's not important?

❧ Do you feel they really do try to understand?

❧ Can you talk to your parents about drugs or sex or violence?

❧ Do you trust your mom and dad?

As you can see, this series of questions begins and ends with trust. By the time she reaches adolescence, your child will not trust you if you lack confidence in her. For parents to have faith in a child doesn't mean they are certain he will do what he says he will do. It means that they refuse to lose sight of their child's core and of their own overriding purpose to enjoy their child.

Judging by the titles of books about the teen years, it's obvious that most parents think they are lucky if they can just get through this period with their sanity intact. The thrust of the literature on adolescents is on how to discipline them, correct them, control them. *Can you imagine any possible way that you could enjoy your spouse if that were your relationship goal?* Trying to change people is at least one sure key to misery. Naturally parents must safeguard their adolescents—that, in fact, we don't do nearly well enough—but trying to change the basic teenage personality at the very time that everything within teenagers is screaming "Become your own person" is insanity.

This list of questions can be a good starting point for a dialogue with your teenager, but notice that it is designed to elicit your kids' feelings about you and so it would indeed be a mistake to use it as the basis of still one more argument with your kid. You may be a very good parent and still your kid may give the "wrong" answer to every one of these questions. If you respond with hurt feelings or with indignation, you will miss a good opportunity to practice seeing and accepting your child. Only if you can accept your children—while still nourishing, guiding, and protecting them—can you enjoy them.

The Joy of Parenting Teenagers is a book that surely will never be written. As a culture we deeply believe that parenting is at best a challenge and more often a nightmare. THIS DOES NOT HAVE TO BE. If you take nothing else from this book, please take the hope that there is a way for you to enjoy your child—at any stage.

This is accomplished by first trusting or having faith in your child's deeper nature. **Trust has nothing—absolutely nothing—to do with how "reliable" or "responsible" you believe your child to be.** After thirty years' experience of dealing with Hugh's memory, Gayle knows that she can't be certain that Hugh will remember an appointment *she has just reminded him of.* And after thirty years of dealing with Gayle's inability to say no, Hugh can't be certain that Gayle won't accept a social invitation without first checking with him. Unless you know some very unusual people, you can probably list several ways right off the top of your head that your partner or a sibling or any number of good friends are not completely reliable and responsible. And yet some of these same people you undoubtedly trust deeply.

One of the sources of the difficulties that parents

have with their teenagers comes from their not realizing (understandably) how dramatically their teenager's priorities have shifted. A child psychiatrist who used to be a neighbor of ours in Santa Fe told us that a survey taken within his specialty had shown that the most frequently reported complaint against teenagers is that they don't take out the trash. One would think that if parents were going to edit out frivolous complaints to anyone, it would be to a child psychiatrist. Why is this universal failing on the part of teenagers so noteworthy that they would take it to their shrink?

We also have heard the trash complaint many times over the years in our own counseling, and it is invariably made in tones of disbelief and irritation. "How could anyone fail to do something so simple as take out the trash?" Consequently, in the parent's mind, the child is being perverse. But in our experience this is rarely the reason.

One dad said that he saves up chicken bones, puts them in the trash, then sets it in his fifteen-year-old's room. Soon the trash starts smelling, but even then his boy usually doesn't take it out on time. We asked him if he eventually took it out. He said yes. We asked him if his son had ever said that he didn't want that duty or that he thought it was unfair he had been given that duty. He said no. We asked him if he had given him that task when he was nine or even twelve, would he have been better about doing it? He said absolutely, then began telling stories about how responsible his son used to be. Why, we asked, did he think he was different now?

"It's a power play," he said. "He's probably testing me. He's turning into his mother [who had left the family several years before]."

In talking to his son, we discovered that the reasons were the same as for most teenagers: He didn't think it was "that" important, and he forgot. He meant to do it but he got busy doing something else.

If parents want to understand their teens, those reasons must be heeded.

First, let's consider trash in terms of teen priorities: If your neck and nose and ears were growing faster than your forehead, eyes, and mouth—now think about it—would trash be important to you? If you were a boy and all your friends' penises were getting longer and their voices were getting deeper but all that was happening to you was that you were getting little pockets of swelling under your nipples, would trash be important to you? If you were a girl and the entire country you lived in was obsessed with large breasts and if many of your career opportunities, your self-esteem, and even the pool of potential mates you could choose from depended on your having large breasts, and yet your breasts were coming in small (or weren't coming in at all!), would trash be important to you? If you went to school and the person who was your best friend yesterday has now decided to hang out with another group of kids—who don't like you—would trash be important to you? If you have finally found someone who will go out with you but now your hormones are kicking in and your face is breaking out in acne, would trash be important to you? If one night you get a call and three of your friends want you to sign a suicide pact with them, would trash be important to you?

You get the point. And we haven't even covered "emerging feelings of intense sexuality," "the tension between staying a child and becoming an adult," "the impact of violent and perverted forces in society," or all the battles (besides taking out the trash) with their parents, schoolteachers, and coaches that teenagers suddenly find themselves enmeshed in.

Meeting faithfully just one small demand such as taking out the trash on certain days or by a certain time of day requires that teenagers share at least a few basic priorities with their parents, and most of these priorities they simply *cannot* share. They can be scared into *appearing* to share them, but their hearts will still not be in it.

For example, pleasing or "honoring" one's parents is no longer a priority for the average teenager. They still love their parents, but they are starting to lose their fear of them. When speaking to their children, if parents use the word "'respect," they usually mean "fear," and children definitely lose "respect" for their parents during adolescence. Earlier in their lives, parents had control over almost everything their children wanted to do. But as kids get older and less dependent, parents lose their leverage. Unless a mom and dad are willing to increase their efforts to terrorize their teenager in the few ways they still can—and many parents do in fact make this mistake—teenagers will not consistently take out the trash solely out of a desire to please, honor, or respect their parents.

Likewise, maintaining a neat, clean house for company or guests is not a priority for children of this age, and probably it wasn't when they were younger. Very often teens don't care if other teens see their room in a mess and they pay very little attention to whether wastebaskets or laundry hampers are full. Mess is so universally an adolescent trait that it's probably an unconscious symbol of freedom and independence.

Being on time—another value necessary to prompt, reliable trash takeout—is certainly not a priority for teenagers, and possibly for similar reasons. Even remembering the plans that include them is often not their priority, as can be seen by how often teens forget or get mixed up about plans they have made with other teens.

Teens and even many tweens live in a world that is radically different from the average adult's world, and they really can't do very much about that. It is up to parents—who, after all, have been through this and should be able to see both worlds fairly clearly—to remember what their teenager cannot be expected to remember:

that God loves them with all the heart of a mother and all the strength of a father and still infinitely more than that. That they will probably get through all of this just fine— although they definitely don't want to be told that. And that there is nothing—including even their forgetting to take out the trash—that can make you, their mother and father on earth, stop loving them or stop being their eternal friend.

IDENTIFYING WITH YOUR ADOLESCENT

Although knowledge of a broad range of possible responses to the common problems that arise between ourselves and our adolescent can give us greater flexibility, it also can be a trap. One of the better indicators of our having fallen into it is how we feel about our kids after having read the parenting book, attended the parenting class, consulted the school counselor, or talked to the schoolteacher. Do we feel more oneness with our child or more separation? Are we standing back and analyzing our child, or do we now feel what our child feels and see what our child sees?

The basic flaw—from a spiritual standpoint—in most of the approaches adopted by schools and social agencies and found within academic textbooks and popular parenting literature is that kids are discussed as if they were a phenomenon apart from ordinary life. If we accept this premise, then we will believe that the teachers, religious counselors, psychologists, and child care professionals who know this species best can give us the most informed parenting rules to follow. It isn't necessary for you even to *try* to use your own love and intuition. In fact, many religious parenting books actually warn you against your "softer" feelings, your silly desire to feed your little lambs rather than beat them, to use your rod to comfort them rather than cause them pain, to use your words to give them peace rather than shame, to suffer your children, to allow them to come to you, to judge them not, to love them as yourself; in fact, to receive them in the name of God.

Obviously you can find very harsh advice to parents in some parts of the Bible. But note that those who build their case on these quotes arbitrarily pick and choose among even these passages. For example, why stop with "beatest him with a rod"? Why not have a "willful and stubborn son" stoned to death as "we are commanded to do" in Deuteronomy 21:18–21? Surely there is no more obvious example of "the letter killeth, the spirit giveth life" than to use holy scripture as an argument that Jesus wanted his followers to beat their children.

Children are not a different life-form. They respond to fairness and unfairness, love and judgment, devotion and betrayal, gentleness and cruelty, appreciation and dismissal, openness and rigidity, in about the same way that adults respond. The main difference is that children, especially younger ones, tend to be more forgiving. Adults often misinterpret this inherent gentleness and conclude that children are unformed, that they don't have egos that react like egos.

Most of the problems we have with our kids indicate our lack of *identification* with their needs, our failure to see that our kids' needs are our own and to treat them as our own. Contrary to what is taught in many parenting classes, especially church-sponsored ones, a deeper identification with our children does not make us more likely to acquiesce to their every whim. We don't do this in meeting our own needs, and we don't do it when we feel our oneness with our child more strongly.

Many impulses pass through our minds daily that we decline to act on. This discrimination is precisely *how* we care for ourselves. We look carefully at the impulse and judge whether it's in our best interests to follow it. Likewise, the policy of blanket indulgence of everything our children think they want comes from too little identification with our kids' needs, not from too much. We don't even care for our pets in this way. Dog owners who identify with their dog don't empty their refrigerators and pantries and lay out all their food before their pet simply because their pet would like this. This would make the dog sick. And it would indicate the owner's *lack* of identification with the dog.

We need a greater experience of oneness and our children need a greater experience of oneness. If we do no more than give a lecture and apply a corrective formula, we probably don't want to bother growing as a parent, at least for now. We simply want our kid's *behavior* to change. Surely, we say, with life being as complicated and burdensome as it is, this is not too much to ask. And yet this attitude is the primary one that makes parenting such a chore.

We believe we can improve the situation by merely changing our child. But our child is what he or she is in *relationship* to us. Our level of learning and our child's level of learning cannot be separated, at least not spiritually.

Most books, talk-show authorities, and articles that offer advice to parents focus on the words you should use and the bodily actions you should take. Their obvious goal is to show you how you can get your child to act the way you want. The word "discipline" is sprinkled throughout these discourses like periods and commas and actually appears in the titles of books on adolescence as often as the word "child."

The obvious implication is that for each problem that arises between you and your children, you can say or do something that will solve it. Most experts pay lip service to concepts such as love, respect, responsibility, and understanding, but these are merely the emotional colors that you should use to paint your words and actions. For example, one authority recommends anger as "the most effective punishment of all," but cautions you to "use it gently" and to word your anger in such a way that your kids will think that it's their behavior, not them, that you are angry at.

Another authority writes that although you might not feel love for your children at the moment you spank them, you let them know that you do love them by not raising your voice or using angry words, and by "calmly" explaining why you are spanking them.

STARTING OVER

We have covered many things in this chapter. Obviously, volumes more could be written. But if you were to carry away just one idea, we would want it to be the knowledge that there is always hope; it is never too late for a breakthrough, even if your child is an adult.

It's true that if you have kept the lines of communication open as your children have approached adolescence, then you are probably now experiencing far fewer problems with your tween or teen than parents who have not managed to do this. But what if you have failed in this respect, or not done as good a job as you would have liked?

Most "teen problems" involve their parents and no one else. Once parents lift the suffocating blanket of their disapproval, the inherent spiritual relationship between parent and child can once again breathe and start to thrive. This process may take a little time, but now it's at least possible. And sometimes the healing can occur very quickly.

When Hugh went to boarding school, first as a day student when he was twelve and thirteen and then going out of state to another one from age fourteen through seventeen, he was struck at how problem-free his and his school friends' lives were once they were away from their parents. This phenomenon is definitely not a sufficient reason for you to send your children off to live somewhere else most of the year, and if you do so as a form of rejection, you will definitely pay a price. Yet it is interesting how well even nine- to twelve-year-olds can function while living outside their parents' home.

child has an advantage over our neighbor's child? This question calls for no detailed position on the thousand political issues and posturings of our time. It calls for an eternal stand, not a tentative opinion that varies with the circumstances of our individual lives and the quality of information we have on a given topic. If we define love by the boundaries of our child's body, it is not an affection that reflects God's love and certainly is no gift to our child.

Instead, we turn away from pettiness and pronounce all children holy in our mind. We allow no shadow to remain across their name within any memory or thought we have of them. We do not ask where to direct our giving, but ask instead if ever there could be a child who deserves to be withheld from. Our heart embraces them all and our body does what it can in the present. Our starting point is where we are and the ones already within our reach.

The time has come for us to move past thinking of children as manipulative egos and bundles of unpleasant little needs. If we haven't already seen, we at least acknowledge the part of each child that flows from the heart of God, and is surrounded by God, and is with God, even until the end of time. Because it is more truthful to do so and because it is our way of worship, we hold all children bright and pure in our mind, the image and likeness of God, proclaimed then, now, and forever to be "very good." We are not arrogant and say we know better than God what any child is at her core, or where she abides, or what his destiny must inevitably be. In the world there are many, but in God—where we look for guidance—there are no ugly children, no dead children, no children who are held back from grace and miracles.

If this is not what we envision and work to bring about under our own roof and under the broader mantle of our lives, all we need is to walk closer to God, to place our hand in God's hand, to place our heart in God's heart, to place our vision in God's eyes. This we can do because it is

If you never experienced this problem-reducing magic at a boarding school, perhaps you got a feel for it at a summer camp or even an overnight field trip. Many people first taste this freedom at eighteen, when they go off to college or even when they get married. Naturally another set of problems takes the place of the old ones within each of these new parent-free circumstances, but most kids find they are no longer "a problem teenager" when there is no parent around who thinks they are.

Yet isn't it sad that for most kids, freedom from being judged, bullied, and manipulated by their parents has to come in this way? But of course it doesn't *have* to. And that is the point.

If you have not kept the lines of trust, love, and communication open with your child, you can start today. This doesn't mean that you stop protecting your child, because you want to do that within your own heart and mind forever, even if you can no longer do it physically. **Adolescents can look a lot more mature than they are.** So don't be fooled by mere size or depth of voice. If your child is walking into real danger, then intervene.

But that circumstance arises during the day very seldom. Nevertheless, the battle of wills, the clashing of egos, the withdrawing and attacking, go on and on. If parents did nothing more than lighten up a little when their kids started to enter puberty, most of what we have been talking about here would be taken care of automatically.

Anyone who reviews the advice that has been given to parents over the last several decades will see that **no consensus has *ever* been formed about how parents should respond in even the simplest and most common predicaments.** You do not know either. Which means you must never try to decide alone. To your ego, parenting is nothing but nagging questions and vague defeats. It's not a lot of fun. But within your stillness and peace you have an unfailing guide out of unhappiness. The voice of Love moves across the surface of your mind like the sounds of morning gliding over the stillness of a lake. There is no more joyous music than the call of your Mother-Father God. It invites you to awake, and nothing more. Awake to your partner. Awake to your parents. Awake to your brothers and sisters. Awake to your child. You have one family—for there is only one—and it enfolds you in certainty. Knowing how to think about your family, how to respond to it, how to heal and be healed by it, can come to you as naturally and joyously as awaking to "the day the Lord hath made." All you have to do is return to your focus of enjoying your child each time you lose it. All you have to do is hold your child in the radiance of God.

MY CHILD, YOU ARE ALWAYS WITH ME, AND ALL I HAVE IS YOURS

This is the ancient, unbreakable commitment that God makes to us. We must now make the same commitment to our children and renew it each day until devotion to them becomes as natural and necessary as breathing. To accomplish this, we ask the question that very few in the world's bitter history have ever bothered to ask: Who are the children in our care?

Certainly they include the children whom we ourselves bring into the world, whether we now have custody of them or not, whether they have turned against us or not, even whether or not they are still alive in bodily form. But are not the remaining children of this world also in our care? How do we honor God—whom we call Father, Mother, Creator, and Source—and make our own parenting a form of worship if we angrily battle for special privilege for our child alone; if we lie, scheme, and attack to ensure that our in our nature. Seeing with the understanding of God comes naturally. We don't generate it or use some dishonest mental process to trick ourselves into believing it; we merely stop resisting it. Disapproval requires constant vigilance and enormous energy to sustain, because it is not in our nature. So we surrender, and gently lay aside all other attitudes, and begin at last the deep and permanent enjoyment of our child and of all the children of the world. Everything we have is theirs because everything we have is God's.

As we find our way back to our own heart and draw near the attitude of God, we feel children as not only our responsibility but our pleasure. Seldom are we called on to intervene on a child's behalf. But when we are, we must not hesitate to respond. Many in our culture are now focusing their attention on how other parents treat their kids at home while at the same time washing their hands of the far more prevalent dangers to kids on our streets and within our schools. Those who include children in their religious practices must not be swayed by trends but only by the call of their own hearts.

The call we neglect to respond to so often is the one for simple compassion for the people whose lives we already touch, for the children in our own family, for the neighborhood kids where we live, for the schoolkids in our district, for the children affected by standards and policies of our own city government, and for the adolescents exploited in ads for products that we ourselves buy.

Nothing ever has to be done in anger, but as adults it is our undeniable function to protect children. That is the basic function of the adult in almost every form of life. Yet we have a higher function as well: to be happy with what God gives us to do today. To sing with the voice of angels as we do the work of angels. To laugh with the laugh of Buddha as we go to our awakening. To extend the arms of Jesus to welcome the presence of children and let them climb into our hearts.

We cannot assume that we love our kids and see them as God sees them while day after day our basic attitude is irritation, impatience, and censure. As deep as any vows we make before God to our partner must be our vows to our children as well. To them we pledge:

❧ I will be your advocate and your friend. I will listen to you deeply. I will guide you when I am able and show you a higher guidance when I am not.

❧ I will never make promises to you lightly. I will remember the promises I make. And I will keep them.

❧ I will not hurt you or shame you—and I will never, never mislead you.

❧ I will respect your needs and give full attention to your desires. I will discount nothing you want merely because you are a child and I am an adult.

❧ Because I wish you to be safe and to feel safe, I will be firm when I must, say no when I must, and intervene when I must.

❧ And still I will provide you with freedom to use your mind, to discover Love's wisdom, to choose and decide, and to make all the mistakes you need to make for your growth.

❧ Above all, I will not forget your innocence. I will remember where it comes from. I will recall it over and over as if my innocence depended on remembering yours.

❧ And in these ways I will love you, and cherish you, and enjoy you so deeply that it will be as if God gave you to me and said, "Please take good care of my beloved child."

Endnotes

1. THE INNOCENT VISION

1. Although you will not find most of them on the shelves of chain bookstores, a number of parenting books have been written that acknowledge the spiritual (and therefore fully developed and fully connected) core in every child. Here are the four we are most familiar with and have used ourselves: *Whole Child/Whole Parent* by Polly Berrien Berends (Harper & Row, 1983); *Teach Only Love* by Gerald G. Jampolsky (Bantam Books, 1983); *Models of Love* by Joyce and Barry Vissell (Ramira Publishing, 1986); and *How to Raise a Child of God* by Tara Singh (Life Action Press, 1983).

2. That was sixteen years ago and nothing else in our life has been associated with the number eight in any unusual way.

2. WHAT ARE PARENTS FOR?

1. In our counseling we have been suggesting a line of questions similar to this for many years. We borrowed the general concept

from Lesson 24 in the *Workbook of a Course in Miracles*. (Most bookstores now carry this three-volumes-in-one book, or it can be ordered from the Foundation for Inner Peace, P.O. Box 635, Tiburon, CA 94920.) A more detailed and very helpful version of this kind of question-and-answer exercise can be found in *Core Transformations* by Connirae Andreas. Andreas is an innovator and leader in the field of NLP (Neuro-Linguistic Programming). Your bookstore can get this book through a distributor or from Real People Press, Box F, Moab, Utah 84532.

3. MEETING YOUR NEEDS

1. John loved the "wars" but decided not to attend any more FCA activities when at one meeting he was asked to pray that the schools have Christian coaches. He has tremendous admiration and affection for his cross-country coach, who is Jewish, and couldn't imagine asking God to replace him, even if he believed Love operated on that level.

4. WHAT ARE CHILDREN FOR?

1. The "folded-towel method" (helping them off with their wet clothing, putting a folded towel over the wet spot, and adding an extra blanket if needed) is one way of dealing with this problem quickly so that your child is not punished by being kept awake too long.

2. For example, making up an excuse so that your child's friends sleep over at your place—where you can discreetly check on your child during the night.

3. See Cultural Assumption #10 in Chapter 10 for more (a lot more) on taking out the trash.

4. Still one of the most accessible, most thorough, and most balanced examinations of the behavior and development of children is the ten-book series from the Gesell Institute. These paperbacks, all reasonably priced, are divided according to age (*Your One-Year-Old, Your Two-Year-Old,* and so on, through *Your Ten- to Fourteen-Year-Old*). Each book provides an abundance of insights and

descriptions of the common characteristics of the stage your child is in now. Most large bookstores keep this series in stock or will order whichever one you need.

6. THE PARENT-CHILD BALANCE

1. For example, from years of counseling and marrying couples, we now know that within most relationships, money is a more powerful symbol of devotion than even sex. In Chapter 12 of *I Will Never Leave You* we discuss money issues in marriage.

2. After this appointment, we did let up on our efforts to get Jordan to try new remedies, and the atmosphere, especially around meal-times, improved greatly. We also noticed that Jordan's anxiety and embarrassment over his physical reactions to food, animals, dust, and so forth, lessened once our own fears lessened. Now at age twelve he has outgrown some of his earlier symptoms and secms reasonably well adjusted to the ones that remain.

3. Jordan started public middle school (grades 6 through 8) one month ago. To date, there has been actual physical activity on only six of the twenty days he has attended physical education class (PE). The remainder of the time has been spent studying and taking tests. This reflects what appears to be a nationwide trend to turn PE into an academic subject.

8. ADOLESCENTS AND FEAR

1. If you are interested in the religious roots of punishment in this country and the effects on children of interpreting the Bible in the narrow and cruel way that many are now choosing, you might want to ask your bookstore to order *Spare the Child* by Dr. Phillip Greven (Vintage Books, Random House, 1990). Also, Dr. Thomas Gordan, the originator of P.E.T. (Parent Effectiveness Training) and T.E.T. (Teacher Effectiveness Training), has a good section on this in his book *Discipline That Works* (Plume Printing, 1991) and gives excel-lent alternatives to a punitive approach to parenting in this and other books. Penelope Leach's book *Your Gowing Child* (Alfred A. Knopf, 1990) is also a very good source of alternatives and suggestions for parenting from babyhood through adolescence.

10. CULTURAL ASSUMPTIONS
ABOUT ADOLESCENTS' NEEDS

1. This story was told to Jerry and Diane by Dr. Elisabeth Kübler-Ross, a physician internationally known for her work in the field of death and dying. The mother went to Dr. Kübler-Ross for help after her son's death.

2. For example, although this aspect of their society has been slowly unraveling over the years, within the more formal culture of Great Britain, adolescents have a more defined path to walk than in the United States and consequently they tend to get sidetracked into destructive activities somewhat less.